T0326644

Print, Politics and the Provincial Press in Modern Britain

Print, Politics and the Provincial Press in Modern Britain

Ian Cawood and Lisa Peters (eds)

PETER LANG

Oxford • Bern • Berlin • Bruxelles • New York • Wien

Bibliographic information published by Die Deutsche Nationalbibliothek.
Die Deutsche Nationalbibliothek lists this publication in the Deutsche
Nationalbibliografie; detailed bibliographic data is available on the Internet at
http://dnb.d-nb.de.

Library of Congress Cataloging-in-Publication Data:

Names: Cawood, Ian, editor. | Peters, Lisa, 1974- editor.
Title: Print, politics and the provincial press in modern Britain / Ian Cawood and
    Lisa Peters (eds).
Description: Oxford ; New York : Peter Lang, [2019] | Includes bibliographical
    references and index.
Identifiers: LCCN 2018050083 | ISBN 9781788744300 (alk. paper)
Subjects: LCSH: Community newspapers--Great Britain. | Local mass media--
    Political aspects--Great Britain. | Communication--Political aspects--Great
    Britain.
Classification: LCC PN5124.C63 P75 2019 | DDC 072--dc23 LC record available
    at https://lccn.loc.gov/2018050083

Cover design by Brian Melville for Peter Lang Ltd.

ISSN 2297-6531
ISBN 978-1-78874-430-0 (print) • ISBN 978-1-78874-461-4 (ePDF)
ISBN 978-1-78874-462-1 (ePub) • ISBN 978-1-78874-463-8 (mobi)

© Peter Lang AG 2019

Published by Peter Lang Ltd, International Academic Publishers,
52 St Giles, Oxford, OX1 3LU, United Kingdom
oxford@peterlang.com, www.peterlang.com

Ian Cawood and Lisa Peters have asserted their right under the Copyright, Designs
and Patents Act, 1988, to be identified as Editors of this Work.

This publication has been peer reviewed.

Printed in Germany

Contents

Figures

Tables

IAN CAWOOD AND LISA PETERS

Introduction

Why do all modern historians, cultural critics and literary analysts (especially those who tread in the swampy, inter-disciplinary mud of 'Victorian Studies') eventually find themselves confronting the intimidating bulk of the newspaper archives? In these days of the 'cultural turn' with its focus on the behaviours, mentalities and representations of life, this is simply because no other source can provide such a rounded view of the priorities, the principles and the prurience of public experience in early modern and modern Britain. The British press can trace its history back to the 'newsbooks' of the English Civil War and, as literacy advanced, newspapers and their readership grew. The lapse of the 1662 Licensing Act, which had restricted printing to London, Oxford, Cambridge, and York, in 1695 paved the way for the creation of newspapers outside these four cities and a provincial press was established. Politicians were quick to recognise the value of supportive newspapers with Robert Harley (1661–1724) and later Robert Walpole (1676–1745) supporting the creation of pro-government newspapers and offering financial subsidies. Politicians also understood that the press was a potential threat and took care to restrict press circulation through the introduction of the 'taxes on knowledge', otherwise known as stamp duty, advertising duty, and paper duty. However, these taxes were never as effective as the government of the day hoped, and even the increase in stamp duty to 2d in 1789 did not stop the production of the pro-revolutionary *Dublin Evening Post*, as discussed in the chapter in this collection by Duncan Frankis. In contrast to the revolutionary fervour of the *Dublin Evening Post*, Catherine Ferris examines the press coverage of musical events in the Dublin press in a six-month period in 1840, using this to examine how political and communal rivalries even divided the social activities of the Irish capital.

Despite the crippling stamp duty, the number of provincial newspapers slowly increased. Numbers rose from around twenty-five in 1735 to thirty-five by 1760 and over fifty by the early 1780s. By 1830 there were over 150 provincial newspapers in England.[1] However, the provincial press displayed a high casualty rate as the 'taxes on knowledge' meant that newspapers were usually only marginally profitable and most nineteenth-century provincial newspaper proprietors were printers whose first concern was their printing business.[2] Some 130 newspapers were launched outside London between 1701 and 1760 but only around half of them lasted for at least five years. Stamp duty fell from 4d to 1d in 1836 and one of the first newspapers to benefit from this reduction in stamp duty was the well-known Chartist newspaper, the *Northern Star*, which was founded in 1837. This newspaper and the political activities of its founder, Feargus O'Connor, contribute two chapters to this collection. Victoria Clarke takes an original approach to the Chartists' leading newspaper, the *Northern Star*, by exploring how it was used as a tool for the formation and maintenance of radical working-class literary identities in the early Victorian period whilst Helen Williams explores the reasons why Dumfries was the centre of radical print politics in mid-nineteenth-century politics and a major hub of Chartist activity.

The 'taxes on knowledge' were repealed over a period of eight years, with the last tax, that on paper, ending in 1861. Frank Manders described the period from the repeal of stamp duty in 1855 to the First World War as the 'great age' of the provincial newspaper.[3] This 'great age' saw the production of yet more newspapers, with newspaper and periodical titles doubling between 1853 and 1913 (albeit with a considerable underestimate of the total number of publications)[4] as more and more of the population looked to the local newspaper for news of local, national, and international events.

---

1   Donald Read, *Press and People, 1790–1850: Opinions in Three English Cities* (London: Edward Arnold, 1961), 59.
2   Read, *Press and People*, 61.
3   Frank Manders, 'History of the Newspaper Press in Northeast England' in Peter Isaac, ed., *Newspapers in the Northeast: the 'Fourth Estate' at work in Northumberland and Durham* (Richmond: Allenholme Press, 1999), 1–14; 8.
4   Alan Lee, *The Origins of the Popular Press* (London: Croom Helm 1976), 131.

Estimates of the number of *provincial* magazines suggested that these trebled between the 1860s and the 1890s.[5] In 1887 the *Journalist* noted that there were several long-lived provincial journals that rivalled the London press, such as Glasgow's *Bailie*, Liverpool's *Porcupine* (1860–1915) and Manchester's *City Lantern* (later the *City Jackdaw*) (1874–1884).[6] This outburst of print culture provides a wealth of source material that has never really been fully exploited by historians and literary scholars. Most of these publications, at the centre of the vibrant urban life of the Victorian era, lie undisturbed in provincial public libraries, archives and record offices, undigitised, unscanned and unread. One of the editors was amazed to be told by the late Chris Upton, a champion of West Midlands history, that at one point in the 1880s, no fewer than four satirical periodicals appeared every week on the streets of Birmingham. On reading the *Dart*, the *Owl*, the *Town Crier* and the *Gridiron*, he was staggered to discover that they presented a far fuller and richer representation of the political and cultural heart of the Victorian age, the cities of provincial Britain, than any more studies of *Punch* or *The Times* could manage.[7]

With the widespread digitising of certain sections of the press, beginning with the *Times Digital Archive* in 2003, the range of journalism available to the historian, both professional and amateur, has considerably expanded and access to this material has become immeasurably easier. There

---

5   See, for example, Simon Gunn, *The Public Culture of the Victorian Middle Class: Ritual and Authority in the English Industrial City, 1840–1914* (Manchester: Manchester University Press, 2000); Henry Miller, 'The Problem With Punch', *Historical Research*, 82, 216 (2009), 285–302; Aled Jones, 'The *Dart* and the Damning of the Sylvan Stream: Journalism and Political Culture in the Late-Victorian City', *Victorian Periodicals Review*, 35: 1 (2002), 2–17.

6   R. R. Dodds, 'Provincial Humorous and Satirical Journals', *The Journalist*, 20 May 1887, 93–4; John K. Walton, 'Porcupine' in Laurel Brake and Marysa DeMoor, eds, *Dictionary of Nineteenth Century Journalism in Great Britain and Ireland* (Ghent: Academia Press, 2009), 556–7.

7   For the results of this discovery, see Ian Cawood and Chris Upton, 'Joseph Chamberlain and the Birmingham Satirical Journals, 1876–1911' in Ian Cawood and Chris Upton, eds, *Joseph Chamberlain, International Statesman, National Leader and Local Icon* (London: Palgrave, 2016), 176–210.

are still serious methodological problems with the study of the press, of course, not least the relatively limited information regarding the proprietors, the journalists and most of all the readers of the press, which only scholars such as Graham Murdock and Peter Goulding, Martyn Lyons and Philip Waller have attempted to investigate.[8] This issue is not helped by the growth in the satirical press in the nineteenth century, where the anonymity of editors and columnists (but oddly not cartoonists) was established and which persists today in publications such as *Private Eye*. Even in more respectable monthly and quarterly periodicals, it was only in the 1860s that magazines such as *Macmillan's Magazine* and the *Fortnightly Review* began to name all their contributors.[9] Many newspapers also published correspondence under pseudonyms, but this is a problem which, as Victoria Clarke demonstrates in her chapter in this collection, can actually provide some valuable material in the self-identification and the values of a newspaper's readership.[10]

Although much is known about such details for the major London newspapers (and periodicals such as *Punch*), the interactions of the provincial, regional and 'underground' press has remained largely unexplored.[11] The comprehensive *Freshest Advices: Early Provincial Newspapers in*

---

8   Graham Murdock and Peter Goulding, 'The Structure, Ownership and Control of the Press, 1914–1976', in George Boyce, James Curran, Pauline Wingate, eds, *Newspaper History from the Seventeenth Century to the Present Day* (London; Constable, 1978), 130–48; Martyn Lyons, 'New Readers in the Nineteenth Century: Women, Children, Workers', in Guglielmo Cavallo and Roger Chartier, eds, *A History of Reading in the West* (Cambridge: Polity, 1999), 313–44; Philip Waller, *Writers, Readers and Reputations* (Oxford: Oxford University Press, 2006).

9   Matthew Rubery, 'Journalism', in Frank O'Gorman, ed., *Cambridge Companion to Victorian Culture* (Cambridge: Cambridge University Press, 2010), 182.

10   Hannah Barker, 'England, 1760–1815', in Hannah Barker and Simon Burrows, eds, *Press, Politics and the Public Sphere in Europe and North America, 1760–1820* (Cambridge: Cambridge University Press, 2002), 94.

11   There have been more recent scholarly investigations of the press in Britain's dominions and Empire than in its localities. See, for example, Simon J. Potter, *News and the British World: The Emergence of an Imperial Press System* (London: Routledge, 2003); Chandrika Kaul, *Reporting the Raj: The British Press and India, c. 1880–1922* (Manchester: Manchester University Press, 2003); Andrew Griffiths, *The New*

England by R. M. Wiles, which covers the early decades of the English provincial press, is now over fifty years old, whilst *Newspapers, Politics and English Society 1695–1855* by Hannah Barker focused on London-produced newspapers. Early influential print historians, such as Arthur Aspinall, dismissed the provincial press as being of little significance, at least until the middle of the nineteenth century, and the pre-millennium scholarly gazetteer of the Victorian press, Vann and Van Arsdel's *Victorian Periodicals and Victorian Society*, included no references to any of the non-London journals of that period.[12] Even Stephen Koss, usually the most fastidious of historians, asserted that he had neglected the provincial press in his surveys of the political press because they were of little lasting significance.[13] Although not quite as dismissive, the 1986 collection, *The Press in English Society*, edited by Alan Lee and Michael Harris, only included a single chapter on a provincial affair and largely curtailed any analysis of the non-London media to the eighteenth century.[14] The pioneering inter-disciplinary studies of the provincial press by post-war scholars such as Asa Briggs and Donald Read were largely forgotten and left to gather dust on the shelves of academic libraries.[15]

Recent research has largely over-turned this London-centred approach however and confirmed the suggestion of Hannah Barker that in this period 'the provincial press was increasingly neither small scale nor amateurish'.[16] It has discovered that the British public tended to buy local media rather

---

Journalism, the New Imperialism and the Fiction of Empire, 1870–1900 (London: Palgrave, 2015).

12   Arthur Aspinall, *Newspapers, Politics and the Press c. 1780–1850* (London: Home and Van Thal, 1949), 350; J. Don Vann and Rosemary Van Arsdel, *Victorian Periodicals and Victorian Society* (Toronto: University of Toronto Press, 1995).

13   Stephen Koss, *The Rise and Fall of the Political Press in Britain Volume Two: The Twentieth Century* (London: Hamilton, 1984), 3.

14   Michael Harris and Alan Lee, eds, *The Press in English Society from the Seventeenth to Nineteenth Centuries* (London: Associated University Press, 1986).

15   Asa Briggs, *Press and Public in Early Nineteenth-Century Birmingham* (Oxford: Dugdale Society, 1949); Read, *Press and People*.

16   Hannah Barker, *Newspapers, Politics and English Society, 1695–1855* (Harlow: Longman, 2000), 112.

than national media (largely owing to the price, the currency and breadth of the news reported and the appreciation of local perspectives on national questions). Scholars such as Andrew Hobbs at the University of Central Lancashire have managed to correct the previously rather peculiarly lop-sided view of the Victorian political media.[17] As Hobbs has recently proved, there were twice as many provincial than metropolitan newspapers in 1800 and more than three times as many in 1900. They also saw far greater circulation figures than the London press, with a largely unstudied paper such as the *North-Eastern Daily Gazette* regularly outselling *The Times* by over 50 per cent. On this basis Hobbs has suggested that, 'using provincial publications as sources for almost any nineteenth century topic, literary or historical, produces a genuinely national picture, often quite different from work based on narrowly metropolitan sources'.[18] With the arrival of Rachel Matthews' valuable introductory text, the scholarly community might, at long last, finally deign to examine the provincial political press on equal terms with that of the London press. After all, as Matthews points out, 'the London daily papers could hardly claim national circulation'; even as late as the 1950s the 'national' titles produced regional editions from locations outside the capital.[19]

The articles in this collection aim to explore the regional identity of the provincial press, as, even in the studies of the national media, there is little understanding of the complex and changing relations between proprietors, editors and readers, to match those between politicians and journalists, which have been well delineated in a number of studies, largely (but not exclusively) focused on the national histories of Wales, Scotland

17   Andrew Hobbs, 'When the Provincial Press was the National Press (c. 1836–c. 1900)', *International Journal of Regional and Local Studies*, 5 (2009), 16–43; Andrew Hobbs, 'Deleterious Dominance of *The Times* in Nineteenth-Century Historiography', *Journal of Victorian Culture*, 18:4 (2013), 472–97.

18   Andrew Hobbs, 'Provincial Periodicals', in Andrew King, Alexis Easley and John Morton, eds, *The Routledge Handbook to Nineteenth Century British Periodicals and Newspapers* (London: Routledge, 2016), 221–6.

19   Rachel Matthews, *The History of the Provincial Press in England* (London: Bloomsbury, 2017), 21.

and Ireland.[20] From its early beginnings, the provincial newspaper was a political instrument, wielded by Tory- or Whig-supporting printers and publishers before the political parties themselves recognised its power and took to using party funds or enlisting the financial help of supportive aristocrats to establish their own newspapers. Lisa Peters examines one such newspaper, the Conservative-supporting *Wrexham Guardian*, as it sought to prevent the dominance of Gladstone's party in north Wales at the pinnacle of the 'Liberal Ascendancy'. The West Midlands, often overlooked, provides a plethora of examples of the link between print culture, newspapers, and politics. Judith Davies' chapter on the print culture in Dudley during the reform crisis and Sue Thomas' chapter on the press battles between Radicals and Tories in 1830s Birmingham illustrate that there is much yet to be explored in the history of the region before the coming of the 'Civic Gospel'. Equally, James Brennan and Ian Cawood's chapter on the ferocious newspaper battles in West Midlands towns in the years following the First World War offers clear evidence that regional political identities did survive the war, with the local press the chief means of sustaining these. Moving away from political party skirmishes, Paul Wilson looks at two expressions of working-class utopianism in the manufacturing town of Keighley, spiritualism and Esperanto, in the late nineteenth and

20 For recent examples, see Lisa Peters, *Politics, Publishing and Personalities: Wrexham Newspapers, 1848–1914* (Chester: University of Chester, Press 2011); Aled Jones, *Press, Politics and Society: A History of Journalism in Wales* (Cardiff: University of Wales Press, 1993); Marie-Louise Legg, *Newspapers and Nationalism: The Irish Provincial Press, 1850–1892* (Dublin: Four Courts Press, 1999); Kevin Rafter, ed., *Irish Journalism before Independence: More a Disease than a Profession* (Manchester: Manchester University Press, 2011); Alex Benchimol, Rhona Brown and David Shuttleton, eds, *Before Blackwood's: Scottish Journalism in the Age of the Enlightenment* (London: Pickering and Chatto, 2015); Michael Dawson, 'Party Politics and the Provincial Press in Early Twentieth Century England: The Case of the South West', *Twentieth Century British History*, 9:2 (1998), 201–18; Paul Gliddon, 'Politics for Better or Worse: Political Nonconformity, the Gambling Dilemma and the North of England Newspaper Company, 1903–1914', *History*, 286 (2002), 227–44; Jonathan Barry, 'The Press and the Politics of Culture in Bristol, 1660–1775', in Jeremy Black and Jeremy Gregory, eds, *Culture, Politics, and Society in Britain, 1660–1800* (Manchester: Manchester University Press, 1991), 49–81.

early twentieth centuries and how print culture sought to promote the idealism of a 'universal language'.

Different methodologies, a wide variety of sources and a sustained scholarly analysis feature in all the chapters in this collection, offered by a range of established and emerging scholars. Yet all the chapters focus exclusively on the provincial media and they attempt to fulfil Barker's hope that we should 'explain the appeal' of the local press, in light of our rediscovered appreciation of its central position in the lives of the modern British reader and the politics in his or her local environment.[21]

---

21   Barker, *Newspapers, Politics and English Society*, 112.

DUNCAN FRANKIS

1   'That Nefarious Newspaper': The *Dublin Evening Post*, 1789–1794

Within a decade of the outbreak of revolution in France in 1789, there were similar rebellions in Batavia (in the Netherlands), Brabant, Ireland, Scotland, Haiti, Liège and Poland. The simultaneity of these events has led some historians to argue that the French Revolution and the 1798 Irish rebellion were part of a wider revolutionary wave which swept across much of Europe, as well as the Americas, during the second half of the eighteenth century: an *Atlantic*, or *Democratic* revolution.[1] Games, however, highlights that attempts to write a Braudelian Atlantic history that connects the entire region and its revolutions, remain elusive. This is in part due to methodological limitations and disciplinary divisions, as well as the difficulty of finding a point of view that is not limited to a single place.[2] This research explores ways in which to address some of these issues and reveals a new insight into eighteenth-century Irish radicalism and its roots, by examining the content of the *Dublin Evening Post*. Ireland, geographically isolated from mainland Europe, found itself amid the revolutionary climate, but to what extent was it influenced by rebels in other countries? It is too simple to call the phenomena a domino effect; the spreading influence and ideologies of one nation upon another were far more complex. However, it is evident that people in one area of the world had a profound impact upon movements in different regions – separated by land, sea, language and social convention. This work explores the relationship between the

---

1   Hugh Gough and David Dickson, eds, *Ireland and the French Revolution* (Dublin: Irish Academic Press, 1990), 1.

2   Alison Games, 'Atlantic History: Definitions, Challenges, and Opportunities', *American Historical Review*, 111/3 (2006), 741.

French Revolution and Irish radicalism through print culture, using two methods outlined by Armitage: a trans-Atlantic approach to determine the effects of the French Revolution upon the growing dissatisfaction of the Irish nation during the 1790s, and a cis-Atlantic approach to examine the uniqueness of the Irish entity.[3]

The historiography of the 1798 rebellion, its origins, and Irish radicalism has divided academics. Early twentieth-century historians Hayden and Moonan believed that the uprising was fundamentally an insular phenomenon, a result of population increase, an increasingly literate populace and the availability of radical publications.[4] They believed that the existing dissatisfaction regarding living conditions for the working class, and an inherited xenophobic attitude towards the British passed down through generations, created an environment in which radicalism and revolution flourished.[5] These ideas, as well as the belief that Francophobia was never truly absent in Ireland during the eighteenth century,[6] has led many to dismiss the idea that the French Revolution had a significant impact on the rise of Irish radicals. More recently Canny and Beckett have contested this image of an isolated Irish society and placed increased significance upon the influence of French Revolutionary ideals. Beckett argued that, until the importation of French philosophy at the end of the eighteenth century, there was no sign of any political move against the Irish government.[7] Canny attributes the increase in radicalism to 'accident, or the excesses of state, or foreign intervention.'[8] Print culture allows us to test the validity of

---

3   David Armitage, and Michael Braddick, eds, *The British Atlantic World, 1500–1800* (New York: Palgrave MacMillan, 2009), 18.

4   Mary Hayden, and George Moonan, eds, *A Short History of the Irish People from the Earliest Times to 1920* (Dublin: Longmans, Green), 8.

5   Hayden and Moonan, *A Short History of the Irish People*, 8.

6   Gerard O'Brien, 'Francophobia in Later Eighteenth-Century Irish History', in Hugh Gough and David Dickson, eds, *Ireland and the French Revolution* (Dublin: Irish Academic Press, 1990), 47.

7   James Beckett, *The Anglo-Irish Tradition* (London: Faber and Faber, 2008), 82.

8   Nicholas Canny, 'Irish Resistance to Empire? 1641, 1690 and 1798', in Lawrence Stone, ed., *An Imperial State at War: Britain from 1689 to 1815* (London: Routledge, 1994), 316.

these different claims and assess which is more accurate, giving us a greater context and understanding of the 1798 Irish rebellion and its origins.

Studying the hypothetical influence of a heterogeneous revolution upon a collective consciousness provides its own set of challenges: how is it possible to tangibly measure impact? Smyth concludes that the concept of *influence* is too simple, because it implies that there was an importation of ready-made French ideas by Ireland and other countries.[9] However, the absence of a defined consensus should not deter historians from trying to understand the process and influence of French social and political thought. One way to do so is to study print culture, which was crucial in forming public opinion. Ó Ciosáin believes that mass literacy is crucial for large-scale nationalist mobilisation and one of the most significant developments in political history and radicalism is improved literacy. He highlights that the ability to access and understand print culture creates an ideological awareness and identity between communities of similar mentality and interests.[10] The social revolutions that took place in France, the Americas and throughout Europe were presented to the Irish public through newspapers, pamphlets and organised or independent propaganda. These structures of communication allowed for the diffusion of nationalistic sentiments and emphasised the empathetic characteristics of those movements.[11]

Considering the increasingly significant role that that newspapers had in forming and expressing public opinion during the eighteenth century, it is surprising to find that there is an absence of comprehensive studies exploring the relationship between individual Irish newspapers and radicalism in this period. The Irish press was, until recently, a neglected source for historians and students of literature. Now, however, the role of newspapers has been emphasised for research into the development of Irish politics and society. In an introductory essay included in a microfilm collection

9   Jim Smyth, ed., *Revolution, Counter Revolution, and Union, Ireland in the 1790s* (Cambridge: Cambridge University Press, 2000), 15.

10 Niall Ó Ciosáin, *Print and Popular Culture in Ireland, 1750–1850* (London: Macmillan Press, 1997), 185.

11 Louis Cullen, *The Emergence of Modern Ireland, 1600–1900* (New York: Holmes & Meier, 1981), 238.

of Irish newspapers, Legg highlighted the work of Bew, Comerford and Donnelly to elucidate this trend.[12] During the late eighteenth century there was a variety of newspapers that had a sizeable circulation within Ireland, but Powell believed that there is still an over-reliance upon two books regarding the Irish radical press: Inglis's *The Freedom of the Press in Ireland, 1784–1841* and Munter's *The History of the Irish Newspaper, 1685–1760*.[13] Radical newspapers in the late eighteenth century included the *Post*, *The Volunteer's Journal* and the United Irishmen's *Northern Star*. Some of these publications have received academic attention already,[14] which resulted in the choice to research the *Post*, which has received little attention in comparison. Despite generally being ignored by the historiography, Tutty revealed that after 1778 it built up a substantial circulation and believed that it was one of the most influential newspapers in Dublin.[15] The opinion that the newspaper was influential was also the view held by Chief Secretary to Ireland, Robert Peel. In 1813 Peel wrote that 'most of the dissatisfaction in this country arises from the immense circulation of that nefarious paper the *Dublin Evening Post*. It is sent gratuitously into many parts of the country and read by those who can read to those who cannot; and, as it is written with a certain degree of ability, and a style which suits those upon whom it is intended to work, it does, no doubt, great mischief'.[16] The newspaper had a reputation for radical and incendiary views, due to its infamous and eccentric proprietor, John Magee, who had been tried for libel on numerous occasions.[17] An examination of the content of the *Post*

---

12   Mary-Louise Legg, *Ireland: Politics and Society through the Press, 1760–1922* (Andover: Primary Source Microfilm, 2010).

13   Martin Powell, 'The Volunteer Evening Post and Patriotic Print Culture in Late Eighteenth-Century Ireland', in Mark Williams and Stephen Forrest, eds, *Constructing the Past, Writing Irish History, 1600–1800* (Woodbridge: The Boydell Press, 2010), 113.

14   Gillian O'Brien, 'Spirit, Impartiality and Independence: The Northern Star, 1792–1979', *Eighteenth Century Ireland/Iris an dá chultúr* 13/1 (1998), 25.

15   Michael Tutty, 'The Dublin Evening Post 1826', *Dublin Historical Record*, 24/2 (1971), 15.

16   Tutty, 'The Dublin Evening Post', 15.

17   Transcript of *The Trial of John Magee, Proprietor of the Dublin Evening Post, for Publishing an Historical Review of The Duke of Richmond's Administration in Ireland* (Dublin, 26 July 1813).

during the French Revolution will show how it covered events and how its stance changed over time.

To understand the significance of the *Post's* reaction to events in France some context to the newspaper's pre-revolution content must first be established. In 1789 the newspaper was published three times a week (Tuesday, Thursday and Saturday) and was structured similarly in each issue. The front page consisted of various advertisements, infrequently there would be a local story, but most issues would save news for the second, third and fourth pages. There was a maximum of five pages in total. The *Post* was noticeably insular in its content with foreign news usually being restricted to a few columns in each edition. French affairs were rarely mentioned in the first half of 1789 and most of the international news coverage was concerned with the Russo-Swedish War and Russia's ongoing tension with the Ottoman Empire. These issues were covered with an air of indifference however, with little interest or consequence connected to Ireland. The newspaper was predominantly concerned with local politics, events and smear campaigns against rival newspapers, most notably the *Freeman's Journal*. The penultimate pages were mainly dedicated to miscellaneous advertisements for books, wholesale items and fashions. The final page consisted of a section entitled 'The Postscript', which contained a variety of opinion pieces from the consistently nationalistic public. Not all contributions were positive regarding the French Revolution, but inflammatory rhetoric against frameworks of government became more frequent. This section was unpredictable and varied, containing risqué, salacious letters sent in from a wide spectrum of individuals. However, liberty, constitutionalism, and Irish freedom were regular themes to be found in the Postscript. The Postscript was an open forum in which radical thoughts, musings and grievances were presented to the reader for interpretation. The *Post's* content prior to the French Revolution supports the vision of an insular Ireland, as depicted by Moonan and Hayden. Articles under the title of *The Irish Revolutionist* and *Friends of this Independent Nation* were published, and Irish socio-politics was the dominant topic, as well as an open disdain for the British government. The nefarious, meddlesome and manipulative image referred to by Peel is evidently not an inaccurate statement. If read to the uneducated, ill-informed or easily convinced, it is easy to see the effect it could have and how far reaching its influence could be. The standard of writing was generally relatively high and produced by seemingly well-educated authors: vocabulary was broad and complicated subject matters were analysed in detail. However, the content was still accessible and clear, but also undeniably manipulative and biased, twisting facts and events to fit an agenda. The vague talk of conspiracies and the British threat were rarely specific, and the *Post* failed to offer practical suggestions to achieve democracy. Romanticized visions of social revolution were included alongside passages about liberty, constitution, the rights of man and the freedom of the press. This research traces the opinion of the *Post* as the grim realities of revolution were revealed throughout continental Europe and the Atlantic World.

Gough proposed that there were distinct periods of the relationship between non-French revolutionaries and the French Revolution: beginning with initial enthusiasm until April 1792 and the French invasion of Austria, followed by hostility until the summer of 1793, culminating in fear following the rise of the Jacobins.[18] The concept is at odds with the idea of a revolutionary or democratic wave, suggesting that the spread of Revolutionary France beyond its own borders may have eventually acted as a deterrent. A study of the *Post* tests the validity of this concept in Ireland through a micro-history focused on its coverage. Upon the outbreak of revolution, the theory holds weight, the pages of the newspaper were flooded with overwhelmingly supportive and enthusiastic coverage. The *Post* declared that the men of the National Assembly were the 'ablest men of one of the most enlightened nations in the universe'.[19] A change in content and structure took place within the pages of the *Post* quickly after the convening of the Estates-General. Coverage of events in France increased throughout July 1789 and by August there was not a page untouched by articles entitled 'Affairs in France', 'National Assembly' or simply 'Paris'. The French Revolution dominated the newspaper, which was a stark change from regional stories and advertisements. The storming of the Bastille was first reported in July 1789 and, following the events, seven consecutive editions of the paper had their front page dedicated

18   Gough, *Ireland the French Revolution*, 1–14.
19   *Dublin Evening Post*, 6 August 1789.

to coverage of Parisian news. The newspaper revelled in the fall of the political elite and nobility of France, as well as the clergy. Criticism of the 'lofty pretensions'[20] of the nobility and derision of the 'plump, pampered'[21] clergymen quickly become prominent themes, and parallels were drawn to Irish society. Kearny concluded that French Revolution of 1789 was ready for exportation.[22] It is evident from the beginning of the Revolution that the *Post* was enthusiastic about a variety of the supposed universal ideas stemming from France.

The repealing of the Navigation Acts in 1779 and new Corn Laws in 1784 had led to a brief boom in the Irish economy,[23] which had led to some stability for the population (although mainly the land-owning classes), as well as a trend towards leniency for the Catholic and Gaelic elements of the population. Despite this, the universalism of the ideas stemming from the Revolution in France evidently provoked the writers at the *Post* to recall the famine of the 1740s, religious sectarianism and the unequal distribution of taxation. The newly formed National Assembly's debates on topics such as clerical tithes and nobility privileges were all printed in detail and reignited old grievances were discussed in the *Post*:

> The National Assembly of France, have in an early instance of their revolutionary system, shown a proper sense of the intolerable burden of Clerical Tithes on the people, and they have therefore suppressed them [...] they wisely see the oppressions under which other countries labour, and are resolved to prevent them in their own [...] the Roman Catholics of this country, who form nine tenths of the peasantry, look with eagerness to the establishment of peace and good order.[24]

20   *Dublin Evening Post*, 6 June 1789.
21   *Dublin Evening Post*, 12 September 1789.
22   Richard Kearny, 'The Irish Heritage of the French Revolution: The Rights of the People and the Rights of Man', in Patrick Rafroidi, Barbara Hayley, and Christopher Murray, eds, *Ireland and France, a Bountiful Friendship: Literature, History and Ideas* (New York: Barnes & Noble, 1992), 30.
23   Eric Evans, *The Forging of the Modern State: Early Industrial Britain, 1783–1870* (New York: Routledge, 2013), 118.
24   *Dublin Evening Post*, 27 August 1789.

Some of the main themes developed within the *Post* in the early months of the French Revolution included the need for reform within the Church's hierarchy, particularly with regards to the collection of clerical tithes. The importance of the freedom of the press was evident, as was the need to reform corrupt law enforcement, as well as the need to reform taxation systems. These aims mirrored many of the French revolutionaries' goals. The newspaper demonstrated an open disdain for many judicial bodies within Ireland and saw the National Assembly as a beacon of hope and proof that legitimate change was possible: 'We see in France at this moment, after overturning the idols of political superstition, and bursting the shackles of oppression, gradually subsiding from the anarchy ever attendant on great and sudden revolutions, into a constitutional grandeur that promises to become the astonishment and admiration of the earth'.[25] Comparing revolutionary France to Ireland, the authors of the *Post* asked their readership: 'what do we behold at this moment in this country? – A system of bribery and corruption, of interest and influence of tyranny, and oppression; of cruelty and injustice, set up in opposition to the sacred principles on which alone the basis of our constitution can be secured'.[26]

It is evident that the *Post* believed the French Revolution to be the beginning of a global movement, regularly referencing the interconnectedness of the international community, a theme which is vital to the historiography of the Atlantic World.[27] The writers of the *Post* seemed convinced that revolution would reach the shores of Ireland, and they welcomed it wholeheartedly. In August 1789 they adopted, and continued to use, a metaphor for the spreading revolutionary vigour to be found in the Atlantic World, taking inspiration from another revolutionary country the *Post* used Benjamin Franklin's studies of electricity as an allegoric device commenting that 'The spirit of Liberty which appeared so conspicuous in America, seems as if conveyed to them by that philosophical Franklin's electrical fire ... The French, while assisting them, caught the glowing flame [...] it is likely

---

25   *Dublin Evening Post*, 17 September 1789.
26   *Dublin Evening Post*, 17 September 1789.
27   Eliga Gould, 'Revolution and Counter-Revolution', in Armitage and Braddick, eds, *The British Atlantic World, 1500–1800*, 214.

to diffuse itself through all despotic monarchies of Europe'.[28] Historians may debate the extent to which the Atlantic revolutions were connected, but it is evident that at least some contemporaries in Ireland had already drawn parallels between similar movements.

The electricity metaphor continued to be used throughout 1789 to track revolutionary movements outside of France. In December it was reported that the French sparks of liberty are 'beginning to kindle up a blaze, in the very heart of Spain [...] Corsica has declared itself independent'.[29] The *Post's* view that the French Revolution influenced events in Corsica has been reiterated in recent studies as well; Ramsay argued that the taking of the Bastille in July 1789 was the first revolutionary event to influence Corsicans, highlighting how there was a spontaneous outburst of enthusiasm when news reached the island.[30] In 1790 the *Post* covered the revolution in Brabant as well, which made front page news. Before the French Revolution, the Austrian-Netherlands (modern-day Belgium) had received little more than a paragraph dedicated to it. Reports of the Brabant Patriots' struggles against the Holy Roman Emperor, Joseph II, and his Imperial army in Brussels contained obvious bias in support of the Brabant rebels with allegations of atrocities against the civilian population by Austrian forces.[31] The language used when referring to the opposing sides in Belgium was both manipulative and brazenly partisan in support of the rebel patriots: 'though liberty may be finally triumphant, it is inconceivable that the Emperor will abandon these fine provinces [...] the opposition of well-disciplined troops, and experienced generals, to a numerous body of raw forces, supported by a generous spirit of freedom, must inevitably produce a frightful contest'.[32] Polasky concluded that the revolutionary movements in Brabant came as a surprise to the rest of Europe and caused more shock when the Belgian army succeeded in driving the Austrian troops from their

---

28 *Dublin Evening Post*, 6 August 1789.
29 *Dublin Evening Post*, 10 December 1789.
30 Robert Ramsay, *The Corsican Time Bomb* (Manchester: Manchester University Press, 1983), 7.
31 *Dublin Evening Post*, 2 January 1790.
32 *Dublin Evening Post*, 2 January 1790.

provinces.[33] Movements such as the Brabant and Corsican revolutions were covered in great detail by the newspaper and cemented the *Post's* belief that a diffusion of revolutionary ideas was spreading and, against all odds, was becoming successful. The coverage of these events directly contradicts the idea that Irish radicalism was isolated and unaffected by international mechanisms. It is evident the *Post* saw the spread of revolutions throughout Europe as inevitable, concluding that 'the era of perfect liberty seems to be fast approaching [...] it is now a question among politicians, which of the nations in Europe will be first to imitate the example of France by a total demolition of those feudal tenures which ignorance and folly have represented as essential to human society'.[34]

If Gough's model regarding Europe's relationship with the French Revolution is correct, the initial enthusiasm of 1789 should have continued throughout 1790 and 1791 and begun to diminish in 1792 as French internal violence continued to escalate.[35] The *Post* however, remained enthusiastic about the French Revolution until at least 1794, but the accuracy of the coverage became increasingly unreliable, unclear and fragmented. Several challenges to the French Revolution emerged throughout 1790–1794, such as the role of Louis XVI, foreign aggression and the divisions between revolutionary movements but despite the difficulties facing French revolutionaries, the *Post* remained optimistic amid the chaotic scenes in France. In fact, much of the bloodshed and anarchy was omitted entirely, a tactic many revolutionary sympathisers, such as Rudé have used (during the Revolution and in retrospect).[36] It is impossible to gauge if the *Post* implemented a similar tactic, ignoring the worst qualities of revolutionary France for the sake of their own argument, but there seemed to be a tangible softening of coverage for violent events attributed to French revolutionaries. Many

---

33   Janet Polasky, 'Women in Revolutionary Brussels: The Source of Our Greatest Strength', in Harriet Applewhite, and Darline Levy, eds, *Women and Politics in the Age of the Democratic Revolution* (Flint: The University of Michigan Press, 1993), 148.
34   *Dublin Evening Post*, 21 October 1790.
35   Gough, *Ireland the French Revolution*, 1–14.
36   Ferenc Feher, *The French Revolution and the Birth of Modernity* (Berkeley, CA: University of California Press, 1990), 157.

violent events committed in the name of the Revolution were treated by
sections of the French population, as well as the *Post*, with indifference,
such as the slaughter of prisoners and violence against the Roman Catholic
Church in August and September 1792.[37] The death of 250 prisoners in
one Parisian prison received as much coverage by the *Post* as the arrest of
a local Dublin handkerchief thief in the same issue: both stories receiving
one column each.[38]

The most controversial element of the French Revolution was unargu-
ably the execution of Louis XVI and, given Louis' liberal use of his veto
prerogative to block the Legislative Assembly's progress, as well as the Old
Regime which he represented, it would be easy to assume that the *Post*
would be critical of the monarch. However, coverage of the deteriorating
relationship between king and executive body was unpredictable, if not
surprisingly sporadic. The newspaper even on occasions defended the king,
one time concluding that: 'the will of the king is an integral part of the constitution in such circumstances, and ministers must respect it, or despise the
constitution.'[39] It is clear that constitutionalism was of the utmost importance to the *Post*, but there was a difficult paradox that existed regarding
the Constitution of 1791; it was bound to collapse because the king wanted
it to, but removing the king from it could also destroy it.[40] The *Post* had
supported the National Constituent Assembly and continued to support
the Legislative Assembly through their relationship with the king, and one
evening it reported with joy that 'the session of this evening was one of the
most splendid that has lately marked the progress of the Assembly. At its
opening a deputation from the foreign residents in Paris, the Irish, English,
Dutch ... presented their address of congratulations to the Assembly, on the
success of its labours, and in the prospect which it opened to the human
race, of a new era of happiness and freedom.'[41] Despite the progress that

37   Patrice Higonnet, *Goodness Beyond Virtue: Jacobins During the French Revolution*
      (Boston, MA: Harvard University Press, 1998), 37.
38   *Dublin Evening Post*, 15 September 1792.
39   *Dublin Evening Post*, 10 July 1792.
40   C. J. Mitchell, *The French Legislative Assembly of 1791* (Leiden: E. J. Brill, 1988), 208.
41   *Dublin Evening Post*, 3 June 1790.

had been made by the Assembly, the constitutional monarchy failed and upon the execution of Louis XVI the *Post* responded with delight, reporting that 'Yesterday evening the cause of liberty received a most honourable testimony of approbation from the citizens of Dublin. The expulsion of Despots and Despotism from France had been for some time a favourite wish of those people ... Ample testimony at the general joy at the great events that have established liberty in France'.[42] Regardless of the victory for freedom, the *Post* was not without sympathy for Louis however, referring to him as an unfortunate victim to a greater cause at the hands of an 'exasperated people'.[43] Despite the *Post*'s earlier assertion that Louis XVI was an integral part of the constitution he was quickly forgotten in the coverage of events and contradiction became increasingly common. In the same week, or same issue on occasions, completely paradoxical accounts of Paris were included. In September 1792 'deplorable'[44] social unrest was covered simultaneously to reports of 'perfect tranquillity in Paris'.[45] The newspaper struggled to produce a clear and consistent picture of events in France in 1792 and 1793, possibly because, as Morris believed, 'radicalism was born of paradox, sustained by paradox, and in the end, confounded by paradox [...] a selective memory invested this tradition'.[46] Despite this throughout the most controversial and violent aspects of the search for French constitutionalism the *Post* was still overwhelmingly supportive of Revolutionary France past Gough's suggested 1792 date.[47]

There could be several reasons for such contradictory and fragmented reports: selective memory, possibly because of the individual internal conflicts of the authors, or confusion surrounding the rapidly changing events in France. Another factor must be considered however: following the outbreak of war with Austria there was a physical breakdown in

---

42   *Dublin Evening Post*, 31 January 1793.
43   *Dublin Evening Post*, 31 January 1793.
44   *Dublin Evening Post*, 15 September 1792.
45   *Dublin Evening Post*, 15 September 1792.
46   Anthony Morris, *Edwardian Radicalism: Some Aspects of British Radicalism* (London: Routledge, 1974), 2.
47   Gough, *Ireland the French Revolution*, 1–14.

communication between Ireland and continental Europe. This may account for the continued enthusiasm for revolutionary France in Ireland, whilst the rest of Europe's revolutionaries became disillusioned. Rossides believed that with radicalism, the role of communication was evidently significant but difficult to determine exactly how and why.[48] The enormous expansion of the European economy had generated new kinds of individuals and had thrown them together, but they remained geographically separate, which created miscommunication and confusion. It was reported in the *Post* that 'the stoppage of all intercourse between France and these Kingdoms through Dover and Calais packet boats, has caused great consternation in the commercial, and great surmises in the political'.[49] The newspaper received various accounts of what was occurring in Europe and was forced to concede that 'the French and Austrian Generals send contradictory accounts of actions, of which there were many thousands of witnesses in both armies to contradict whatever is wrong in either statement'.[50] This led to numerous amendments and clarifications being produced within the newspaper. As time passed and hostilities between England and France heightened, a complete breakdown in communications occurred. This added fuel to the fire that was anti-British sentiment. Despite regular communication problems it becomes evident that whatever sources the *Post* used for its information, there was an inclination to trust French information over others. The Austrians were regularly referred to as *enemies* and derogatory language was used to undermine the quality of writing within Austrian newspapers as shown by the *Post*'s comment that 'the following article, from the Austrian Gazette, published at Brussels, is evidently garbled'.[51] In contrast, information obtained from the French military was optimistic and complimentary: 'our accounts from the French army contain little news, but give us great hopes of news; and we are as impatient as if no

48 Daniel Rossides, *Communication, Media, and American Society: A Critical Introduction* (London: Rowman & Littlefield, 2003), 31.
49 *Dublin Evening Post*, 2 April 1793.
50 *Dublin Evening Post*, 23 June 1792.
51 *Dublin Evening Post*, 9 June 1792.

news is good news were not peculiarly applicable to our situation.'[52] Even when news was difficult to piece together, the *Post* continued to support the French Revolution and described information from the French military as 'wisdom for the ages'.[53]

Despite its continued support for revolution, there was an increasing amount of frustration evident within the writings of the *Post*. Constitutionalism seemed unworkable and several revolutionary movements had failed entirely. McDowell believed that whilst it is evident that many people in Ireland sympathised with the objectives, and methods, of the Atlantic and continental revolutions, it is also clear that the French Revolution provoked some feelings of trepidation.[54] This apprehension is not present in the Postscript of the *Post*, but if there were members of the public who were concerned about events in France the *Post* could do little to alleviate their fears.

Many of the revolutions occurring were failing or being brutally suppressed. The new French government struggled to find a constitution that universally satisfied their people, and in the Polish-Lithuanian Commonwealth, efforts by the laity to shake the nobility out of its mental cul-de-sac had failed.[55] The Brabant Revolution became contained as well and coverage of it began to dwindle, failed revolutions received little attention in the *Post*. It was replaced with enthusiasm and encouragement for unrest in Switzerland and constitutional reform in the Polish-Lithuanian Commonwealth. Regular updates from Warsaw appeared in the *Post* and the 1791 May Constitution was received positively by the newspaper. The *Post* lauded that 'this new constitution of Poland totally changes its Government, by wresting the destructive sword of power out of the irregular hands of a turbulent Nobility, whose contentions, at every new election of a King, preserved a continual civil warfare in the bowels of the Kingdom;

52   *Dublin Evening Post*, 25 September 1792.
53   *Dublin Evening Post*, 25 September 1792.
54   Robert McDowell, *Irish Public Opinion, 1750–1800* (London: Faber and Faber, 1975), 149.
55   Jerzy Lukowski, *Disorderly Liberty: The Political Culture of the Polish-Lithuanian Commonwealth Constitution* (London: Continuum, 2010), 255.

and to whom the greatest part of the country people, farmers, as well as labourers, were in a state of pure vassalage'.[56] Despite the enthusiasm for the Polish-Lithuanian Commonwealth and its search for a constitution, the nation was ruthlessly crushed by the forces of Russia.

Whilst the coverage of violence by revolutionaries had been limited, those who suppressed revolutions were depicted by the *Post* as monsters: Catherine the Great received some of the most scathing criticism: 'to some it might have been sufficient, to have ascended a throne on the removal of a husband; to have reigned over a numerous people, and to have kept even a son, long after his arrival to manhood, out of inheritance belonging to him [...] but ambition must be fed, if not satisfied'.[57] The newspaper covered the destruction of Poland's constitution by Russia with anxiety: 'the fact is atrocious; but the precedent is alarming. In the ruin of one helpless inoffensive nation, the other states of Europe [...] ought to see an example and a warning of the principles and practice of ambition, which they may experience in their turn'.[58] Whilst the *Post* had welcomed the spread of revolutionary vigour, there was also a fear of the threat from foreign despots intervening in other country's affairs. The parallels between Catherine's relationship with the Polish-Lithuanian Commonwealth and Oliver Cromwell's treatment of Ireland were clear.[59] Esdaile concluded that Russia's stranglehold over Poland meant that Catherine was able to maintain the archaic social and political structure that reduced the latter to a de facto Russian protectorate.[60] This familiar relationship with an oppressive external threat struck a nerve with the newspaper, as fear grew that perhaps the spread of revolution was not certain after all.

The *Post*'s obvious dislike of absolutist monarchs intensified throughout the early 1790s and absolutism was portrayed as the single greatest threat to liberty and constitutional reform. When Gustav III of Sweden was assassinated, the *Post* declared that 'those who will compare the history

---

56 *Dublin Evening Post*, 2 August 1792.
57 *Dublin Evening Post*, 26 July 1792.
58 *Dublin Evening Post*, 18 October 1792.
59 *Dublin Evening Post*, 20 October 1792.
60 Charles Esdaile, *The French Wars 1792–1815* (London: Routledge, 2001), 5.

and constitution of Sweden with the conduct of Gustav the Third, will
not wonder at the misfortune which has befallen him'.[61] Bisztray highlighted the manner of Gustav's death, which provided much amusement
around the continent, including within the *Post*: 'Ironically in tune with
the murder of Gustav III in his beloved Opera at a masquerade ball, the
King's excessive preoccupation with roles and individuals foreshadowed
a more conscious utilisation of romantic irony'.[62] The *Post* revelled in the
failure of monarchs and became noticeably bolder and more critical in its
views as revolutions became more frequent (and unsuccessful). The radicalisation of an already radical publication is evident to the reader, and as
the relationship between the oppressed laity and the absolutist oppressors
developed in continental Europe, comparisons were drawn between the
Irish and the English: 'are our improvements in constitution owing to our
intercourse with England? No – she had reduced our legislative assembly
to the rank of a colonial council [...] to our intercourse with Britain we
owe an immense annual drain, by which our country is exhausted to support absentee landlords in the luxuries of a foreign court'.[63] The revolutions
throughout Europe, as well as the behaviour of authoritarian monarchs,
governments and regimes were clearly, and tangibly stirring anti-British
sentiment in radical sections of the Irish population. The widely distributed
Post continued to print incendiary coverage of British rule: 'Reports of a
coalition of parties in England, and a consequent change of Administration
in this country, become more and more strong [...] what party forever rules
in Britain – ENGLISH SUPREMECY [*sic*] will still be the object of the
ruling party here'.[64]

Of all the revolutions that took place in the 1790s, there was only one
that did not receive support from the *Post*, that of the French Caribbean
colony of Saint Domingo. Davis concluded that the Haitian Revolution
'evoked little applause from whites, even those who rejoiced over European

---

61   *Dublin Evening Post*, Thursday, 26 April 1792.
62   George Bisztray, 'Romantic Trends in Scandinavian Drama', in Gerald Gillespie, ed.,
       Romantic Drama (Amsterdam: John Benjamins Publishing Company, 1994), 317.
63   *Dublin Evening Post*, 23 August 1792.
64   *Dublin Evening Post*, 17 November 1792.

and Latin American movements on national liberation'.[65] When reading the *Post* this assertion seems to be accurate; the enthusiasm extended to Corsican, Brabantian and Polish revolutionaries is noticeably absent with regards to the Haitian rebels. The death sentences enforced by the French government on the revolutionaries were covered with scorn for the slaves: 'The two leaders of the disturbances in St Domingo have been broke on the wheel, and nearly 200 of their misguided adherents have received sentence of death'.[66] Articles from the *Jamaican Royal Gazette* were published in May 1791, and provided a stark contrast with the usual support for revolutionary movements: 'These unhappy wretches considered as the leaders of the rebellion at Hispaniola, are condemned to terminate their existence on the gallows'.[67] Before the French Revolution, however, the *Post* had described the slave trade as 'disgraceful to humanity'.[68] The negative effect the Haitian Revolution had upon Revolutionary France appeared to have had a significant effect on public opinion in Ireland. Davis hypothesises that the Haitian Revolution reinforced the belief that slave emancipation in any form would lead to economic turmoil and the massacre of white populations.[69] Whether the authors of the *Post* feared massacre is unknown, but the concern over economic turmoil was evident: 'Nothing can exceed the consternation which this news has raised among the trading people in France; for St Domingo was by much the richest settlement in the West Indies; and the produce of sugar, cotton, and indigo, which is sent to France, was immense – The value of the articles destroyed, will be felt most heavily in that Kingdom, and in some respects, all over Europe'.[70] Despite this claim, Rodgers highlighted that although many Irishmen had connections with slavery, very little of the slave trade profits actually stimulated the Irish economy or significantly increased

---

65   David Davis, *Inhuman Bondage: The Rise and Fall of Slavery in the New World* (Oxford: Oxford University Press, 2006), 159.

66   *Dublin Evening Post*, 10 May 1791

67   *Dublin Evening Post*, 14 May 1791.

68   *Dublin Evening Post*, 23 May 1789.

69   Davis, *Inhuman Bondage: The Rise and Fall of Slavery in the New World*, 158.

70   *Dublin Evening Post*, 19 November 1791.

the wealth of many individuals residing in Ireland.[71] The economic justi-
fication for a lack of sympathy to the plight of the Haitian slave populace
underlines a specific support for European revolution, not the spread of
universal rebellion. Despite this the similar aims of the Haitian people to
Irish radicals is evident in a speech printed in the *Post* by '*one of the negro
leaders*'.[72] His address attacks the same oppressive regimes, and unequal
systems of social governance that the *Post* had criticised extensively: 'We
have heard our masters for years exhort us to obedience. They have told
us, that all men cannot be Governors, though all that govern should be
good – Some, therefore, must necessarily command, and the rest obey. Our
masters have taken our powers into their service, until our sweat has been
blood [...] we obeyed, for so they told us did they themselves have master,
the Great King'.[73] The irony is evident, the spread of French revolutionary vigour that the *Post* had been championing had crossed the Atlantic
and was having an unexpectedly detrimental effect on France, and in turn
Ireland. However, more so than despotic monarchs or slave rebellions,
the revolutionaries within France began to provide a problem for the pro-
French Revolution newspaper.

Mcllwain concluded that the incompetence of constitutional governments in Europe led to their replacements by despotism. He argued that
weak leadership was no guarantee of constitutionalism, in fact it was usually
the cause of its failure.[74] The rise of the Jacobins in the political vacuum following the death of Louis and the trial of the Girondins mirrored a familiar
European tyranny that tarnished the reputation of French revolutionaries
for many foreign sympathisers. Gough's theory that the non-French radicals'
enthusiasm for the French Revolution had turned to hostility in 1792,[75]
proved to be inaccurate with regards to the *Post*. However, his assertion

71   Nini Rodgers, *Ireland, Slavery and Anti-Slavery, 1612–1865* (New York: Palgrave
     MacMillan, 2007), 390.
72   *Dublin Evening Post*, 31 July 1790.
73   *Dublin Evening Post*, 31 July 1790.
74   Charles Mcllwain, *Constitutionalism: Ancient and Modern* (New York: The Lawbook
     Exchange, 2006), 127.
75   Gough, *Ireland the French Revolution*, 1–14.

that by 1794 there was a universal fear of the Jacobins[76] proves to be more accurate. Whilst not fearing the Jacobins, the *Post* became disillusioned with the Jacobin Committee of Public Safety and was vocal in its criticism of Robespierre. It was printed that he was 'born without genius, could not create circumstances, but profited by them [...] to the profound hypocrisy of Cromwell, he joined Sylla, without possessing any of the great military and political qualities of either'.[77] It is important to note however, the criticism of the French Revolutionary government in 1793–1794 did not discourage the newspaper from being pro-revolution. There was a distinction made between the Jacobins and the Revolution, which were portrayed as two separate entities, and the *Post* urged that fear of the Jacobins should not allow revolutionary vigour to dwindle in Ireland. Throughout the height of the violence, republicanism (not specifically French Republicanism, however) was still championed: 'The debates of the Convention serve to illustrate the true position of the country, and from them we learn that the jealousies between the parties remain in all their violence; but though they tear one another like tigers they most [*sic*] cordially agree in the measures necessary to preserve the Republic'.[78]

For the majority of 1793 the *Post* rarely addressed the escalating violence, or political assassinations and executions, until the executions of Charlotte Corday and Marie Antoinette which caused a change in attitude. Corday was hailed by the *Post* as a 'heroic woman'[79], which described her trial in romanticised overtones: 'none but spectators of this assisting scene can conceive the majestic picture of the immortal Corday – who for a perfect sense of rectitude and independent spirit deliberately sacrificed her own life for what she conceived would be the redemption of her country – and enlighten the seduced minds of those wretches who adhered to the seditious doctrines of Marat'.[80] Marat, the radical journalist she had murdered, could have been seen as a natural ally to the *Post*, but his Jacobin sympathies left

76   Gough, *Ireland the French Revolution*, 1–14.
77   *Dublin Evening Post*, 4 September 1794.
78   *Dublin Evening Post*, 25 May 1793.
79   *Dublin Evening Post*, 15 August 1793.
80   *Dublin Evening Post*, 15 August 1793.

him exposed to criticism and he was depicted as a traitor to the Revolution. The execution of Marie Antoinette, received similar coverage, according to information the *Post* received from Brussels marked 12 October: 'the day before yesterday arrived a courier, with the melancholy news, that the ill-fated French Queen has been immolated by her tyrants'.[81] Whilst this information can be proved erroneous in retrospect (her execution was not until the 16 October), the reaction to the news was overwhelmingly critical of the French government. The *Post* reported that 'thus died, by the hands of the most relentless monsters, Marie Antoinette, of Austria and Lorraine'.[82] The executions proved to be a turning point in the *Post's* coverage of the French Revolution.

It is evident from the coverage of the trials of Marie Antoinette and Corday that the newspaper saw the trials as unfair and corrupt: 'Kings and placemen are not yet satisfied, and the country is to be drained to the last [...] to indulge the insatiable lust after power. Jacobin extermination is therefore the order of the day for some time longer ... to prevent the revival of the Bastille or inquisition – and in the end to secure themselves the blessings of a free constitution, and the benefit of a trial by an honest jury'.[83] The pre-determined trials in France drew parallels with the 1781 suspension of Habeas Corpus in Ireland: 'The suspension of the Habeas Corpus Act having recently taken place – we lay before the Public the following sketch of it – The purpose of this Act will easily appear to have been that of securing this subject against the attacks of power, without it he can have no security for his freedom – nothing to protect him against the most wicked and wanton persecutions'.[84] Hussain highlighted the significance of Habeas Corpus and its implications upon a society by concluding that 'whether in its origins as a facilitation of sovereign power or in its subsequent and modern guise as a check on the executive, whether used to intern or to free, habeas corpus is a mode of binding

---

81   *Dublin Evening Post*, 31 October 1793.
82   *Dublin Evening Post*, 9 November 1793.
83   *Dublin Evening Post*, 17 July 1794.
84   *Dublin Evening Post*, 29 May 1794.

subjects to the law and to its economies of power'.[85] The judicial bodies of Ireland, influenced by the English, or the Jacobin zeal for execution in France were both expressions of oppression, and as a result the Jacobin party began to represent everything the newspaper had always criticised. The conduct of the Jacobins drew comparisons to the Old Regime that the revolutionaries were in theory fighting: 'The vast numbers of men of great property who either emigrated or fell by the guillotine, or in the insurrections against the convention, have thrown an immense mass of property into the hands of those that rule the nation'.[86] In the eyes of the *Post* the Jacobins had failed to replace oppression, decadence and corruption with a representational constitution. It was the trials of the Committee of Public Safety that ended the *Post*'s enthusiasm for the French Revolutionary political groups.

Puntscher-Riekmann argued that since the eighteenth century, constitutionalism has relied on the public to legitimise the political order created by representative bodies, that in turn must demonstrate that their product bears the imprint of the people.[87] The Jacobins had failed to represent the people, and as a result the *Post*'s support for French politics had found its limits. For them the systematic execution of political opponents resembled the tyranny it had replaced. Despite the newspaper losing faith in the French Revolution, the Revolution had galvanized it into publishing years of coverage championing revolutionary ideas, anti-British sentiment and Irish nationalism. The *Post* had remained optimistic throughout the failure of revolutions in Brabant and Poland, throughout the execution of a monarch, through the slave rebellion against France in St Domingo. Even after the rise of the Jacobins the newspaper continued to support people fighting oppressive rulers (whoever they may be): 'The people of France act upon principles of which they never lose sight – parties may

85   Nasser Hussain, *The Jurisprudence of Emergency: Colonialism and the Rule of Law* (Flint: The University of Michigan Press, 2009), 70.

86   *Dublin Evening Post*, 5 December 1793.

87   Sonja Puntscher-Riekmann, 'Constitutionalism and Representation', in Petra Dobner and Martin Loughlin, eds, *The Twilight of Constitutionalism?* (Oxford: Oxford University Press, 2010), 121.

destroy each other but they will always act with regard to LIBERTY AND EQUALITY'.[88] Ireland had unique socio-political circumstances that may have led to rebellion, but, when reading the newspapers of the time, the French Revolution was evidently a catalyst that brought old tensions to the forefront of the national political consciousness. The provincial press of Dublin provided the people of Ireland with a window into a radical new world order, and within four years of 1794 Ireland would begin a rebellion of its own.

88   *Dublin Evening Post*, 23 August 1794.

JUDITH DAVIES

2   A 'Paper War': John Rann, George Walters and the Political Print Culture in Dudley, Worcestershire, c. 1814–1832

This chapter examines the political, religious and social changes that affected Dudley in the decades following the end of the Napoleonic wars. By studying the effects of these changes, it is hoped that it will be possible to build a micro-history of Dudley that extends our understanding of regional and national developments. In particular, this chapter concentrates on the struggle between 'reaction' and 'reform' and shows that, with print media becoming increasingly available to both sides, the reform agitation took the form of a 'paper war'.[1] The discussion centres on the work of two printers from opposite sides of the argument. John Rann was credited with being the first man to start printing in Dudley in about 1788 and he soon became the printer for the town's establishment.[2] On the other side of the political divide was George Walters, who operated as a printer in Dudley for thirty-eight years (c. 1812–1850). He was described by George Barnsby, the Marxist historian, as 'a radical publisher who deserves further study'.[3] Yet, one of the questions to be asked about Walters is whether he was himself a radical or merely printed radical material for others. This chapter addresses that question and considers the work of both printers in the context of the upheavals that threatened the town's status quo.

1   The expression 'paper war' was used by George Walters. The National Archives (TNA), George Walters, Affidavit to the Court of King's Bench, 1820, TS 11/80/253.
2   *Staffordshire Advertiser*, 28 January 1854, 5; British Book Trade Index (BBTI), Rann, John (1788–1819), <http://bbti.bodleian.ox.ac.uk>, accessed 17 January 2018.
3   George J. Barnsby, *The Dudley Working Class Movement, 1750 to 1860* (Dudley: Dudley Leisure Services, 1986), 9.

It also analyses the main protagonists who were exploiting print on both sides of the divide. It considers their contribution to key moments in the controversy and shows how the post-Napoleonic situation in Dudley, both reflected and inter-connected with wider regional and national events.

In common with the rest of the Black Country, Dudley had expanded with the development of its coal and iron industries but, despite its growing population, the town offered little opportunity for popular politics.[4] Its only parliamentary representation was as part of the two-member Worcestershire constituency. The local aristocrats, the Ward family, remained powerful and the only local government came from self-perpetuating oligarchies such as the Court Leet and the Town Commissioners, both dominated by a Tory hierarchy of major industrialists and Anglican clergymen. Chief among the latter was the vicar of Dudley, Reverend Luke Booker, a formidable opponent of political reform and a man who appreciated the power of print for good and ill. Booker was a prolific author, especially of religious works and poetry.[5] One of Booker's sermons, dated 1791, seems to be Rann's earliest surviving publication.[6] Rann attended the Free Grammar School in Birmingham, worked at *Aris's Birmingham Gazette* and then moved to Dudley in about 1784.[7] He remained the town's only printer until William Maurice, a Unitarian, set up in 1807 and they were joined by George Walters in about 1812.[8] However, neither of the new arrivals challenged Rann's position as the establishment's printer of choice and Rann was increasingly accepted as part of that establishment. He was elected

4   Dudley's population rose from 13,925 in 1811 to 23,043 in 1831. Online Historical Population Reports, <http://www.histpop.org>, accessed 24 February 2017.

5   For instance: Luke Booker, *Poems on Subjects Sacred, Moral and Entertaining, 2 volumes* (Wolverhampton: J. Smart, 1785); *Malvern, a Descriptive and Historical Poem* (Dudley: J. Rann, 1798); *The Springs of Plynlimmon* (Wolverhampton: William Parke, 1834).

6   Luke Booker, *Sermon, Preached at St Edmund's Church, in Dudley; and Published for the Purpose of Erecting a Monument, within the Said Church, to the Memory of its Pious Founder, Mr George Bradley, who died Dec. 8, 1721* (Dudley: J. Rann, 1791).

7   *Staffordshire Advertiser*, 28 January 1854, 5; *Wolverhampton Chronicle*, 24 June 1846, 3.

8   BBTI, Maurice, William (1807–1841); TS 11/80/253, 1820.

a member of the Dudley Pitt Club shortly after its inauguration in 1813; he served on the Court Leet and became a Town Commissioner in 1827.[9] The few poll books that survive show Rann voting for Tory candidates and he signed pro-Tory petitions in the early 1830s.[10] He was also at the centre of a scandal that broke in July 1814. The controversy concerned a £26 5s 5d bill for sixteen months' worth of printing that Rann presented to 'the Overseers of the Poor of the Parish of Dudley'. Some of the more controversial items arose from celebrations held to mark Napoleon's defeat in spring 1814. The inappropriateness of using poor rates for items such as two packs of playing cards and '200 epitaphs on Bonaparte', caused local concern and the issue was raised at a meeting of the overseers on 29 July. There are no records of the meeting but an anonymous handbill, printed in Birmingham, claimed that even the revised bill accepted by the overseers had not been approved by the magistrates and echoed a call for the bill to be paid by 'voluntary subscription'.[11]

The following year, the campaigner William Cobbett delighted in publicising the scandal over Rann's bill in his *Political Register*.[12] Purporting to address American 'Back-woods' Men', Cobbett trumpeted the affair as an example of 'John Bull's press' and how it was used to give John Bull 'instruction in the science of politics, and to guard his political morality from adulteration, as well as to quicken and keep alive his loyalty'. Cobbett provided details of the defence of Rann's bill, including Rann's claim that he had presented it to the overseers for them to decide what parts should be paid out of the poor rates, not expecting full payment. The three overseers,

---

9   Dudley Archives and Local History Service (DALHS), Records of the Dudley Pitt Club, 1813, DSCAM/6/2/7/1–5; DALHS, Dudley Manor Court Book, 1798–1866, DE/3/3/1/28; DALHS, Dudley Town Commissioners' Minutes, Volume 1, 1791–1832 (no reference number).

10 See for example: Worcestershire Archives and Archaeology Service (WAAS), Stourbridge division, poll book, 1832, 1/7/4/2; DALHS, *Dudley. April 21, 1831. We the Undersigned* (Dudley?: n p, 1831), PO/475

11 DALHS, *The Following is an Exact Copy of the Bill first Presented by Mr Rann* (Birmingham: J. Belcher and Son, 1814?), PO/478.

12 *Cobbett's Weekly Political Register*, 19 August 1815, 194–208. Some details discussed by Cobbett cannot be corroborated from other sources.

all powerful coal or iron masters led by the combative Thomas Badger, were unrepentant. They seemingly claimed that any defects in the bill had been corrected and that neighbouring towns, such as Birmingham, paid higher sums for printing and stationery from their poor rates. Cobbett reproduced what he said was Rann's revised bill which was the same as the first, except that the celebratory material had been replaced by 500 'bills to preserve the peace'. In Cobbett's opinion nothing in either bill represented legitimate expenditure from poor rates.[13] Rann's original bill was later re-printed in the radical *Monthly Magazine* where it was lambasted for corruptly 'abstracting sums, for party purposes, from the poor-rates, and consequently from the poor!' It did not say what was considered 'party purposes' but this probably included loyalist material such as '200 requisitions on addressing Prince Regent on his speech'.[14] This incident shows Dudley's establishment uniting against opposition and highlights an important connection between print and politics. Men in positions of authority in the town had developed an enthusiasm for using printed materials for political purposes without the proper mechanisms to pay for them. The incident also suggests that opposition to the loyalists within Dudley at this time was less vociferous than it was nationally. The only surviving complaint from within the town was anonymous and although this may well have been the source that caught Cobbett's attention there are no records to show that Cobbett's article, or that in the *Monthly Magazine*, drew any more support from within Dudley. After Waterloo, Rann reinforced his loyalist credentials by printing an extremely patriotic ballad, 'The king and the prince of the island'.[15]

The large, public meeting at St Peter's Field, Manchester on 16 August 1819 formed part of the ongoing reform debate. The violent attack on the peaceful crowd by the forces of law and order, subsequently condoned by the government, enraged radical opinion across the country and polarised political positions in towns such as Dudley. As a magistrate, Booker sought

13   *Cobbett's Weekly Political Register*, 19 August 1815, 194, 203–8.
14   *Monthly Magazine*, No. 275, 1 November 1815, 377–8.
15   Broadside Ballads Online, Bod18451, Roud Number: V4298, 'The king and the prince of the island'. <http://ballads.bodleian.ox.ac.uk/search/printer/Rann%2C%20J>, accessed 19 January 2018.

to restrict the circulation of 'seditious papers' by reminding Dudley's publicans of their legal responsibilities.[16] However, 'a scurrilous letter' addressed to Booker from 'Mithra', and a copy of the first issue of Richard Carlile's *Republican*, strongly condemning the Peterloo 'massacre', were thrown into the vicarage garden. Booker made good use of government contacts. He went through the paper marking the passages he deemed 'highly seditious if not treasonable' and sent both it, and a copy of the letter, to the Home Secretary, Lord Sidmouth. As a chaplain to the Prince Regent, Booker proudly wore buttons featuring the royal monogram, GPR, but the Prince Regent was reviled by radicals, particularly after thanking the Peterloo magistrates for keeping order. Mithra railed at Booker: 'You bear the initials of tyranny on your buttons and madly mix religion with politics'. Mithra also questioned Booker's success in preventing the spread of radical material, telling him that 'publications which tend to destroy your craft circulate with avidity even under the sacred vaulted roof'. Booker thought that he had been targeted partly for 'ordering a travelling hawker of sedition to be properly taken notice of'.[17]

Boyd Hilton noted that the Home Office reaction to Peterloo was to 'mobilize a loyal press' and encourage local meetings to make public declarations of loyalty.[18] The authorities in Dudley obligingly called a meeting on 1 October 1819 to send a loyal address to the Prince Regent and express abhorrence of 'seditious and blasphemous publications so industriously disseminated ... under the pretext of REFORM'.[19] Radicals tried to disrupt the meeting which they claimed was rigged by the loyalists and it was followed by what George Walters called 'a paper war'.[20] The radical attack was led by Francis Finch, who later became Walsall's first radical

---

16   TNA, Luke Booker to Lord Sidmouth, 15 September 1819; *The Republican*, 27 August 1819, folio 33–43, 1819, HO 42/194.

17   HO 42/194, 1819.

18   Boyd Hilton, *A Mad, Bad, and Dangerous People? England 1783–1846* (Oxford: Oxford University Press, 2006), 252.

19   *Meeting at Dudley* (Birmingham, J. Belcher & Son, 1819?), 1–2. Published anonymously but subsequently claimed by Finch.

20   TS 11/80/253, 1820.

MP. A business man with connections to a well-known Unitarian family in Dudley, Finch was the first of the combatants to produce a pamphlet.[21] Finch's pamphlets were printed in Birmingham, at Belcher & Son's, the same firm that had printed the anonymous handbill denouncing Rann's bill.

In December 1819, inspired by the formation of 'the Birmingham Loyal Association', Dudley's loyalists founded a society 'for the suppression of blasphemy and sedition', supported by annual subscriptions of a guinea per member.[22] Soon renamed 'the Dudley constitutional association for the suppression of disloyalty, blasphemy and sedition', its remit was wide enough to include taking part in the propaganda battle. Some of the subscription money was used to pay Rann for printing 500 copies each of two pamphlets to counter two by Finch.[23] Rann was not a subscriber but the society's funds prevented a repetition of the embarrassment seen in 1814. The first loyalist pamphlet included the names of those at the meeting who had supported the loyal address, including Rann.[24] His support for the Tory establishment was noted by the radicals. Their last pamphlet in this particular dispute was a spoof purporting to be written by a member of the Dudley Pitt Club.[25] One satirical suggestion was that the club was going to produce a comprehensive and lengthy denunciation of Thomas Paine's *Age of Reason* to rival a famous work by Bishop Watson.[26] Anyone wishing to have more details was referred to 'Mr John Rann, the publisher'.[27]

21 *Meeting at Dudley*, 1819?

22 DALHS, Dudley Constitutional Association, resolutions, 1819, DSCAM 6/2/2/2; TNA, Birmingham Loyal Association, statement of purpose, folio 103, 1819, HO 42/199.

23 DALHS, J Rann's bill to the Dudley Constitutional Association, 1819, DSCAM 6/2/2/12.

24 *Dudley Meeting* (Dudley: J. Rann, 1819?), 16.

25 *A Defence of the Loyal Inhabitants of Dudley by a Member of the Pitt Club* (London: S. Fawcett, 1820).

26 *A Defence of the Loyal Inhabitants of Dudley*, 6–9; Richard Watson, *An Apology for the Bible, in a Series of Letters Addressed to Thomas Paine, Author of a Book Entitled, The age of reason* (New edition of Part II, London: F. C. & J. Rivington, 1819).

27 *A Defence of the Loyal Inhabitants of Dudley*, 8.

Apart from the spoof, the pamphlet battle was lacklustre, being preoccupied with allegations regarding speeches at the meeting, interspersed with genteel bickering. Finch came from the upper echelons of Dudley society and the anonymous pamphleteers who responded probably had similar backgrounds. However, a second front was soon opened up by two men from a different background. George Walters and John Wallace enraged the loyalist establishment by producing a radical paper, *The Patriot*, in their midst. Little is known about either man's private life. Walters was probably born in Walsall and baptised in 1788.[28] He married in Birmingham in 1810 and about two years later began printing in Dudley which was, apparently, his wife's home-town.[29] However, the business seems to have been only moderately successful.[30] Declared bankrupt in 1838, he managed to restart and struggled on till he went bankrupt again in 1849.[31] He left the town shortly afterwards and never printed again.[32] John Wallace was the son of Robert Wallace, a Scot who had moved to Dudley and who was variously described as a pawnbroker, draper or shopkeeper. The Wallace family was originally Presbyterian, but in Dudley they had embraced Unitarianism.[33] John was an artist who moved to Birmingham before emigrating to New Zealand in 1841.[34] Joseph Payton, a member of the Pitt Club and 'Constable of Dudley', made the uncorroborated claim that Wallace had 'long been

28 England and Wales Census, 1851, Islington, Middlesex, 23; St Matthew's, Walsall, baptisms, 1788, <https://www.freereg.org.uk>, accessed 13 March 2018.: Recorded as 'George Walter'. Father's occupation not given.
29 St Martin's, Birmingham, marriages, 1810, <https://www.ancestrylibraryedition. co.uk>, accessed 17 March 2018.: Surname recorded as 'Waters'; TS 11/80/253, 1820; Census, 1851, Islington, Middlesex, 23.
30 In 1820 he claimed he had suffered 'great losses'. TS 11/80/253, 1820.
31 *Wolverhampton Chronicle*, 14 November 1838, 1.
32 *Birmingham Journal*, 30 March 1850, 4.
33 R K Webb, 'Wallace, Robert (1791–1850)', *Oxford Dictionary of National Biography* (2004–2008), <http://www.oxforddnb.com/view/article/28540>, accessed 9 May 2017
34 'WALLACE, John FSA 1788–1880', in Una Platts, *Nineteenth century New Zealand Artists: a Guide & Handbook* (Christchurch, NZ: Avon Fine Prints, 1980), 245.

known to the police as 'a very active agent in the formation of union societies in this town and neighbourhood'.[35]

Barnsby wrote that the *Patriot* was 'the only local radical paper known
to have been published in the Black Country'.[36] The first issue, priced 2d,
appeared on 6 November 1819, stating that it was 'a weekly publication:
printed and published for J. Wallace'.[37] Payton quickly sent a copy to Lord
Sidmouth, together with a letter claiming that 'the loyal inhabitants of
Dudley have had the "Patriot" suspended upon a gibbet at the Market
Cross all this afternoon & it has this evening been publickly burnt'.[38] Similar
treatment had been meted out to an effigy of Napoleon a few years previously and the authorities were using this theatrical display to send out the
message that, far from being a patriot, this paper was classed as an enemy
or a traitor.[39] To make their point more widely, the story about the gibbet
was fed to several sympathetic newspapers such as the *Morning Post* and
the *Worcester Journal*.[40]

In Barnsby's opinion, 'a publication less subversive or seditious than the
Patriot to modern eyes would be difficult to find'.[41] However, at the time,
with the government preparing further legislation to try and curb radical
journals, there was plenty in the *Patriot* that might have concerned the
authorities.[42] On the front page was a quotation, 'God armeth the patriot',
which possibly appealed to Wallace because it was a motto identified with
his namesake, William Wallace, but it was also one that had appeared
amongst the banners at Peterloo.[43] Although not mentioned by name, the
first issue included much condemnation of Peterloo, together with what

---

35   TNA, Joseph Payton to Lord Sidmouth, letter and paper, folios 111–16, 1819. HO
      42/198.

36   Barnsby, *The Dudley Working Class Movement*, 9.

37   *The Patriot*, No. 1, 6 November 1819.

38   HO 42/198, 111–16, 1819.

39   *The Patriot*, No. 2, 13 November 1819, 15–16.

40   *The Morning Post*, 9 November 1819, 3; *Worcester Journal*, 11 November 1819, 3.

41   Barnsby, *The Dudley Working Class Movement*, 9.

42   'Peterloo and the Six Acts, 1819', <http://www.historyofparliamentonline.org/
      themes/politics/peterloo-and-the-six-acts-1819>, accessed 18 February 2018.

43   'Express from Manchester', *The Times*, 19 August 1819, 2.

could be taken as a call to arms. Wallace wrote: 'as we have converted our swords into plough-shares, and our spears into pruning-hooks, that were employed against our neighbours abroad; so must we transmute our pipes into pistols, and our cups into cannons, to defend our liberties at home'.[44] At a time when 'seditious libel' could include anything likely to cause the people to question the government, some of Wallace's language might seem reckless and inflammatory. He wrote: 'The people cry out, oppression, – oppression, – oppression, – and their rulers answer, chains, – chains, – chains, – and a dungeon'.[45] At the very least, this portrayed the government as repressive and unfeeling. Wallace's apparent attack on the rule of law and the Church of England was similarly provocative:

> What is the law of the land? The law of the land is a compound of priestcraft and knavery, made up of mysticism and subtleties; unintelligible to every one that has common sense, united with honesty; and intelligible only to those who have *uncommon* sense, united with craft. It consists of dogmas and doctrines, invented for the purpose of binding both body and soul; and is exercised upon the poor by the rich, for the purpose of making the poor poorer, and the rich richer, both here and hereafter. It has two branches of equal magnitude – the one deriving its existence from the superstition of mankind – the other from their fears and their follies: the first exercised by things called priests – the other by reptiles called lawyers – both of them animals of prey – that live upon the vitals of their country ...[46]

Such polemical portrayals of class hostility and anti-clericalism, similar in tone to the scathing writings of the radical, William Hone, might have proved popular in London or larger towns and cities but it seems to have been too strident for Dudley.[47] Wallace persevered, discussing common radical concerns such as the working of the poor laws, the unjust division of society and the fear that the government was becoming 'a military despotism'.[48] Yet only four issues of the paper appeared. As with the first,

---

44   *The Patriot*, No. 1, 6 November 1819, 2.
45   *The Patriot*, No. 1, 6 November 1819, 5.
46   *The Patriot*, No. 1, 6 November 1819, 5–6.
47   William Hone, *The Political House that Jack Built* (London: William Hone, 1819); TS 11/80/253, 1820.
48   *The Patriot*, No. 2, 13 November 1819, 9–12; No. 4, 27 November 1819, 25–32.

copies of the second and fourth issues were sent to the Home Office by Dudley's loyalists.[49] They also lobbied the Home Office to prosecute those responsible for the *Patriot*.[50] To their disappointment, no action was taken against Wallace because of insufficient evidence that he was the author.[51] Prosecuting Walters was easier. His imprint was on the *Patriot* and James Hillman, a serjeant of the Court Leet, testified that Walters had sold him a copy.[52] Walters was arrested at the end of January 1820 'for printing a seditious and libellous paper' and struggled to find bail.[53] The apparent unfairness of Walters shouldering all the blame might explain why one of the men who eventually provided bail was Wallace's father, together with another man also connected to the Unitarian chapel.[54]

Walters's submission to the Court of King's Bench is one of the rare cases where he recorded his views, though it has to be seen in the context of a man who feared losing both his liberty and livelihood. Whilst sound-ing naïve and apologetic, he did not completely submit. Walters claimed that, 'Such a work as the *Patriot* would never have been thought of but for the party spirit excited in the town of Dudley by the meeting of the first of October last'. He explained why some objected both to the meeting and to the treatment given to Finch, 'a gentleman of the highest respectability and character'. Walters also distanced himself from Wallace who, he said, had attended the meeting 'unfortunately under the influence of excited and irritated political feeling'. As to himself, Walters said 'he never had nor did he wish to interfere in political matters'. Walters claimed that he had been reluctant to print the paper and only agreed because Wallace persisted and led Walters to believe that it would be 'merely a political squib' covering local matters. Walters said he had no intention 'to make it the vehicle of

49   TNA, Cases and copies of *The Patriot*, numbers 2 and 4 (1819–1820), TS 11/156/506–507. There are no known copies of number 3.
50   DALHS, Correspondence between the Dudley Constitutional Association and Home Office officials, 1819–1820, DSCAM 6/2/2/22–31.
51   DSCAM 6/2/2/24, 25, 30, 1819–1820.
52   DSCAM 6/2/2/23, 1819.
53   Rex v Walters, DSCAM 6/2/2/29–30, 1820; *Public Ledger and Daily Advertiser*, 12 February 1820, 3.
54   *Public Ledger and Daily Advertiser*, 12 February 1820, 3.

blasphemy and sedition or to libel the King and constitution' and he presented a carefully worded apology. Walters seemed particularly disingenuous when claiming that he had neither read the papers that he printed nor realised 'that a printer was liable for the doctrines and contents of a work of which he was not the author'. Walters hoped that he exonerated himself by putting Wallace's name 'on the face of the work'.[55]

Despite this taking place at a time when the government was extending the range of 'gagging' acts and several high-profile trials for seditious libel, such as that of Richard Carlile, being keenly reported, Walters's prosecution was apparently allowed to fizzle out.[56] Considering the *Patriot*'s overall significance, it certainly changed the degree and tone of the political debate in Dudley but it was a very short-lived phenomenon that mainly reflected the anger caused by Peterloo. According to Walters, over a third of the papers did not sell and those that did were 'principally purchased from motives of curiosity'.[57] Although it marked an advance in radicalism in Dudley, it was a comparatively small one. Walters received little overt assistance and the loyalists used the production to rally the faithful. However, if Walters had been cowed by the experience, he had recovered sufficiently by the time that the Queen Caroline affair reached its height in December 1820 to reprint an address to the King from the Lord Mayor, Aldermen and Commons of the City of London which sided with 'her Majesty'.[58]

After the Queen Caroline affair, radical agitation in Britain died down till the renewed demand for parliamentary reform in the early 1830s. Before considering that next wave of radicalism, it is useful to note changes in

---

55   TS 11/80/253, 1820.
56   E. P. Thompson, *The Making of the English Working Class* (Harmondsworth: Penguin Books, revised edn, 1968), 768; Boyd Hilton, *A Mad, Bad, and Dangerous People? England 1783–1846* (Oxford: Oxford University Press, 2006), 252–3; Philip W. Martin, 'Carlile, Richard (1790–1843)', *Oxford Dictionary of National Biography*, <http://www.oxforddnb.com/view/10.1093/odnb/9780192683120.001.0001/odnb-9780192683120-e-4685>, accessed on 18 February 2018; TS 11/80/253; 11/156/506–7, 1819–1820.
57   TS 11/80/253, 1820.
58   *The Following Address was lately Presented to His Majesty*, n.d. i.e. 1820, DSCAM 6/2/2/5.

Dudley amongst the printers and the chief exponents of print. Rann retired in 1821 and passed the business, including the 'goodwill', to Joseph Hinton.[59] However, Hinton died in 1823 and his will stipulated that the business was to be run by a trust until his two young sons reached their majority.[60] Records are scarce but the executors used a manager, also named John Rann, and probably the nephew of the original owner.[61] The imprint read variously, 'Hinton's', 'Hinton's Office' or 'Hinton's Executors'. With a small exception that is discussed later, Dudley's elite remained loyal to this firm. Concomitantly, there is no evidence of Hinton's producing any 'opposition' literature. Although Walters got a large slice of pro-reform work, he did not get it all. Some of it went to Maurice and some to Joseph Goodwin, another printer who had set up in Dudley.[62]

Whilst Booker remained the chief exponent of print propaganda for the Dudley loyalists after 1819, he came up against a new adversary, Samuel Cook, a radical draper and a passionate advocate of the power of print. Cook soon became the acknowledged leader of Dudley's radicals and remained active till his death in 1861, thus giving the radical cause a stability it had not enjoyed previously. He was born in Trowbridge and only moved to Dudley in 1819. There are no records of his taking part in the controversy that year. The handbill announcing the opening of Cook's shop on 8 May 1819 was printed by Rann, but it is the only surviving item of Cook's prolific output that was produced by the establishment printer.[63]

As well as being on opposite sides of the religious and political divide, Booker and Cook epitomised two divergent strands of the evolving print culture in the town. Although Booker occasionally claimed that he was non-party political, his published sermons and other writings reinforced

---

59   DALHS, Circular concerning the business of J. Rann and Joseph Hinton, October 1821, DSCAM 6/5/3/7.

60   TNA, Will of Joseph Hinton, Printer etc. of Dudley, proved 24 May 1834, PROB 11/1831/276.

61   *Birmingham Gazette*, 23 February 1835, 3.

62   BBTI, Goodwin, Joseph (1833–1862); DALHS, *To the Friends of Reform and Captain Spencer* (Dudley: J. Goodwin, 1831?), PO/396. This is of a committee meeting dated 6 May 1831, so earlier than Goodwin's start date given by BBTI.

63   Reproduced in: Barnsby, *The Dudley Working Class Movement*, 12.

the loyalist agenda of 'King and Country', the pre-eminence of the Anglican church and acceptance of traditional hierarchies. A firm advocate of law and order, he played a pivotal role in organising the society for the suppression of blasphemy and sedition. In opposition, Cook made himself the voice of dissent and nonconformism. Unlike Booker's carefully drafted writings, Cook specialised in pithy handbills, often using sarcasm and invective, with eye-catching headlines. He frequently got into trouble with the authorities through his persistent practice of displaying radical material in a window of his shop which was at the top of the High Street, close to the parish church. Cook copied items from many papers to disseminate news and ideas and urged radicals to read radical papers, even if shared.[64] For this to benefit the lower classes there needed to be improved literacy. Cook advocated both universal education and self-help amongst the working classes.[65] In his long career he used many printers, including some in Birmingham, but in the 1820s and early 1830s much of his output was printed by Walters.

Cook's earliest surviving dated, political handbill was printed by Walters in January 1823 (see Figure 2.1).[66] It is a quintessential example of Cook's work, detailing a scandal that he had unearthed concerning the Church of England in Dudley and complaining that he had not been allowed to inspect the vestry minute book. He added 'extracts from a standard law authority' and advised churchwardens to discharge their duties 'with firmness and impartiality, and not from the dictation of a JUNTO'.[67] A further collaboration between Cook and Walters came in 1827 when Cook was himself tried for 'alleged seditious libel' for displaying a notice that blamed the government for widespread starvation whilst spending large sums on church extensions and the refurbishment of Windsor Castle.[68]

---

64 DALHS, SC/55, Every one, two or three radical families (Samuel Cook, attributed, handwritten, n.d.).

65 DALHS, Samuel Cook, *Some of the Principles of Dudley Radicalism* (Dudley: Joseph Goodwin, 1834?), SC/23; *Birmingham Journal*, 13 August 1842, 5.

66 DALHS, Samuel Cook, *The Vestry Book, and the Celebrated Secret Order* (Dudley: G. Walters, 1823?), SC/106.

67 SC/106, 1823?

68 DALHS, *S. Cook's Case* (Dudley: Walters, n.d.), SC/112.

To Cook's delight, he was only bound over to keep the peace and Walters then printed a transcript of the trial.[69] As such, they could safely repeat the seditious sentences that Cook had been indicted for, thus making them available to a much wider readership. Cook took out advertisements in newspapers such as the *Birmingham Journal* to help maximise sales.[70]

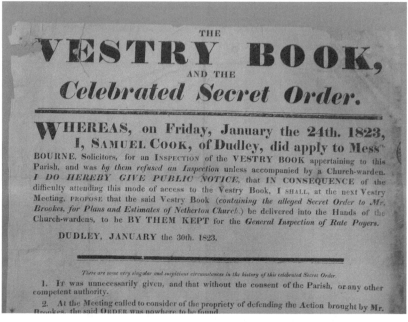

THE

VESTRY BOOK,
AND THE
Celebrated Secret Order.

WHEREAS, on Friday, January the 24th. 1823, I, SAMUEL COOK, of Dudley, did apply to Mess" BOURNE, Solicitors, for an INSPECTION of the VESTRY BOOK appertaining to this Parish, and was *by them refused an Inspection* unless accompanied by a Church-warden. *I DO HEREBY GIVE PUBLIC NOTICE*, that IN CONSEQUENCE of the difficulty attending this mode of access to the Vestry Book, I SHALL, at the next Vestry Meeting, PROPOSE that the said Vestry Book (*containing the alleged Secret Order to Mr. Brookes, for Plans and Estimates of Netherton Church.*) be delivered into the Hands of the Church-wardens, to be BY THEM KEPT for the *General Inspection of Rate Payers.*

DUDLEY, JANUARY the 30th. 1823.

There are some very singular and suspicious circumstances in the history of this celebrated Secret Order.

1. It was unnecessarily given, and that without the consent of the Parish, or any other competent authority.
2. At the Meeting called to consider of the propriety of defending the Action brought by Mr. Brookes, the said ORDER was nowhere to be found.

Figure 2.1. *The vestry book and the celebrated secret order* (Dudley: G. Walters, 1823?) (detail). Reproduced with permission of Dudley Archives and Local History Service.

Walters's contributions were mainly practical but some were less tangible. The former included collecting signatures and subscriptions, disseminating political information and producing propaganda. More nebulous, but

69   *A Full Report of the Trial of Samuel Cook, Draper, Dudley, for an Alleged Seditious Libel, Tried at Worcester, August 1 1827, before Mr Justice Littledale* etc. (Dudley: G. Walters, 1827).
70   *Birmingham Journal*, 20 October 1827, 1.

still significant, was the attention-grabbing sense of urgency and excite-ment that he managed to engender into his best work. Another aspect was his helping to extend the sphere of what was considered 'political' in the town. The claim that Walters had made in 1820 about not wanting 'to interfere in political matters' therefore became increasingly untenable.[71] Yet it is not clear from most of his output whether the material he printed represented his own views or those of customers. There are no payment records for any of his work so it is not known how much of it was com-missioned and how much, if any, he produced for the good of the cause. Some of the handbills are clearly attributed to an individual or a committee but some carry a generic by-line (such as 'a Townsman') or, occasionally, a pseudonym. Many others are completely anonymous. However, Walters's argument, noted above, that he thought he distanced himself from the contents of the *Patriot* by clearly putting Wallace's name on it, could be used to argue that by producing so much material anonymously, it might be assumed that either Walters wrote it himself or that he was prepared to be associated with the views expressed.

The first signs of renewed radical activity in Dudley came in the summer of 1830, following the July Revolution in France. Cook and Thomas Parkin, a London radical with business interests in Dudley, organised a meeting to celebrate the revolution.[72] Parkin, a member of the council of the Birmingham Political Union (BPU) since May 1830, provided a useful link between Dudley's reformers and their counterparts in Birmingham, some of whom attended the meeting.[73] Cook, Walters and the reform-minded grocer, John Twamley, made their shops available for collecting subscriptions to send to General Lafayette.[74] Resolutions passed at the

71 TS 11/80/253, 1820.

72 DALHS, Samuel Cook & Thomas Parkin, *French Independence and English Sympathy!* (Dudley: G. Walters, 1830), PO/154

73 Carlos Flick, *The Birmingham Political Union and the Movements for Reform in Britain, 1830–1839* (Hamden, CT: Archon Books; Folkestone: Dawson, 1978), 39–41.

74 DALHS, *French Independence. At a Public Meeting* (Dudley: G. Walters, 1830), PO/458.

meeting included criticisms of the English government.[75] A report in the *Birmingham Argus* suggested that the Dudley radicals were thinking of setting up their own political union, though it is not known exactly when the Dudley Political Union (DPU) was founded.[76] Parkin later claimed responsibility for drawing up its objectives but Cook was always its chairman.[77] Parkin was an enthusiastic user of print who had his own press in London. He also edited a radical paper called the *Christian Corrector* which was controversial in both its treatment of politics and religion.[78] In a letter to the *Morning Advertiser*, Parkin suggested that he was considering moving its production to Dudley, though that never happened.[79]

A print war flared up in February 1831 when Rev. Booker headed up a requisition to the mayor to call a meeting to promote *moderate* parliamentary reform.[80] This was clearly a pre-emptive bid and was immediately countered by an anonymous handbill printed by Walters, which concentrated on the merits of voting by ballot.[81] The outcome was open to question. The 'moderate reformers' sent copies of their resolutions to local papers but Walters claimed victory and printed two celebratory handbills, including a satirical attack on Anglican clergy.[82] This was an early example of the propaganda battle to come and of the immediacy that often characterised Walters's work. When a general election on the reform

---

75   PO/458, 1830.

76   *Birmingham Argus*, 3 September 1830, 143–4.

77   *Christian Corrector*, No. 33, 15 October 1831, 264.

78   *Christian Corrector* (London, Thomas Parkin, May 1829 – June 1832 with gaps). In religion, Parkin claimed to be a Sandemanean [*sic*] and his writings often had an anti-clerical bias. He also wrote millenarian articles, used apocalyptic language in his political writing and described the *Book of Revelation* as 'highly political'. *Christian Corrector*, No. 21, 27 March 1830, 169; No. 43, 25 January 1831 [i.e. 1832], 329–31; No. 52, 28 March 1832, 389–91; No. 63, 20 June, 1832, 469.

79   *Morning Advertiser*, 27 August 1830, 2.

80   DALHS, *To J. C. Brettell, Esq., Mayor of Dudley* (Dudley: Hinton's office, 1831), PO/468.

81   DALHS, *Vote by Ballot* (Dudley: G. Walters, 1831), PO/433.

82   *Wolverhampton Chronicle* 16 February 1831, 2: DALHS, *The Requisition Defeated* (Dudley: G. Walters, 1831), PO/424; DALHS, *Lost, Several Clergymen of the Established Church* (Dudley: G. Walters, 1831), PO/472.

question was called in May 1831, the Tories rallied around the reactionary, sitting MP for Worcestershire, Henry Beauchamp Lygon. Walters issued a pro-reform, anti-Lygon petition which already had over 300 signatures and was to lie at Walters's shop to gather more.[83] It was countered by a Booker-led petition in favour of Lygon who had apparently agreed to support 'moderate reform'.[84]

Walters furthered the radicals' election campaign by printing the manifesto for the new Reform candidate, Frederick Spencer, younger brother of Viscount Althorp.[85] The Dudley radicals were particularly enthusiastic about helping to get Spencer elected in place of Lygon. Walters's handbill announcing their victory was one of his most ebullient (see Figure 2.2).[86] It contained the usual foolery expected of a political squib and a suggestion that the Tories had tried to buy the election. Walters also provided data, giving the voting figures for each candidate on each day of the poll. A less pleasant side to the election was reflected in a handbill by Booker hotly denying that he had accepted corrupt payments and complaining that, whilst conducting a burial service, he had been jeered by 'those under the influence of political delusion'.[87] This well fits with the description of the febrile atmosphere of the election as described by Michael Brock and also with Brock's assertion that: 'Virtually all the intimidation was exercised by reformers.'[88]

With the general election giving the Whigs a majority, their proposed Reform bill passed through the Commons and attention switched to delaying tactics in the Lords. Walters continued to disseminate political information, firstly by reprinting an important anti-Reform speech by

83   DALHS, *Reform. We, the Undersigned Freeholders* (Dudley: G. Walters, 1831), PO/490.

84   PO/475, 1831.

85   DALHS, Frederick Spencer, *To the Worthy & Independent Freeholders* (Dudley: G. Walters, 1831), PO/189.

86   The two Reform candidates were elected with the sitting MP, Thomas Henry Foley, topping the poll. Lygon retired towards the end of the scheduled poll. DALHS, *Rejoice! Rejoice!! Glorious Victory!* (Dudley: Walters, 1831), PO/244A.

87   DALHS, The Vicar of Dudley, that is, Luke Booker, *To the Inhabitants of the Parish of Dudley* (Dudley: Hinton's Office, 1831), PO/333.

88   Michael Brock, *The Great Reform Act* (London: Hutchinson & co., 1973), 198.

Figure 2.2. *Rejoice! Rejoice!! Glorious Victory!* (Dudley: Walters, 1831).
Reproduced with permission of Dudley Archives and Local History Service.

the Earl of Dudley.[89] Following the Lords' rejection of the Reform bill in October and the violence that ensued in cities such as Nottingham and Bristol, members of the BPU, led by the chairman, Thomas Attwood, prepared a statement urging the people to be patient and law-abiding.[90] Copies were sent to other towns and cities, including one to Dudley, which Walters reprinted immediately, just changing the names of the town and personnel to make it applicable to Dudley.[91] The political unions wanted to be seen to have a role in calming down the situation and this may have helped to encourage what looks like a short lull in Dudley's print war which led to Walters getting his only known commissions from the establishment.[92]

The situation in mid-November 1831 was particularly tense. On top of the fear of riots, cholera had been confirmed in the north of Britain and there was a serious strike brewing amongst the colliers in the Dudley area.[93] A petition was drawn up, 'to keep this place and neighbourhood in peace and safety, without any view whatever being had to politics or party feeling'.[94] The notice included a request for 'respectable inhabitants' to be sworn in as special constables.[95] As usual, Booker's was the first name on the

89   DALHS, *Lord Dudley turned Republican!* (Dudley: G. Walters, 1831), PO/98A.

90   Flick, *The Birmingham Political Union*, 65; DALHS, *Address of the Council of the Birmingham Political Union* (Birmingham, Midland Representative Office, 1831), PO/71.

91   DALHS, *Address of the Council of the Dudley Political Union* (Dudley: G. Walters, 1831), PO/21.

92   Flick, *The Birmingham Political Union*, 64–6; Nancy D. LoPatin, *Political Unions, Popular Politics and the Great Reform Act of 1832* (Basingstoke: Macmillan, 1999), 99–117.

93   DALHS, *To Colliers and Miners* (Dudley: Hinton's Office, 1831), PO/217A. Eric Hobsbawm, writing of the situation in Britain up to the passing of the Reform Act of 1832, argued that: 'this period is probably the only one in modern history ... where something not unlike a revolutionary situation might have developed'. E. J. Hobsbawm, *The Age of Revolution: Europe 1789–1848* (London: Weidenfeld and Nicolson, 1962), 110–11.

94   DALHS, *To the Magistrates of the County of Worcester* (Dudley: G. Walters, 1831), PO/81.

95   PO/81, 1831.

list of requisitionists but the second name was Cook's.[96] The arrangement of names looks like a deliberate attempt to show the coming together of the different parties and that Walters was asked to print this cross-party handbill reinforces the impression that it marked some sort of truce. On the same day, Walters printed another official notice, calling a meeting to discuss precautionary measures against cholera.[97] Cook, for the DPU, issued a handbill lamenting the recent riots and vowing to do their utmost to preserve 'peace, order and tranquillity'.[98]

If there was something of a rapprochement between the two sides in mid-November, it was short-lived. By the end of the month, Hinton's had printed a sermon of Booker's in which he blamed 'national sin' for 'national distress' and included a condemnation of strikers, as well as reprinting a harsh piece on rioters and rick-burners previously sent to the *Wolverhampton Chronicle*.[99] There was a fear that the Swing riots might be starting up again with new incidents of incendiarism in the Swindon area receiving wide coverage. One such report in the *Midland Representative* was headed: 'Terrible progress of "Swing"'.[100] The *Worcester Journal* subsequently reported that:

> An address numerously and respectably signed has been transmitted to the King from the town of Dudley expressing approbation of the Royal Proclamation for the suppression of Political Unions, and a determination to support, by all constitutional means, his Majesty and his Government in putting down such dangerous and illegal associations.[101]

The colliers' strikes spread into many parts of the Black Country and the authorities had to employ several military units to suppress them.

---

96   PO/81, 1831.
97   DALHS, *The Churchwardens and Overseers of the Poor* (Dudley: G. Walters, 1831), PO/330.
98   DAHLS, *Preservation of the Peace* (Dudley: G. Walters, 1831), PO/181A.
99   Luke Booker, *The Cause and Cure of National Distress: Stated in a Sermon, Preached at Dudley* (Dudley: Hinton's Executors, 1831), 5–6, 11, 21–2; *Wolverhampton Chronicle*, 23 November 1831, 2.
100 *Midland Representative*, 19 November 1831, 1.
101 *Worcester Journal*, 1 December 1831, 3.

The Lieutenant-Colonel of the Worcestershire Yeomanry Cavalry, Lord Lyttelton, personally rode with his men in a show of strength to help subdue the miners in the Stourbridge and Dudley area. Radicals in Birmingham and Dudley were soon protesting at what they saw as unfair treatment of some of the men arrested during the troubles.[102]

The DPU was responsible for a lot of the printed material produced in Dudley during the Reform crisis but at the height of the tension, in the so-called 'days of May', a split appeared in their ranks with some of the more moderate reformers starting a new society, confusingly also called the Dudley Political Union. Walters printed a handbill for the new Union and his shop was one of only two that collected names and subscriptions, but he also printed handbills for Cook and the original Union, celebrating Lord Grey's return to government and the assurance that the third Reform bill would pass.[103]

The national crisis, from April to June 1832 and the social divisions it caused, was mirrored in Dudley by the parish vestry becoming politicised to an unprecedented degree.[104] The election of churchwarden that year provides a good example of Walters operating in the thick of the action and helping to expand the accepted sphere of politics. The Church of England party thought that their candidate, Joseph Bennitt, had been elected churchwarden, by traditional means on 24 April 1832.[105] However, the result was overturned on a technicality and the election had to be re-run. The vestry meeting on 1 June decided to hold a public poll beginning at

102 DALHS, *To the Inhabitants of Dudley and its Vicinity* (Dudley: J. Goodwin, 1831?), PO/63B.

103 DALHS, *Objects, Rules & Regulations of the Dudley Political Union Established May 14, 1832* (Dudley: G. Walters, 1832?), PO/196; DALHS, *Dudley Political Union Established 14 May, 1832* (Dudley: J. Goodwin, 1832?), PO/226; DALHS, *Earl Grey is again Minister!! Reform Triumphant!!* (Dudley: G. Walters, 1832), PO/64; DALHS, Samuel Cook, *Lord Grey is Prime Minister with Sufficient Power to Carry the Reform Bill* (Dudley: G. Walters, 1832), SC/109; DALHS, Samuel Cook, *To the Labouring Classes of Dudley* (Dudley: G. Walters, 1832), SC/114.

104 Smith (ed.), *Reform or Revolution?*, 111–12; A. J. Ware, *Dudley Parish Order Book, 1821–1856* (Dudley: typescript, 1992), 53–7.

105 Ware, *Dudley Parish Order Book*, 53–4.

3 pm the same day.[106] Walters immediately issued a handbill announcing the poll and campaigning for the radical candidate, Thomas Hill, a non-conformist shoe-dealer and one of Walters's closest neighbours.[107] The handbill urged: 'Vote Hill, and retrenchment'. At close of poll, Walters issued another handbill telling ratepayers that, 'the aristocratic provisions of the *Sturges Bourne's Act*, has given your rich opponents a small majority on the first day's Poll'.[108] Casting itself as a political campaign, the handbill was published, 'by order of Mr Hill's committee'.[109] The following day, Walters issued another handbill, ascribed to 'an independent voter', asking rate-payers to, 'Vote for Mr Hill, the Reform candidate'.[110] Walters must have been responsible for this handbill for it carried a veiled threat that he would publish lists giving the names of those who voted and which candidate they voted for.[111] He resorted to this tactic over the next few years but there are no surviving lists for this particular election. After a four-day poll, Bennitt was finally elected by a majority of 210.[112]

The royal assent to the Reform bill on 7 June 1832 guaranteed that Dudley became a single-member parliamentary constituency and the first election took place that December. By the terms of the Reform Act, men living in boroughs who met the forty-shilling freehold qualification, but did not have the requisite property worth ten pounds to secure the borough franchise, were allowed a vote in their county constituency. For men in Dudley, that meant the new constituency of East Worcestershire. The part of the East Worcestershire campaign that took place in Dudley was at times even more fraught than the borough election, mainly because the Tory candidate was J. S. Pakington who had previously been Lygon's chief agent and he re-awakened old enmities. On one handbill by Walters,

---

106 Ware, *Dudley Parish Order Book*, 55.
107 DALHS, *Rate-Payers of Dudley, Vote for Hill* (Dudley: G. Walters, 1832), PO/17; TNA, England and Wales Census 1841, Worcestershire, Dudley, PRO HO 107.
108 DALHS, *To the Rate-Payers of Dudley* (Dudley: G. Walters, 1832), PO/255. A sliding scale gave wealthier landowners extra votes, to a maximum of six.
109 PO/255, 1832.
110 DALHS, *No Slavery!* (Dudley: G. Walters, 1832), PO/15B.
111 PO/15B, 1832.
112 Ware, *Dudley Parish Order Book*, 55.

Pakington's supporters were described as 'ruffians on horseback'.[113] In the borough election, Sir Horace St Paul, a wealthy ironmaster and a Tory MP who had voted against reform, stood against the Reform candidate, the lawyer, John Campbell. Walters collected subscriptions for Campbell and printed some of his election material, but not all of it.[114]

More divergences appeared amongst Dudley's reformers. Thomas Parkin, the most radical of all, who resisted anything short of universal suffrage, had fallen out with Attwood and other moderate members of the BPU.[115] Parkin found nothing to choose between Whigs and Tories, calling them all 'public plunderers'.[116] This view was not reflected in the last handbills that Walters printed in the election campaign, however. One in particular, attributed to 'a Reform Elector', called on Whigs, Liberals and all Reformers to unite against the Tories.[117] Significantly, it also took a more national standpoint than had been customary in elections at local level. It listed the perceived failures of recent Tory governments and finishing with the exhortation: 'The contest is not *particular*, but GENERAL! it is not *provincial* but NATIONAL!!!'[118] Both sides ended their campaigns by urging a peaceful election. In a 'secular pastoral address', Booker called for moderation and 'fair play' on both sides.[119]

Walters's reporting of the first borough poll, as it happened, is a notable example of his acting as public information provider and of the immediacy that characterised his most powerful work. Using data supplied by the Whig committee, he produced three updates on 'the state of the poll' during the election and capped it with a jubilant handbill the following day to celebrate

---

113 DALHS, *Public meeting. The Meeting. The Meeting of the Town and Parish of Dudley* (Dudley: G. Walters, 1832), PO/159.

114 DALHS, Thomas Lester, *At a Meeting of the Committee and Friends of Mr Campbell* (Dudley: W. Maurice, 1832), PO/112B.

115 *Christian Corrector*, 13 June 1832, 465–7; 20 June 1832, 469–71.

116 DALHS, *To the Non-Electors of Dudley* (London: Parkin, 1832), PO/25A.

117 DALHS, *Reformers of All Classes; Whigs and Liberals!* (Dudley: Walters, 1832), PO/61B.

118 PO/61B, 1832.

119 DALHS, The Vicar of Dudley, that is, Luke Booker, *A Secular Pastoral Address* (Dudley: The Office of Hinton's Executors, 1832), PO/32B.

Campbell's success.[120] This is one of the few surviving handbills that made a direct connection between the borough election and the county election taking place the following week. Walters ended his coverage of the first borough election by printing lists, priced 6d, of those who voted for each candidate 'in the memorable and glorious contest'. Unsurprisingly, Booker and both Ranns had voted for the Tory, whilst Cook and Walters, newly enfranchised, had voted for the Reform candidate.[121]

In conclusion, in the forty-four years since Rann first began printing in Dudley in 1788, the town had become a vibrant hub of modern print culture, only lacking its own town newspaper.[122] Printed materials were ideally suited to the adversarial politics of post-1815 and rather than merely reflecting debates, they helped to set the agenda. The increasing availability, and importance, of print to both sides accompanied a significant shift in the balance of power in Dudley. From the ending of the Napoleonic wars, the traditional dominance of the Tory, loyalist elite began to be eroded. Occasional upsurges of radicalism strengthened to produce better sustained support which, together with a sometimes uneasy alliance with moderate reformers, was enough to defeat the Tory candidates in 1831 and 1832. The influence of reformers probably peaked in 1832 and Booker would be credited with helping to rally conservative interests to defeat Campbell at a by-election as early as February 1834. The 'paper war' also reflected changes caused by the growth of the town, including the transforming role of incomers such as Booker, Rann, Walters, Finch, Cook and Parkin. Booker and Cook, in particular, had their own networks that helped to tie Dudley into regional, national and even international affairs. The 'paper war' in

120 DALHS, *Dudley Election. State of the Poll, First Day, Quarter past Ten AM*, PO/388A; *Dudley Election. State of the Poll, First Day, Twelve O'Clock* (Dudley: G. Walters, 1832), PO/388B; DALHS, *Dudley Election. Gross State of the Poll, First Day* (Dudley: G. Walters, 1832), PO/242B; DALHS, *Borough of Dudley. Principle Again Triumphant!* (Dudley: G. Walters, 1832), PO/92. Sir Horace retired overnight, thus precluding a second day of polling.
121 DALHS, *A List of the Electors of Dudley who Voted* (Dudley: G. Walters, 1832), PO/60.
122 The earliest Dudley newspaper was the *Dudley Weekly Times* produced in 1856, but it was short-lived. *Dudley Archives Journal*, Winter 2009, 4.

Dudley fully reflected the agitation seen across the rest of the country but also helped to extend what was considered 'political' within the town.

As to the conundrum of trying to determine Walters's own political beliefs, there are no easy answers. His career as the publisher of a radical paper was extremely short-lived and the explanation he gave to the authorities looked very naïve. He never repeated that experiment but he was responsible for a large proportion of the radical material that was printed in Dudley during the reform agitation of 1830–1832 and much of it was done with a verve and panache that suggests that Walters must have personally supported the cause. Despite his claim not to want to 'interfere in political matters', he played a full part in airing the political debate and disseminating information to the general public. Printing was at the heart of the battle for reform in Dudley and Walters was at the heart of the print war, possibly inadvertently in 1819, but much more deliberately in 1830–1832.

In so far as this chapter can be seen as a tale of two printers, the ending seems particularly unfair. John Rann senior spent over thirty years in comfortable retirement, an esteemed member of Dudley society till he died in 1854, aged ninety-eight.[123] George Walters's fate could not have been more different. In 1862 he was committed to the County Asylum in Maidstone, Kent, as a pauper and a lunatic and as such he died in 1864, aged about seventy-six.[124] His committal record gave 'the supposed cause of insanity' as 'reverse of fortune'.[125]

123 C. F. G. Clark, *Curiosities of Dudley and the Black Country from 1800 to 1860 etc.* (Birmingham: Buckler Brothers, 1881), 172.

124 United Kingdom, Lunacy patients admissions registers, 1862, <https://www.ancestrylibraryedition.co.uk>, accessed 28 February 2018.

125 Kent History and Library Centre, Barming Hospital admission register, 1862–1864, MH/Md2/Ap 1/4.

SUSAN THOMAS

3 'One of the Most Extraordinary Publications Which Has Ever Appeared ...': George Edmonds v the *Monthly Argus*

The historian Asa Briggs' 1949 article 'Press and Public in Early Nineteenth-Century Birmingham' described the symbiotic relationship that exists between a local press and its readership and argued that studying such local publications would allow historians to learn a great deal about the society they served. Briggs described the plethora of newspapers and magazines published in Birmingham between 1815 and 1832 and the way in which they both reflected and contributed to a lively literary and political culture. The town was in the throes of social transition and industrial growth; its press reflected the turbulence of society. This was a town that expressed local pride and had a zeal for improvement. Politics was taken seriously, and religious affiliation was important. At the same time the press reported on the theatre, concerts and other amusements.[1]

This chapter analyses the same magazine that was central to Briggs' article, the *Monthly Argus and Public Censor*, and explores a particular episode in its existence. In 1831 the *Monthly Argus* was involved in a locally celebrated libel case which ended with the editor and printer both being jailed. The dispute shines a light on aspects of Birmingham society and the political tensions running through it, on ambitions, pretensions and on gender and class relations. The affair also throws up questions of accountability, regulation and press freedom which have a contemporary resonance. What should be the balance between freedom of expression

---

1   Asa Briggs, 'Press and Public in Early Nineteenth-Century Birmingham', in A. Briggs, *The Collected Essays of Asa Briggs, Vol. 1* (Brighton: Harvester, 1985), 106–37, originally *Occasional Papers of the Dugdale Society* No. 8 (1949).

and the right of individuals to defend their reputation? At what point does 'fair comment' become outright libel? How does possession of power and money impact on the relationship between the law and the press?

By the late 1820s, Birmingham supported several local newspapers and magazines. The leading weekly paper, *Aris's Gazette*, was generally a supporter of Church and State, although not openly aligned with either Tory or Whig interest.[2] From 1825, the *Birmingham Journal* joined the *Gazette* as a weekly, Saturday morning paper: it included London news received up to the previous evening, reflecting the town's appetite for commercial and political connection with the capital.[3] Originally under Tory editorship, the *Journal* became closely associated with the campaign for political reform from 1829 onwards.[4] As for periodicals, there were at least thirty produced at various times between 1815 and 1832. Many of these were extremely short-lived. They included literary criticism, miscellaneous essays and poetry. The theatre was a favourite topic, covered by the *Birmingham Spectator*, the *Mousetrap* and the *Theatrical John Bull*.[5]

These local publications, together with the national press, were sold by many small booksellers and read in a number of newsrooms, both private and public.[6] The newsroom in Waterloo Street, which opened in July 1825, claimed to provide the leading London, provincial and foreign newspapers, shipping, commercial and law intelligence as well as local journals.[7] Such newsrooms were mostly middle-class institutions but there were alternatives. Some booksellers and printers kept rooms, while George Edmonds, one of the protagonists in this story, kept 'Coffee Rooms' in Union Street in the early 1820s. Here he sold the radical press such as Cobbett's *Political Register* and Mrs Edmonds supplemented the family's precarious income by trading

---

2   Briggs, 'Press and Public', 109–10.
3   R. K. Dent, *Old and New Birmingham, Volume Two from 1760–1832* (Wakefield, MA: E. P. Publishing, 1973) (originally 1878–1880), 418–19.
4   Briggs, 'Press and Public', 111–12.
5   Briggs, 'Press and Public', 119; T. Harman, and W. Showell, *Showell's Dictionary of Birmingham* (Birmingham: Cornish Brothers, 1885), Dodo Reprint, 318–19.
6   J. A. Langford, *A Century of Birmingham Life from 1741 to 1841 Vol. 2* (Birmingham: E. C. Osborne, 1868), 496–7.
7   Dent, *Old and New Birmingham, Vol. Two*, 430.

in boots and shoes.[8] Added to these reading venues were Birmingham's pubs, the chief social and debating venues of the day, which also stocked the press. When James Guest began to sell unstamped newspapers in defiance of the law in 1830, he offered them to publicans 'with the newspapers of the week'.[9] In this context it is hardly surprising that estimates suggest every newspaper could be read by ten to twenty people.[10] Newspapers might also be read aloud, further increasing their reach.[11]

Clearly there was a reading public which included middle- and working-class individuals. Although overall literacy rates were still restricted (29 per cent of bridegrooms and 47 per cent of brides still 'made their mark' on the register in the 1840s), there was a big enough pool of educated workers to sustain two Artisans Libraries, with another attached to the Mechanics Institute. Sunday schools, especially those of the dissenting churches, educated children and young adults.[12]

This vibrant print culture intersected with a sometimes turbulent political scene. Birmingham was not incorporated and had no council of its own. The press reported on the many local civic and commercial institutions which ran the town: the High and Low Bailiffs, the oligarchic Street Commissioners and the Poor Law Guardians who were elected by wealthier ratepayers. These institutions, run by the town's elite and, by convention, shared between Anglicans and dissenters, resisted public scrutiny but gradually had to accede to it.[13] Despite this, Birmingham's nonconformists

8   *Edmonds, Weekly Register*, No. 19, 8 January 1820; Library of Birmingham, Archives and Collections, *Report of the Proceedings of the Public Dinner Given in Honour of Mr Wooler on his Liberation from Warwick Gaol* (Birmingham, 1822) in Birmingham Miscellaneous D/7.

9   James Guest, 'A Free Press and How it Became Free', bound with W. Hutton, *A History of Birmingham*, 6th edition (Birmingham: James Guest, n.d.), 495.

10 Briggs, Press and Public, 117.

11 Rachel Matthews, *The History of the Provincial Press in England* (London: Bloomsbury, 2017,) 63.

12 Eric Hopkins, *The Rise of the Manufacturing Town: Birmingham and the Industrial Revolution* (Stroud: Sutton Publishing, 1998, revised edn), 161, 165–7.

13 Roger Ward, *City-State and Nation: Birmingham's Political History 1830–1940* (Chichester: Phillimore, 2005), 15–17; *Birmingham Journal*, 16 April 1831.

were the junior partner in the institutions and so had most interest in the town gaining borough status. Political debate had become increasingly focused on the need for parliamentary reform, especially as Birmingham had no MPs of its own. The campaign waxed and waned: in the difficult years immediately after the Napoleonic wars, the middle class had shown little enthusiasm. Leadership of the campaign fell to the Birmingham Hampden Club, chaired by George Edmonds, and made up of artisans, school teachers and shopkeepers. This group adhered to the programme of popular radicalism: manhood suffrage, an end to 'old corruption', removal of unjust taxes and opposition to repressive legislation.[14] Supporters of the Hampden Club sold the radical press and sometimes produced their own, such as *Edmonds' Weekly Register*. They engaged in a pamphlet war with Tory propagandists who advocated common-sense adherence to the status quo, fearing revolutionary outbreaks inspired by French experience. Several radical booksellers such as George Ragg and Joseph Russell were prosecuted for selling banned literature such as *The Republican* and the *Black Book*.[15] The period had culminated in a great meeting on Newhall Hill in July 1819, to elect Sir Charles Wolseley as a 'Legislatorial Attorney' – a substitute MP. Although the meeting had passed off without incident, escaping the fate of the one at St Peter's Field in Manchester that followed, its organisers had been charged with seditious conspiracy. George Edmonds consequently spent nine months in Warwick Gaol.[16]

The campaign for reform declined in the 1820s but resurfaced towards the end of the decade. Middle-class supporters of reform united around attempts to have parliamentary seats transferred to Birmingham and other industrial towns in the region. The Whig-leaning Unitarian lawyer Joseph Parkes, another protagonist in this story, played a role in this campaign. These early attempts failed and eventually, against a background of renewed distress, the banker and currency reformer Thomas Attwood took a lead. He gathered together a coalition of his own supporters and others he thought necessary to build a successful campaign; one of these was George

14   Ward, *City-State and Nation*, 20–1.
15   Dent, *Old and New Birmingham, Vol. Two*, 360.
16   Ward, *City-State and Nation*, 20–1.

Edmonds whose presence was considered essential to win working-class support. In January 1830 the Birmingham Political Union (BPU) was launched. Over the following two years the BPU was to play a significant role in the movement for parliamentary reform which dominated local and national political life until the passing of the Great Reform Act of 1832.[17]

The town was full of contrasts; there were innumerable examples of philanthropic endeavour and peaceful co-operation between those of different denominations and political persuasions. But at the same time differences could spill over into unruly behaviour. Any issue concerning the privileged place of the established Church was potentially divisive. The payment of church rates to the Anglican churches was a running source of resentment and the 1830s were punctuated by rowdy meetings in St Martins.[18] The town generated rival petitions on the issue of Catholic Emancipation, the one against being much better supported, and Daniel O'Connell was greeted by a 'No Popery' mob in 1828.[19] The town's workers supported innumerable Friendly Societies, which provided basic mutual support and insurance, but once trade unions were freed from legal shackles a burst of activity followed, with bargaining, strikes and opposing lock-outs by employers.[20]

The Birmingham Cooperative Society, formed in 1828 by William Pare, promoted the ideas of Robert Owen, and produced its own *Birmingham Cooperative Herald*.[21] This organisation deliberately encouraged the participation of women in what was otherwise a very male-dominated political and cultural scene. At its first anniversary, Pare presided over a tea party and meeting of over a hundred, including 'wives and children'.[22] Despite limited opportunities for female engagement, the late 1820s and early 1830s saw a gradual change. The Ladies' Society for the Relief of

17   Ibid., 21–2.
18   R. K. Dent, *The Making of Birmingham* (London: Simkin and Marshall, 1894), 407.
19   Ward, *City State and Nation*, 13.
20   Langford, *A Century of Birmingham Life*, 465–6.
21   *Birmingham Cooperative Herald*, April 1829–October 1830, L62.53.
22   E. W. Hampton, *Early Cooperation in Birmingham and District* (Birmingham: Birmingham Cooperative Society, 1928), L62.53, 18.

Negro Slaves brought a group of largely middle-class women into political campaigning. Women were active in the campaign for press freedom and repeal of the stamp duties. They attended the large reform public meetings although they did not have their own reform organisation until later in the 1830s.[23]

Birmingham was, therefore, a town with a habit of discussion and independent thought. Debate on the printed page or in the pubs and clubs was usually good-humoured but often sharp and sometimes full of invective. It was against this background of an effervescent print culture and frequently turbulent politics that the *Monthly Argus* appeared.

Asa Briggs called the *Argus*, 'one of the most extraordinary publications which has ever appeared in any city at any time'. The *Birmingham*, then *Monthly Argus and Public Censor*, was published from 1828 to 1834, at first as a weekly, but from 1829 onwards as a monthly magazine, a format that avoided newspaper taxes. There are no circulation figures, but its very survival in the face of libel charges and court cases testifies to the popularity of its diet of local news, literary comment and scandal. 'Tory–Radical in politics, vigorously anti-Catholic and anti-Dissent in religion, the *Argus* revelled in vituperation'.[24] As Briggs noted, the *Argus* reflected both the local political scene and a lively social life; the town was growing fast but it was still a tightly knit community, at least for the middling sort who probably made up most of the *Argus*'s readership.[25]

The *Argus*'s motto, an epigram from Alexander Pope, clearly situated it in a satirical tradition, but with a potentially unpleasant twist.

> Yes I am proud! I must be proud to see
> Men not afraid of God, afraid of me.

These two sides of the *Argus* co-existed: on the one hand the magazine delighted in deflating egos and attacking hypocrisy, on the other it could

---

23   Helen Rogers, '"What Right Have Women to Interfere with Politics?": The Address of the Female Political Union to the Women of England (1838)', in T. Ashplant and G. Smyth, *Explorations in Cultural History* (London: Pluto Press, 2001), 80–2.

24   Briggs, 'Press and Public', 120.

25   Briggs, 'Press and Public', 121–2.

threaten serious damage to reputations and did not refrain from exposing family scandals. The first volume of the magazine, suggested the compilers of *Showell's Dictionary of Birmingham*, was a 'tolerably well-conducted sheet of literary miscellany, [with] prominence being given to local theatrical matters and similar subjects', but from July 1830 onwards, unpleasant gossip began to outweigh other content.[26]

The owner of the *Argus* was Joseph Allday (1798–1861), who was originally a partner with his brothers in a small metal business. Allday fell out with the family and struck out as a news magazine publisher, first producing the short-lived *Mousetrap* in 1824. To escape libel charges Allday always tried to keep in the background and avoided being called the editor, leaving his printers to carry the can. The printer who finally fell foul of the law was William Chidlow who had to bear the brunt of attacks such as being horse-whipped by metal manufacturer George Frederick Muntz.[27] Allday was a Tory and a loyalist, a supporter of the established Church and the monarchy. Reporting on a 'Birmingham Protestant Meeting', the *Argus* applauded those who opposed Catholic Emancipation and inveighed against the 'Irish bog-trotter', Reverend McDonnell, who spoke in support of the measure.[28] Evangelists of any persuasion were a favourite target: even Church of England priests might find themselves lampooned if they were 'new-light' clergymen.[29]

'Socinians' – Allday's preferred, faintly abusive term for dissenters who did not accept the idea of the trinity – also came in for their share of attack. Many Unitarians from the Old and New Meeting were prominent in Birmingham's business and civic community in this period. The *Argus* disliked Unitarians for their theology and liberals for their politics so the 'Cabal', a Whig-leaning group of Unitarians around the lawyers Joseph Parkes and William Redfern, was another regular target.[30]

26   Harman and Showell, *Showell's Dictionary of Birmingham*, 318.
27   Harman and Showell, *Showell's Dictionary of Birmingham*, 319.
28   *Birmingham Argus and Public Censor*, Vol. 2, 1 March 1829, 135.
29   *Monthly Argus and Public Censor*, Vol. 1, December 1829, 206.
30   *Monthly Argus*, Vol. 2, December 1830, 322–5.

Women might be treated with chivalry and sentimental regard but were expected to stay in their place. The *Argus* reflected the common view that women would be best employed making a decent home and here it blamed employers rather than the women themselves. The employment of girls was particularly castigated: they would miss out on education, fail to learn housewifely arts and be thrown in harm's way, 'What can we expect from such girls? Can we hope to find them honest, industrious servants? Can a poor man hope to find an economical housewife, who will look to his comforts and those of his family?'[31] This genuine, but thoroughly patriarchal, concern for the well-being of poorer classes is typical of Allday's Tory-radical views. Any middle-class woman flouting societal norms might expect to be noticed by the *Argus*. In 'Lies of the Day', a regular satirical column, a more vicious side of Allday's lampooning emerges 'It is not true that the daughter of a ci-devant chronicler (commonly called *The Jew*) has yet got a husband by means of the collecting carriage, but it is true that she longs for a helpmate, eagerly anticipating the bridal hour.'[32] There is enough information here for identification. The men that Allday attacked might be able to challenge him in conversation, on the street or, eventually, in court. Women had no such recourse, so this was a particularly unpleasant form of satire. Women of an evangelical bent who were active in the public sphere offended twice over: the 'canting' daughters of Benjamin Guest were criticised for collecting for a missionary school.[33] Such middle-class women were operating outside the sphere of the home. Here Allday anticipates Dickens, whose Mrs Jellyby in *Bleak House* spent more time concerned with the poor in Africa than her own family.

Like other Tory radicals, Allday's support for Church and State did not mean he defended all aspects of the status quo. He supported a number of social reforms. The *Argus* uncovered abuses in the management of the Birmingham workhouse, campaigned to improve conditions in the Court of Requests gaol and opposed the 'barbarous' use of corporal punishment at

31   *Monthly Argus*, Vol. 1, August 1829, 23–4.
32   *Monthly Argus*, Vol. 1, August 1829, 25.
33   *Monthly Argus*, Vol. 2, December 1830, 325.

the Quarter Sessions.[34] In 1833, the *Argus* launched an attack on the practice of 'sand-wheeling', which the Birmingham Guardians had launched as employment for paupers. Just as with Oastler's campaign against child labour in the textile factories, it attacked the hypocrisy of those who condemned slavery abroad but tolerated it at home.[35] Allday's own attitude to the abolition movement was equivocal. He opposed slavery but his Tory loyalties ensured that he favoured compensating the slave-owners. He echoed their argument that black people would not work without compulsion: 'indolence is the main character of his [the black man's] nature and we would be glad to hear from the anti-slavery associations how the colonies are to be cultivated if the slaves be freed.'[36] Another characteristic of Allday's Tory-radical suggestions for improvements were that they depended on employers and civic leaders behaving better: his was a paternal approach to social reform. Plebian associations such as the Birmingham Cooperative Society received short shrift; it would be 'conducive to riot and disturbance, bickering and squabbling and subversive, not only of the Christian faith, but social union'.[37] Despite the apparent respectability of the tea-drinking Co-operative Society, Allday undoubtedly saw its Owenite ideology as a threat. If those from the lower classes could organise improvements for themselves, then old hierarchies could not survive.

Wherever the ground was shifting with regards to gender or class relations, Allday expressed an attitude of unease, and the same applied when it came to political change. The *Argus's* attitude towards political reform typified the approach of Tory-radicals in the unenfranchised towns. Allday was in favour of a moderate degree of political reform and especially Birmingham's right to representation. He was, at first, a cautious supporter of the Birmingham Political Union and applauded the fact that, with Thomas Attwood in charge, the Whigs would not dominate Birmingham's

34 *Monthly Argus* Vol. 1, January 1830, 297; Vol. 1, February 1830, 338; Vol. 4, November 1832, 386.

35 *Monthly Argus*, Vol. 5, January 1833, 194.

36 *Monthly Argus*, Vol. 2, November 1830, 286.

37 *Monthly Argus*, Vol. 1, February 1830, 389–41.

reform movement: 'The Cabal ought not to be at the helm'.[38] However, once the popular character of the BPU emerged, Allday took fright. In August 1830, the *Argus* deplored the re-election of three members of the BPU's Political Council, 'one an atheist and seller of radical literature, one a demagogue and poacher on the legal profession, the third a cooperator, a great man at the Mechanical Institute and known for levelling principles' – these were Joseph Russell, George Edmonds and William Pare, respectively.[39] Still worse was a meeting called to celebrate the July Revolution in France, which was supported by both the Political Council and the 'Cabal'.[40] In January 1831, the *Argus* declared that 'the Church has been assailed, the State has been traduced, Protestants have been vilified'.[41] It had turned its back on Attwood and the BPU altogether and in doing so, expressed the concerns of Birmingham Tories and Anglicans about the Political Union's growing power in the town.[42]

The dramatic quarrel between the *Monthly Argus* and George Edmonds resulted in Allday's incarceration and contributed to Edmonds' financial difficulties in the early 1830s. Edmonds, with his radical background and credentials as an imprisoned popular leader, was perhaps an inevitable target. Edmonds came from a predominantly artisan family: his father was a jeweller turned Baptist minister whose congregation was drawn from workers and small traders in the manufacturing district. Besides chairing the Hampden Club and organising popular meetings, he had published radical journals between 1819 and 1820, *Edmonds' Weekly Recorder* and *Edmonds' Weekly Register*. He had successfully campaigned against corruption in the Workhouse and been elected to the Board of Guardians.[43] Despite

---

38   *Monthly Argus* Vol. 1, December 1829, 207.

39   *Monthly Argus*, Vol. 2, August 1830, 93–4.

40   *Monthly Argus*, Vol. 2, September 1830, 159–60.

41   *Monthly Argus*, Vol. 2, January 1831, 370.

42   Ian Cawood and Chris Upton, 'Joseph Chamberlain and the Birmingham Satirical Journals 1876–1911', in Ian Cawood and Chris Upton, eds, *Joseph Chamberlain: International Statesman, National leader, Local Icon* (Basingstoke: Palgrave Macmillan, 2016), 180.

43   Susan Thomas, 'Edmonds, George (1788–1868), radical and philologist', *Oxford Dictionary of National Biography*, <http://www.oxforddnb.com/view/10.1093/ref:odnb/9780198614128.001.0001/odnb-9780198614128-e-74226>, accessed 1 April 2018.

this shared opposition to corruption, Edmonds' radicalism was of a very different stripe from Allday's Tory-radical politics. He was an advocate of manhood, or at least household, suffrage, he was a fervent opponent of slavery, he opposed the privileges of the established Church and supported Catholic Emancipation. He represented everything Allday opposed.

The *Argus*'s first attacks on Edmonds were not on this radical reputation, but on his attempts to join the legal profession. By 1828, Edmonds had abandoned his life as a schoolmaster. 'He longed for more active duties and a larger sphere of work', suggested his contemporary Eliezer Edwards. Edmonds took advantage of the fact that there were no strict rules over who could appear as a 'Representative' in court. He began to appear regularly in the local Police or Magistrates Court and the Court of Requests, which dealt with local debt cases.[44] However, at the same time as Edmonds was pursuing this goal, senior lawyers were anxious to regularise and control access to the profession. The Birmingham Law Society, formed in 1818, was keen to do just this.[45] It took a particularly dim view of upstart amateur lawyers. In 1828 it upbraided one of its own members, the lawyer Joseph Parkes, for allowing Edmonds to act at the Quarter Sessions in his own name.[46] The *Argus* was not generally a fan of lawyers, but it was happy to join in criticism of Edmonds' ambitions. In February 1828 it expressed astonishment that Edmonds was being allowed to practise in both the local magistrates and debtors courts 'as though he were a regular bred attorney'. How could those on the bench tolerate this?

> If professional gentlemen pay for their education, they certainly ought to be permitted to derive every lawful advantage from their practice, and not be superseded therein by intruders, totally unauthorised, and certainly unqualified, to occupy their

44   E. Edwards, 'George Edmonds' in *Personal Recollections of Birmingham and Birmingham Men* (Birmingham: Midland Educational Trading, 1877), reproduced by The Echo Library, 2007.

45   *Birmingham Law Society Bulletin*, 2006, 6.

46   Library of Birmingham, Archives and Collections, *Records and Minutes of the Birmingham Law Society*, Minute Book A, 26 March 1828, 8 April 1828 and 23 August 1828, MSS 2830.

stations. We hope those gentlemen will take this hint, and assert their authority, in regulating the professional practice in these courts, and thus protect the interests of the suitors therein.[47]

In Allday's class-conscious view, Edmonds had upset the natural order of society: he was an 'intruder' without the breeding needed to become a professional lawyer; nor had he paid for his education. The sons of poor Baptist ministers ought not to have the temerity to try to join a gentlemanly occupation. Even when Edmonds tried to regularise his position by becoming an articled clerk, the *Argus* continuing to refer to him as a 'poacher' on the legal profession.[48]

Edmonds became one of the town characters that the *Argus* loved to satirise, especially if he evinced any hint of social pretensions. In 'Lies of the Day', dated June 1830, it suggested that it was 'not true that GE has had a full-length portrait of himself taken – for the purpose of handing down to posterity the form and fashion of his tremendous cloak. It is not true that this fat Narcissus of 50 sleeps in said cloak'.[49] This satire took a sharper turn in the second half of 1830. Earlier in the year, the *Argus* had still been disposed to praise Edmonds when it suited its political purpose. It had been generous when Edmonds had launched into the local Whigs, Redfern and Parkes, for opposing the formation of the BPU: 'Mr E. was fully awake to (Parkes's) sophistry in a powerful and well-managed speech, which had an astonishing effect upon the meeting, and opened the eyes of those Joseph Parkes wished to delude'.[50] Such praise vanished as Allday became more critical of the reformers and as Edmonds' role became more prominent. The *Argus* suggested he was acting as a hidden editor of the *Birmingham Journal*. When Edmonds denied he had such a role, the *Argus* acknowledged he had one fact on his side. It had seen a handwritten piece by Edmonds with such poor spelling that he could not possibly be acting

47   *Birmingham Argus and Public Censor*, Vol. 2, No. 7, 1 February 1829, 103.
48   *Pigot's Directory of Birmingham*, 1829; *Monthly Argus*, Vol. 2, August 1830, 94.
49   *Monthly Argus*, Vol. 1, June 1830, 519. Edmonds was forty-four.
50   *Monthly Argus*, Vol. 1, February 1830, 349.

in any journalistic capacity![51] This was of course a criticism guaranteed to needle Edmonds, the ex-schoolmaster, journalist and would-be lawyer.

By August 1830, the *Argus* was keen to remind readers of Edmonds' radical political record: the 'roaring demagogue' had been left at home when the leadership of the BPU attended an election meeting in Warwick because 'only a few years have lapsed since he was a prisoner in the gaol at W. for similar meddling in elections', a reference to his incarceration following the July 1819 Newhall Hill meeting.[52] From November 1830, the *Argus* adopted the epithet 'Munchausen Edmonds; in other words, a boastful teller of tall tales or outright liar.[53] Edmonds was, as *Showell's Dictionary of Birmingham* put it, 'none too tender-tongued himself'.[54] His political invective was sharp and his use of irony consistent, whether in court or on a public platform. He was used to being called a demagogue, and had matters rested there, the case against the *Argus* might not have proceeded.

But by this point, the *Argus* was sharpening more than its political attacks. *Showell's Dictionary* dated a coarsening of approach from the new series starting in July 1830. 'The publication became nothing better than the receptacle of rancour, spite, and calumny, public men and private individuals alike being attacked, and often in the most scurrilous manner'.[55] A seriously unpleasant aspect of the *Argus's* method began to surface: individuals were being approached to pay 'hush money' so that stories shaming themselves or their families would not appear.[56] A flavour of what the *Argus* could deliver came in the November 1830 issue. It delivered 'a hint to a certain tall lady of a rosy countenance that she was seen going into an accommodating house with a gentleman not her husband. She is warned'.[57]

George Edmonds' brother Edward also came under the spotlight. Edward Edmonds' London journalistic career had stalled, suggested the

51 *Monthly Argus*, Vol. 2, July 1830, 4.
52 *Monthly Argus*, Vol. 2, August 1830, 121.
53 *Monthly Argus*, Vol. 2, November 1830, 225.
54 Harman and Showell, *Showell's Dictionary of Birmingham*, 319.
55 Ibid.
56 *Birmingham Journal*, 19 February 1831.
57 *Monthly Argus*, Vol. 2, November 1830, 224.

Argus, and he now practised 'like Munchausen in our Birmingham Office – as clerk to some battered, broken-down, vagabond limb of the law'. More seriously it accused him of malpractice in a well-known case concerning the death of a prize-fighter.[58] By the end of 1830, not only had relations between Allday and various reformers worsened, but the *Argus* had become despised and feared by an increasing number of citizens. At this point Parkes had begun investigations to prove that Allday was the editor of the journal.[59] Matters came to a head at a Town's Meeting called to support political reform in December 1830. The *Journal* reported that Allday had been spotted at the back of the meeting and pushed forward to jeers from the crowd. Edmonds called out, 'let the wretch come forward who eats the dirty bread of slander' and Joseph Parkes openly accused him of being the editor of the *Argus*. Allday admitted writing for the *Argus* but denied being the editor and was able to escape.[60]

The February 1831 *Argus* contained several references to Edmonds. One was a typical Allday fabrication and Edmonds seems to have ignored it. A small item suggested that Edmonds had been a follower of the millenarian visionary Joanna Southcott in 1813.[61] What might be the origin of this claim? The Southcottians did indeed have a church in Birmingham in that period and conducted a debate with some Baptists in May 1812. Edmonds was moderator of the last debate and had begun by stating his intentions to act fairly; he wanted Southcott's adherents to explain their faith. In his closing remarks, however, he had stuck to Baptist orthodoxy and read out an article from the *Evangelical Magazine* of 1805 which rejected Southcott's teachings as a blasphemous 'confused mass of materials'.[62] He was certainly no follower of Southcott. Another reference to Edmonds was much more serious, however. Under the heading 'Munchausen Unmasked', the *Argus* published a letter which suggested that Edmonds had, some

58   *Monthly Argus*, Vol. 2, December 1830, 326–8.
59   Jessie Buckley, *Joseph Parkes of Birmingham* (London: Methuen, 1926), 50–1.
60   *Birmingham Journal*, 18 December 1830.
61   *Monthly Argus*, Vol. 3, February 1831, 31–2.
62   Cadbury Research Library, University of Birmingham, *Diary of Joseph Dixon* Vol. I, MS 14.1, 174–80; *Evangelical Magazine*, Vol. 13, 1805.

years earlier, left his post at a school in Blockley, near Chipping Campden in Gloucestershire, fleeing debt. Specifically, he had avoided payment to a poor woman huckster. The letter acknowledged that the school had been respectable and well-attended; Edmonds had secured the position from Mr Smith, a Baptist minister and friend of his father's. However, he had ruined the life of the poor woman who was still complaining about her treatment years later (see Appendix).[63] It was this accusation which finally provoked Edmonds to bring a libel case. The charge may have been too serious to ignore. It is also possible that Edmonds and Parkes, acting in concert, were waiting for a suitable case to take against Allday.

On Monday, 7 February, 'considerable interest was shown at the Birmingham Public Office when it was understood that Mr George Edmonds was about to apply for a warrant against Chidlow for various libels'.[64] In a characteristic piece of showmanship, Edmonds told the magistrates he had an application to make of a somewhat novel nature. The *Argus* had attacked the characters of many respectable citizens, he declared, and he himself had passed over many gross attacks. It was time for the authorities to put down such a vile publication. He suggested that the magistrates had the power to take cognisance of libel, hold the offender to bail and commit him in default of sureties. After some hesitation, the justices agreed. Edmonds read two articles, one an 'Epitaph' which had compared his character to that of Richard III and the other the letter headed 'Munchausen Unmasked'. Edmonds declared the whole story an invention. He had not known such a woman in Blockley nor had he left the village a sixpence in debt.[65] A warrant was issued and taken to Chidlow's printing shop in Great Charles Street, where the officers eventually broke in. The unfortunate printer was handcuffed and taken to the Public Office gaol. 'During this ignominious perambulation, the crowd on more than one occasion, evinced the most boisterous exhultation [*sic*]', reported the *Birmingham Journal*, clearly in a celebratory mood itself. Chidlow was put in the jail yard, not with the male thieves but in 'appropriate accommodation

63   *Monthly Argus* Vol. 3, February 1831, 41.
64   *Birmingham Journal*, 12 February 1831.
65   *Birmingham Journal*, 12 February 1831.

with the common prostitutes'.[66] Sureties were allowed the next day. Over the following days several other individuals came forward, alleging libel by the *Argus*. A week later it was Allday's turn. Joseph Parkes appeared before the magistrates, producing evidence of Allday's involvement in the *Argus*. When Allday appeared it became apparent that some members of the public had already meted out rough justice: 'Allday appeared with his head and face horribly disfigured. His nose, eyes and cheeks were of various hues and his appearance most ghastly'.[67] The libel cases were now applied to him as well as Chidlow. Meanwhile Chidlow's printing press and manuscript copies of the *Argus* were seized.[68]

Of all the characters who had been maligned by Allday, why was it Edmonds who came forward? Certainly he had been a particular target: the ambitious son of a Baptist minister, a convicted radical who was gaining prominence in the town as a member of the Political Council of the BPU. Edmonds perhaps had less to lose and more to gain from taking Allday to court. Others faced losing their respectable character if Allday's slurs became the subject of such public discussion. Edmonds also possessed both a considerable ego and genuine courage. He had the audacity to take Allday on but did not (and probably could not) do this alone. He needed the backing, connections and resources that Parkes, the respectable Unitarian lawyer, could access. This compact was further revealed in the trial that followed.

The libel cases were heard at the Warwick Easter Sessions, beginning on the 5 April 1831. They had been delayed a week because Edmonds had fallen ill, the strain of the case possibly telling. Before any business had been transacted, Joseph Allday and his brother John were bound over to keep the peace after an incident in which they threatened Joseph Parkes in the Hall of the Court.[69] Matthew Davenport Hill, a member of a leading family of Birmingham educationalists and a rising lawyer, conducted the cases

66   *Birmingham Journal*, 12 February 1831.
67   *Birmingham Journal*, 19 February 1831.
68   *Birmingham Journal*, 19 February 1831.
69   *Birmingham Journal*, 9 April 1831.

against Chidlow and Allday.[70] Hill had connections to both Parkes and Edmonds: Parkes was a fellow Unitarian and Benthamite reformer, while Edmonds had been a youthful debating companion.[71] Hill had defended Edmonds in his 1820 trial for seditious conspiracy after the Newhall Hill meeting and had made a name for himself despite losing the case.

The first case was brought by Samuel Morris, a Birmingham wine merchant. The *Argus* had implied that Morris had refused to pay for his son-in-law's coffin and attempted to interfere with a family inheritance. Hill took the opportunity to lay out his general case against the *Argus*. He stressed the threat that the magazine posed to respectable citizens-an approach designed to get the jury on side. No publication had approached the *Argus* in libel in the history of printing, 'It directed its attention to no branch of literature or science but ... was conducted for no other purpose than the introduction of as many names of the middle class as could offensively and libellously cram into the publication'. Witnesses were called to show that Chidlow was the printer and Allday the editor, the libel was quickly established and the jury found against the defendants after five minutes deliberation.[72]

Joseph Parkes' case was taken the following day. Various libellous statements were cited including the designation of Parkes as 'a bully, a braggart, a trembler and a coward'. Parkes was unlikely to have been seriously troubled by these epithets. It became clear that the real point of this trial from the point of view of the prosecutors was to establish beyond doubt that Allday was the real controller of the *Argus*. Shelton Mackenzie, a previous employee, was called as a witness and declared that Allday was the real editor. Once again the jury found the libel proved. At this point Edmonds offered to stop his prosecution if the defendants would plead guilty and promised not to renew publication. Chidlow took these terms

---

70 The family of Thomas Wright Hill ran a progressive school in Birmingham. Penny Post founder Rowland Hill was another member.

71 Rosamond and Florence Davenport Hill, *The Recorder of Birmingham: a Memoir of Matthew Davenport Hill* (London: Macmillan, 1878), 11, 25.

72 *Birmingham Journal*, 9 April 1831.

but Allday refused and his case came up the following day.[73] Matthew Hill's conduct of Edmonds' case showed great concern to establish Edmonds' respectable character; after all, the last time he and Edmonds had been together in Warwick Court, Hill had been defending Edmonds for his role in organising the July 1819 Newhall Hill meeting. Hill's opening stressed the importance of character to Edmonds who was seeking a career in the law late in life but with every chance of success. Character was indispensable to a member of the law. Edmonds had a political role in the neighbour-hood: 'It was no dishonour to impute a political character to him. But this article exposed his private character'. Hill reminded the jury that there was no need to prove the falsehood of the libel, but Edmonds was anxious to expose its falsehood and would give evidence to that effect.[74] Edmonds agreed he had resided in Blockley but knew no such person as the coster-woman referred to and owed £10 to no one. Matthew Hill had to step in when Edmonds declared that he was proud of having served nine months for seditious conspiracy. 'I must check your pride', Hill interjected. Allday made a long and extraordinary speech in which he attacked Hill's politics, Parkes's religion and Mackenzie's treachery, but at the end admitted that the jury had no choice but to find him guilty and 'solemnly disavowed the editorship of the work'. The jury gave the guilty verdict without hesita-tion.[75] Allday was sentenced to a total of ten months and Chidlow to six.

The *Birmingham Journal*, perhaps now feeling slightly sorry for its crowing tone two months before, commented that this was 'a severe pun-ishment however deserved'. It explained that imprisonment was inevitable given Allday's inability to pay any damages and that the editor had made matters worse by his behaviour in court.[76] A few days later, the *Birmingham Journal* expressed 'the obligation of the inhabitants to those gentlemen who have fearlessly come forward to expose this monster of calumny and malig-nant slander'.[77] A testimonial was launched for Edmonds which garnered

73   *Birmingham Journal*, 9 April 1831.
74   *Birmingham Journal*, 9 April 1831
75   *Birmingham Journal*, 9 April 1831.
76   *Birmingham Journal*, 9 April 1831.
77   *Birmingham Journal*, 9 April 1831.

wide support. While some of that support might have been in response to his campaigning work for the BPU, other donations probably expressed the gratitude of neighbours relieved from Allday's attentions. On 21 March 1831 a letter had already appeared in *Aris's Gazette* describing Edmonds as 'a laborious, indefatigable and disinterested servant of the town', who was facing heavy loss from his challenge to the 'that disgusting monthly publication'. The letter suggested that some leading men should come forward, while the writer, 'a Ratepayer' would be glad to help collect the smaller donations.[78] A meeting of the 'Friends of George Edmonds' duly took place on 23 April 1831 at the Globe Tavern with John Betts in the chair. The Reverend T. M. McDonnell successfully proposed

> That Mr George Edmonds, by his superior talents, by the tried integrity, the intrepid spirit, and the persevering industry with which he has for a long series of years devoted himself to the great cause of public liberty, and more especially to the rights, privileges and welfare of his fellow townsmen, has established a just claim to their approbation and esteem.[79]

The *Argus* was forced to close but re-emerged in June 1832, soon after Allday's release. Showell noted that from then on 'the vile scurrility of the earlier paper was abandoned to a great extent, it was permitted to appear as long as customers could be found to support it, ultimately dying out with the last month of 1834'.[80]

Edmonds was able to win his libel case without proving the *Argus's* story untrue, but it would be interesting to find out if there was any basis to the tale. Did Edmonds, a radical politician critical of powerful interests, exploit a poor shopkeeper? Or was Allday prepared to simply invent a story to keep up his circulation? His technique had been demonstrated in relation to the Joanna Southcott story, to take an old report and weave a new fabrication around it.

In court, Edmonds agreed that he had been in Blockley. There was indeed a Baptist Church in the town, whose Meeting House was opened

---

78   *Aris's Gazette*, 16 March 1831.
79   *Aris's Gazette*, 16 May 1831.
80   Harman and Showell, *Showell's Dictionary of Birmingham*, 319.

in 1794. Its minister was the Reverend Elias Smith, a pastor of some note. The Baptist presence in the area could be traced back to dissenters of the late seventeenth century but had been augmented by silk-weavers moving to the area from Coventry, some of whom became mill-owners.[81] The connection between Elias Smith and George Edmonds' father, who was pastor of the Birmingham Bond Street Chapel was highly probable. Both had studied at the Baptist Bristol Academy about 1780 and both were supported in their early preaching years by local minister Reverend James Butterworth.[82] It is very likely that, as a young man, George would be sent to keep school under the eye of Reverend Smith. It is not possible to trace the school: it is unlikely to have been the main one in the village whose building still stands next to the Anglican Church, but was more likely to have been a separate day school aimed at the children of the Baptist congregation – mill owners and silk weavers. There is simply no way of verifying or disproving the story of the poor huckster, as, of course, Allday must have known.

It is also difficult to pinpoint an exact date for Edmonds' presence in Blockley. His suggestion in court that he had been there twenty years before puts the date at about 1810–1811. However, there is some evidence that he was connected with Blockley a little earlier. In November 1809 the banns were read in St Peter's Church, Harborne, near Birmingham for the marriage of George Whitfield Edmonds and Sophia Figgures.[83] The latter was the daughter of Thomas and Hannah Figgures, nee Peyton, of Blockley.[84] The Figgures and Peyton families were significant inhabitants of Blockley. The Peytons were a Baptist mill-owning family and related to

81   H. E. M. Icely, revised and updated by Jeremy Bourne, *Blockley through Twelve Centuries: Analysis of a Cotswold Parish* (Blockley: Blockley Heritage Society, 1974/2013), 107–14.

82   Icely, *Blockley through Twelve Centuries*, 10; A. Langley, *Birmingham Baptists Past and Present* (London, Kingsgate Press, 1939), 81–2.

83   George Whitfield Edmonds and Sophia Figures, Record of Banns, 5–19 November 1809, Harborne St Peter, Library of Birmingham, *Birmingham, Church of England Marriages and Banns, 1754–1937*, DRO 61, 552.

84   Sophia Figgures, baptised 8 April 1791; Gloucestershire Archives, Gloucester, *Gloucestershire Parish Registers*; P52 IN 1/1. Figgures is spelt in a variety of ways.

minister Elias Smith.[85] The marriage between George and Sophia did not take place; perhaps family intervention prevented it.

By early 1811, Edmonds was in Shrewsbury, associating with fellow Baptists and working on the problem of constructing a new type-making machine. His friend, Joseph Dixon, visited him in March of that year with a view to manufacturing this machine.[86] This project seems to have come to nothing and by 1812 Edmonds was back in Birmingham.[87]

All the principal characters in this affair went on to have respectable careers. Joseph Parkes moved to London and became secretary of the commission on municipal corporations and a parliamentary solicitor.[88] George Edmonds overcame many hurdles to pursue his legal career and became Clerk of the Peace in 1839 in the Court of Quarter Sessions for the new Borough of Birmingham, while Matthew Hill became the first Recorder for the same Court.[89] Joseph Allday became a town councillor in the new Borough, serving from 1849 to 1859.

These men all continued as radicals of one variant or another. Joseph Parkes was one of the circle of philosophical radicals who espoused Benthamite ideas of improvement, Matthew Hill campaigned for penal reform and Edmonds became the grand old man of many liberal causes in Birmingham, besides inventing a new Universal Language and Alphabet.[90] Allday continued to battle corruption and mismanagement, in particular exposing poor treatment in the borough gaol. He was also a founder of the Ratepayers' Protection Society, whose aim was to keep borough spending in check. His brand of Tory radicalism led him to become a key member of the conservative 'Woodman council', notoriously opposed to spending

85   Icely, *Blockley through Twelve Centuries*, 84–5, 113.

86   Cadbury Research Library, *Diary of Joseph Dixon*, Vol. 1, MS 14.1, 6–29.

87   Library of Birmingham, Archives and Collections, *A Report of the Proceedings of the Artisans of Birmingham*, 1812, D19/A.

88   Buckley, *Joseph Parkes of Birmingham*, 116–33.

89   R. K. Dent, *The Making of Birmingham* (London: Simkin and Marshall, 1894), 381.

90   Buckley, *Joseph Parkes of Birmingham*, 169–77; R. and F. Hill, *The Recorder of Birmingham*, 176–218; Thomas, *George Edmonds*, *Oxford Dictionary of National Biography*.

public money on improvements, who were eventually ousted by Joseph Chamberlain's radical Liberals in 1873.

What do we learn from the brief journalistic career of Allday about early nineteenth-century provincial society, its attitudes and its press? This was a boisterous society where insults could be cheerfully traded, but its leading characters could not tolerate serious threats to their reputation any more than those of today. However, challenging libel was a difficult business risking reputation, health and finances. In the end, it took someone from outside established middle-class ranks to take Allday on, backed by those with money and connections.

The line between satire and libel was as hard to tread then as now. Were Allday's critics, many of whom supported press freedom and opposed stamp duty, being hypocritical when they attacked him? Possibly, but Allday's was a particularly unpleasant form of satire, often aimed at those with no ability to reply, and increasingly accompanied by attempts at blackmail.

The episode also confirms Briggs' judgements that in early nineteenth-century Birmingham, politics was taken seriously and religious affiliation remained significant. By the turn of 1830–1831, the movement for political reform had moved centre-stage in political life. A Tory, even a Tory-radical like Allday, might now feel threatened. The ground was shifting under his feet. The old certainties of church and state were being challenged. The outcome of the trial confirmed that radical and nonconformist identities were now accorded more tolerance in provincial Britain. In contrast, a supporter of the status quo and of Anglican monopoly power such as Allday could no longer rely on the very hierarchy he defended. This episode was one small harbinger of things to come. Only a year after Allday's trial, the country experienced the turbulence of the 'Days of May' and the passing of the Great Reform Act.

Finally, these events reflect changing social relations. Allday came from a small-trader background, Edmonds from an artisan one. Both were able to overcome vicissitudes and maintain themselves, albeit precariously, within the town's political and social spheres and participate in its print culture. Other social changes are harder to detect because they are partly hidden. Women's voices are hard to trace in this whole affair. Women appear as the object of Allday's pity or prejudice or innuendo. They do not have recourse to the law, or to print, themselves. However, the very fact that the *Argus* was disturbed by the public activities of women indicates that a shift in gender relations might be occurring.

Seventy years on from the publication of Briggs' essay, his observations on the importance of the local press within provincial society, and his championing of it as a source for historians, remain a useful guide. Absences, for instance of women's voices, also need to be noted. The controversies engendered by the press, as well as the original material, can add to our knowledge of those societies.

Appendix

'Munchausen Unmasked', *Monthly Argus and Public Censor*, Vol. 3, No. 1, February 1831:

> To the Editor of the Monthly *Argus*
> Sir: The present is an important era in the Political World, individuals are continually appearing on the stage of politics, some with high-sounding appellations of 'High Church and King Men', Whig, and radical Reformers. Among the partisans of the latter has appeared a man in the name of Edmonds, who of late has cut a pretty considerable figure among the inhabitants of Birmingham, and he appears to have a number of followers among the laborious classes of your townsmen; now I think that as he has set himself up as a leader, and a director of the movements and opinions of the public, that the said public should be a little acquainted with the character and principle of a man before they adopt his opinions, and allow his conduct to be a guide for theirs. I know the movements of the man from the commencement of his public career, and considering that neither his character nor political conduct partakes of that degree of honour and integrity that I should like a man to possess to whom I would look up to or advise with, regarding my actions and conduct, I have taken the liberty of addressing you, and giving you a little information.
>
> I shall commence with his residence in Blockley, a small village about 4 miles from Camden, in Gloucestershire: he there rented a house from Lord Northwick and kept a school, which I considered respectable, and was well-attended, but his dissipated habits kept his purse empty, the consequence was, he got in debt with his landlord,

and various tradespeople; amongst the latter was a poor and almost helpless woman, who for her existence kept a small huckster's shop. He by degrees ran up his bill to £10, under a promise that at the quarter's end all should be paid. The quarter came and he bolted: the Woman had, through her faith in his promises, contracted a debt, under the amount of his bill, with her grocer (I believe, a Mr Mathews of Camden). His conduct rendered her unable to pay him: her credit ruined, she was absolutely obliged to go to the Workhouse! I had the opportunity of seeing her in the year 1828. A complete object distressed in mind and body. She referred to her little cottage, and regretted she had ever seen the schoolmaster, as she called him, who consigned her to the Workhouse. I found that he was introduced to Blockley by a Mr Smith, a Baptist minister, a friend of his late father's, and when he bolted from thence, I find, he went to Shipston-upon-Stour, and from thence also bolted to Birmingham. At the former place I shall commence my narrative. In the mean time

I am, Mr Editor, your obedient servant,

ANTI-HUMBUG

January 14th 1831

4 'Mr O'Connor, Famous Chartist, Visits Town': Reporting Chartism in South-west Scotland

The early years of Victoria's reign were a period of active campaigning for political reform. The Reform Act of 1832 had only provided for a limited widening of the franchise. The campaign to repeal the Corn Laws, which kept the price of bread artificially high, had begun many years earlier, and did not finally achieve its object until 1846. In 1838, the London Working Men's Association drafted the People's Charter, consisting of six demands: universal male suffrage; secret ballot; annual parliamentary elections; constituencies of equal size; salaries for Members of Parliament; and the abolition of the property qualification for MPs. In May 1838 the Scottish campaign for what became the National Petition, presented to Parliament the following year, was launched at a meeting on Glasgow Green which was attended by many thousands of supporters. In the wake of this rally, working men's associations and universal suffrage associations were set up in many areas. The Dumfries Working Men's Association, for example, came into being by August 1838, and over the next three years or so similar associations were set up in towns throughout Scotland's south-western region. The focus of this essay is the period from mid-1838 until the decline of Chartist activism in south-west Scotland following the failure of the second National Petition to Parliament in 1842, as reported in the pages of two local newspapers – the *Dumfries Times*, and the *Dumfries and Galloway Herald and Advertiser*. The third newspaper published in the town, the *Dumfries Courier*, was not available for this study.

The south-western region of Scotland, an area roughly equating to the present county of Dumfries and Galloway, then comprised three counties: Dumfriesshire to the east, with its county town of Dumfries on its western border with the Stewartry of Kirkcudbright; the latter county,

which formed the central part of the region and in the west on the mouth
of the Solway Firth, Wigtownshire. The Royal Burgh of Dumfries was the
largest town in the region and for centuries had been the most important
administrative and marketing centre for the whole region, particularly for
agriculture and by 1830 the town had already acquired the nickname the
'Queen of the South'. In the 1830s and 1840s the town was at the height of
its importance as a trading and cultural centre for the whole region, and
was described as 'the metropolis of the south-west corner of Scotland [...]
Serving as a kind of capital, not only to its own shire, but also a portion
of Galloway'.[1]

There was little industrial activity in the area, although there was some
local manufacturing in trades relating to agricultural produce, such as brew-
eries, tanneries, and the manufacture of hosiery, shoes and hats. The town's
position on the cross-roads of traditional droving routes made it a centre
for livestock markets in particular. Dumfries lay on the main west coast
route between Glasgow south through Kilmarnock to the industrial towns
of Lancashire including Manchester and Liverpool. Roads also led west
from Dumfries to Portpatrick and Stranraer for boats to Ireland, north-
east to Edinburgh via Moffat and more directly towards the eastern border
towns such as Hawick, as well as via Carlisle to Newcastle. In the 1830s,
there were daily mail coaches to Edinburgh, Glasgow and Portpatrick, and
port facilities on the River Nith for the coastal trade and transatlantic sail-
ings. Today, Dumfries has largely been by-passed but in 1830, according to
Robert Chambers, it was considered to be 'the seventh town in Scotland in
point of population, and is certainly the fifth in respect of external appearance [...] In many respects, though of course upon a small scale, it has quite
the appearance of a populous wealthy city. Its principal thoroughfares are
lined with respectable shops'.[2] Dumfries was also the main centre for the
regional printing trade at this period, as well as for the production of local
newspapers. The trade was centred in and around the High Street, where
there were four letterpress print shops in operation for most of the period.

1   *Pigot & Co.'s National and Commercial Directory etc* (London: Pigot & Co., 1837), 351.
2   Robert and William Chambers, *The Gazetteer of Scotland* (Glasgow: Blackie, 1838),
     vol. 1, 217.

There were a number of booksellers in the town, three of which operated circulating libraries. By the end of the 1830s there was also a Law Library, the Dumfries Public Library (a subscription library) and three reading rooms 'supplied with London and provincial newspapers, magazines &c. (the principal one has an excellent billiard table)'.[3]

For most of the period between 1830 and 1850, three weekly newspapers were produced in Dumfries and circulated throughout the region. The titles varied as the proprietors and printers changed. The *Dumfries and Galloway Courier* was founded in 1809 and continued until 1884, when it merged with the *Dumfries and Galloway Herald and Advertiser*, which had itself been founded in 1835. The first proprietor of the *Courier* was Dr Henry Duncan, best known as the promoter of the savings bank movement. This interest was reflected in the *Courier*'s original focus on thrift and social improvement rather than politics. From 1817, its editor was John M'Diarmid, who had come from Edinburgh, where he had been working for a bank while moving in literary circles. M'Diarmid joined the partnership that established the *Scotsman*, but moved to Dumfries before the first issue of the Edinburgh newspaper was published, never writing for the *Scotsman*, although retaining a financial interest in the company. As well as editing the *Courier*, M'Diarmid took over as proprietor in 1837. Under his management, the *Courier* generally favoured Whig politics, and promoted social issues such as prison reform, education and electoral reform. In 1820, for example, M'Diarmid took part in the campaign for the repeal of the Test and Corporation Acts, and in 1829 he supported Catholic Emancipation:

> in opposition to the prejudices and passions of almost a whole community. [...] The circulation of the *Courier* fell off immensely, its office windows were broken, the Editor's effigy burnt, and serious injury to his own person attempted. Mr M'Diarmid's principles were, however, not the fancies of the hour, nor was he the man to flinch from them in the day of trial. He pursued his course calmly and perseveringly.[4]

3   *Pigot & Co.'s National and Commercial Directory etc*, 352.
4   W. R. M'Diarmid, *Memoir of John M'Diarmid, Editor of the Dumfries and Galloway Courier* (Dumfries: Dumfries and Galloway Courier, 1852), 18.

During the 1830s and later 'though he continued a consistent and able advocate of the political principles of his youth, he gradually withdrew from the more disturbed sphere of political agitation'.[5] It was M'Diarmid's qualities as a journalist and editor that led to Dumfries in the 1830s becoming, according to one of the town's historians, 'the chief force in journalism outside Edinburgh and Glasgow'.[6]

The *Dumfries Times* was founded in 1833: according to the 'Prospectus' in its first issue, 'A newspaper of enlarged, liberal, and consistent views has long been a desideratum in the south of Scotland. A wish for newspapers of such a character is generally entertained throughout the kingdom'.[7] The editor for its first two years was Robert K. Douglas 'a careful, laborious, and intelligent coadjutor, of long experience in the best school of newspaper management – the London press'.[8] Douglas later moved south to become the editor of the *Birmingham Journal*, and was prominent in the Chartist movement there. Under both Douglas and its next editor, Thomas Harkness, the *Times* continued to support causes such as universal suffrage, free trade and temperance. However, the newspaper did not support all Chartist principles, supporting, for example, triennial rather than annual parliaments. Of the Dumfries newspapers, the *Times* carried the most extensive reports on local reform activism, although these were not necessarily uncritical, in fulfilment of its promise to 'give to the counties and towns in the South of Scotland all the attention which their mutual connexion demands and deserves'.[9] It ceased in 1843, when Harkness moved the entire operation to Stranraer, where he founded the *Wigtownshire Free Press*.

The other local newspaper which reported on reform activities at this period was the *Dumfries and Galloway Herald and Advertiser*, but the tone of its articles on the subject was consistently critical of reform movements and their aspirations. It had taken the place of the long-established *Dumfries*

---

5   M'Diarmid, *Memoir of John M'Diarmid*, 18.
6   James Anderson Russell, *The Book of Dumfriesshire* (Dumfries: T. C. Farris, 1964), 82.
7   *Dumfries Times*, 10 January 1833, 1.
8   *Dumfries Times*, 10 January 1833, 1.
9   *Dumfries Times*, 10 January 1833, 1.

Weekly Journal, founded in the 1770s, which had ceased publication in 1833: its politics having been described as 'pallid Toryism'.[10] The founders announced in the prospectus that they 'at once identify themselves with that body of the community, who are more anxious to guard the blessings of social order they already enjoy, than disposed to hazard these by sweeping innovation'.[11] The *Herald*'s editor from 1835 to 1863 was the poet Thomas Aird, who had edited the *Edinburgh Weekly Journal*, and was a friend of Thomas Carlyle. The *Herald* generally promoted what have been described as 'High Tory' opinions.[12] It was, for example, a supporter of the continuation of the Corn Laws: in early 1837 it reprinted an item headed 'The London Anti-Corn Law Association' from the *Metropolitan Conservative Journal* which addressed a warning to the 'farmers of England' that 'this illegal committee' included nearly thirty Members of Parliament and exhorting them to keep a 'vigilant watch on the Administration, which is attempting to entrap and betray you'.[13]

The *Times* did not explicitly support the Chartist cause or the local Working Men's Association, but reported on reform demonstrations and other events in support of the People's Charter outside the region with varying degrees of approval. The *Herald*, in contrast, was consistently disapproving of any such demonstrations.

Another weekly newspaper was published in the town in the 1840s, but the *Dumfries and Galloway Standard* was not established until 1843, so falls outside the period. It is no coincidence that it first appeared in the year of the Church of Scotland's Disruption,[14] as the founders, who again included Dr Henry Duncan, wished to support 'the view of the Evangelical majority in the Church'.[15] In general, the newspaper supported

---

10   Russell, *The Book of Dumfriesshire*, 81.
11   'Prospectus' *Dumfries and Galloway Herald and Advertiser*, 23 March, 1835.
12   Russell, *Book of Dumfriesshire*, 83.
13   *Dumfries and Galloway Herald and Advertiser*, 16 October 1837, 2.
14   After around ten years of intense debate, during its General Assembly in 1843, the Church of Scotland split over the question of whether congregations had the right to appoint their own ministers, independently of secular influence or state interference. The result was the formation of the evangelically-inclined Free Church of Scotland.
15   Russell, *Book of Dumfriesshire*, 1.

social reform and broadly liberal politics. The *Standard's* importance in
the context of local Chartist activism lies in the fact that the editor from
1846 was William M'Dowall, who played a prominent part in the local
Working Men's Association and the reform movement generally. M'Dowall
was a native of Dumfries who had been educated at Dumfries Academy
before undertaking an apprenticeship with a local bookbinder. His brother
Robert was a compositor, and active in the Dumfries Typographical Society.
Later, after the Society had become one of the founding branches of the
Scottish Typographical Association in 1853,[16] Robert M'Dowall served as
the branch president for four years. William M'Dowall apparently worked
in Glasgow and London as a bookbinder, before working as a journalist
in Edinburgh for the *Scottish Herald* and then for the *Banner of Ulster* in
Belfast. He retained the post of editor of the *Standard* until his death in
1888. He was active in a range of local institutions, such as the Mechanics'
Institute and the Dumfries and Galloway Natural History and Antiquarian
Society, as well as serving on the Town Council. He was the author of a
number of books, including a history of Dumfries and he also contributed
articles to the *Encyclopaedia Britannica*.[17]

In the western Scottish borders, Dumfries itself and Annan, on the
route to Carlisle, were home to the earliest Working Men's Associations
for the region, dating from 1838. Those in Castle Douglas, Gatehouse of
Fleet, New Galloway and Newton Stewart were established in 1841. There
were also organisations in the eastern borders in Galashiels, Kelso, Selkirk,
Jedburgh, Hawick and Innerleithen which appear to have been associated
with those in Dumfries and the south-west.[18] As the main administrative and marketing centre for the region, the town of Dumfries was focus
for Chartist activism, although it was by no means the largest regional
centre in Scotland. Ayrshire, for example, added 17,000 signatures to the

---

16   The Scottish Typographical Association was the union representing letterpress print-
      ers (compositors and pressmen) in Scotland.

17   David Lockwood, *Dumfries' Story* (Dumfries: T. C. Farries/Nithsdale District
      Council, 1988), 1–2.

18   Alexander Wilson, *Chartist Movement in Scotland* (Manchester: Manchester
      University Press, 1970), 85.

National Petition of 1838 compared with a mere 3,350 from Dumfries and the Borders.[19]

The earliest public meeting in support of the People's Charter took place in Dumfries, about a month after the establishment of the Dumfries Working Men's Association, on 28 September 1838 and was around the time of the annual traditional Rood Fair,[20] when there would have been many people visiting the town from the surrounding region. The *Times* for 3 October reported three demonstrations in the town on that day: the procession of the Dumfries and Maxwelltown Total Abstinence Society, a meeting of the working classes and a procession of journeymen and apprentices.

By far the most column inches were given to the 'Procession of the Dumfries and Maxwelltown Total Abstinence Society', founded about two years previously, and said to have a membership of about 2,000. At noon the town's bells were rung and the procession, including deputations from Carlisle, Annan, Gatehouse, Lockerbie and other towns, as well as bands from Moffat and Annan, moved off from the school yard, where it had been marshalled. Towards the end of the procession, John M'Manus of the *Times* office and John Hamilton of the *Herald*, worked a press on a horse-drawn carriage, decorated with the slogan: 'The Press! We hail it as the terror of the tyrant, the liberator of the slave, and the great promoter of the temperance reformation.'[21] In the early to mid-nineteenth century there are many examples of printers working a press in a carriage as part of a procession: this seems to be the earliest instance of such an event in Dumfries. Unfortunately the carriage is not depicted, nor have any examples of what was actually printed survived. There are later instances, particularly in association with temperance outings and demonstrations, as well as the procession that took place to mark the centenary of the birth of Robert

19 Colin Troup, 'Chartism in Dumfries 1830–1850', *Transactions of the Dumfriesshire & Galloway Natural History Society* (1981), 100; Wilson, *Chartist Movement in Scotland*, 171.

20 Originally a large element of the Rood Fair was the horse sales, and it later became a hiring fair for servants (Lockwood, *Dumfries Story*, 1988, 30).

21 *Dumfries Times*, 3 October 1838, 4.

Burns. Despite the reputation for radicalism held by operative printers, they do not seem to have participated in this way at any political demonstration in Dumfries, irrespective of trade society or print union membership. In the case of these two individuals, both M'Manus and Hamilton were associated with the local typographical society or union, though the former had been expelled for arrears (and since reinstated). Hamilton, after appearing regularly in the list of those fined for non-attendance at meetings, was elected secretary to the typographical society in May 1842.[22] The Total Abstinence Society parade of September 1838 passed through the High Street where it paused for speeches, after which there was a prizegiving. In the evening there was a Soiree in the Assembly Rooms and a Ball at the King's Arms which went on 'with undiminished spirit till about 4 o'clock next morning'.[23]

The same issue of the *Times* reported an event on the Corbelly Hill on the Maxwelltown (south) side of the River Nith on the same day under the heading 'Meeting of the Working Classes'. The meeting took place at four o'clock in the afternoon, between the temperance procession and their evening festivities. To start with there was a small crowd of about a hundred people 'among whom were several women', which grew to 'several hundreds'. The designated chairman of the proceedings, 'Mr Campbell, gunsmith' was not present, and there was confusion about who should take the chair in his absence – several people 'declined the honour'. The chair was eventually taken by Mr Campbell who had arrived late and who announced that 'the meeting had been called to adopt the people's Charter, that the working classes expected no assistance from the aristocracy or any other class in procuring for themselves their rights, they had to look to their own exertions exclusively for emancipation from the evils with which they were oppressed'. Jeremiah Knight then spoke and 'addressed the meeting in a rambling speech of some length in which he endeavoured to repel the objections that had been urged against the extension of the franchise to the working classes'. He was followed by Andrew Wardrop who, among

22   Ewart Library Dumfries (ELD), records of the Dumfries Typographical Society
        (1831–1889), GD25/1 and GD25/2.
23   *Dumfries Times*, 3 October 1838, 4.

other things, warned the meeting 'not to be led away from their object by any agitation for the repeal of the corn laws, denounced the idea of having recourse to physical force [...] and called on them to knock on the door of the House of Commons until their grievances were redressed'. After a vote of thanks to the owner of the field the meeting broke up. The reporter from the *Times* was not impressed, writing that 'Altogether the effect was not calculated to aid the cause'.[24] Of those mentioned as having taken a part in the meeting, the most significant in terms of local support for Chartism was Wardrop, a native of Glasgow, and a recent newcomer to Dumfries, having arrived in 1837 to work as a frame-maker there. Wardrop became secretary to the Dumfries Working Men's Association and in June 1841 stood for election to parliament, apparently winning the hustings on a show of hands, but declined to go to the actual poll as he did not have enough support among the enfranchised electors in the Burgh. Wardrop was also involved in the temperance and, co-operative movements and, before his death in 1869, became a Town Councillor.[25]

The third and shortest report concerned the 'Procession of the Journeymen and Apprentices'. The journeymen and apprentices met at the Trades Hall (also in the High Street) at noon and paraded through the streets:

> 'according to the good old custom' [...] at the time the tee-totallers were walking – we even suppose the processions oftener than once met each other – but the numbers being limited, and appearance not very prepossessing, instead of riveting the attention and respect of the public, they were regarded with callous indifference, or rather we should say awakened, in the breasts of not a few, feelings of disgust. The spectacle, we are of the opinion, added nothing to the credit of our burgh.[26]

Disapproval of such 'traditional' outings, which had no doubt been a feature of the town's annual fairs from time immemorial, was inevitable in the pages of a newspaper which generally supported the cause of temperance.

---

24   *Dumfries Times*, 3 October 1838, 4.
25   Troup, 'Chartism in Dumfries', 106–7; W. Hamish Fraser, *Chartism in Scotland* (Pontypool: Merlin Press, 2010), 225.
26   *Dumfries Times*, 3 October 1838, 4.

As well as reporting these local public meetings, the issue of the *Times* for 3 October 1838 also carried reports on 'Radical Demonstrations (abridged from the *London Courier*)' further afield. Firstly, a meeting in Manchester 'afforded abundant evidence, that if the Whigs are unpopular with the masses, the Tories are infinitely more so'. It was also 'a powerful display of numbers. Some assert there were at least 300,000 present, while others maintain that the numbers did not exceed 100,000': the writer was of the opinion that the truth was somewhere between the two and that it was larger than the 'Peterloo' demonstration of 1819. The speakers showed 'few displays of genuine feeling'.[27] Secondly, a meeting in Liverpool was much smaller, attended by no more than 1,400 people, and suffered from inclement weather. Feargus O'Connor himself gave a 'long and violent address' which 'concluded with strong invectives against gentlemen of the press'. He was followed by another speaker, Mr Acland, whose address diverted onto the topic of the evils of gin. This led to him being booed and hissed by the audience. At a third meeting on Trowle Common, between Trowbridge and Bradford-on-Avon in Wiltshire, resolutions 'similar to those adopted at other demonstrations of the kind were unanimously agreed to' and two processions, one from Bath and one consisting of people from Trowbridge, Bradford and many surrounding villages, met to form the crowd, which was estimated at 30,000.[28] The *Dumfries Times* editorial had some words of warning for those seeking reform that 'the union among the working classes, though scouted by a certain class of politicians as trifling or visionary, is matter of serious concern. We earnestly hope that all influential Reformers will view it in this light'.[29]

Towards the end of October 1838, there was another 'Radical demonstration' in Dumfries, which featured speeches from 'Messrs Duncan of Edinburgh, Lowrey of Newcastle, and Arthur of Carlisle'. Its main theme was the National Petition and those present were called on to join the Working Men's Association. In his speech, Abram Duncan exhorted the meeting 'to cause their voices to be heard within the walls of St Stephens,

27   *Dumfries Times*, 3 October 1838, 2.
28   *Dumfries Times*, 3 October 1838, 2.
29   *Dumfries Times*, 3 October 1838, 4.

and said – if the national petition should receive two millions of signatures it would show that great discontent prevailed, it would make the
Government to set their house in order' and 'After calling on those present to join the Working Men's Association, he concluded his lengthened
address amid great cheering'.[30]

There were some occasions on which both the *Herald* and the *Times*
reported on meetings in the town, and despite their differing political view-
points recorded remarkably similar impressions of the more lively meetings.
The *Herald*, for example, was first to print an account of an Anti-Corn
Law meeting in Maxwelltown in January 1839. According to its reporter:

> A knot of Anti-Corn-Law agitators met this forenoon in Maxwelltown to advance
> their grand nostrum [...] The Chartists, however, had been on the alert; and under
> the leadership, we believe, of Thomas Johnstone, they mustered in such numbers,
> or argued so convincingly, that they overset the meeting altogether, carrying an
> amendment that it was useless for the people to petition for a repeal of the Corn-
> Laws till, by the carrying of Universal Suffrage, they could constitute such a House of
> Commons that not only the Corn-Laws, but every thing else which they considered
> an abuse, would be swept away to a certainty – and no mistake.[31]

The speakers at the meeting included Thomas Harkness, editor of the
Times, John M'Diarmid, editor of the *Courier*, and Andrew Wardrop.
The same meeting was also reported at considerable length in the next
issue of the *Times*, including a more detailed account of the disruption
caused by the supporters of the six points of the Charter. After the Provost,
who was in the chair, declared the meeting dissolved 'amid great uproar
and confusion', the Chartists apparently elected another chairman and
proceeded to pass a resolution of their own, although by this time, the
Times's reporter had left along with 'Many respectable men of business,
wearied with Mr Johnston's long and irrelevant harangue, and otherwise
disgusted with the factious and tumultuous of the meeting'.[32] The *Times*

---

30   *Dumfries Times*, 31 October 1838, 3.
31   'The Dumfries and Maxwelltown Anti-Corn-Law Agitators Defeated by the
      Chartists!!!', *Dumfriesshire and Galloway Herald and Advertiser*, 25 January 1839, 4.
32   *Dumfries Times*, 30 January 1839, 2–3.

continued to report on what it described as 'radical demonstrations' over the next months, alongside reports on Anti-Corn Law agitation. Where the two movements disagreed, the *Times* supported the Anti-Corn-Law movement rather than the Chartists, describing the latter in one article as 'deluded' and 'destitute alike of good feeling, or prudence or decorum – all fury – and coarse brawling faction'.[33] In the issue dated 3 May 1841, the *Times* reprinted in full an item from the *Leeds Times*, described as 'an able Radical Journal', in which the writer declares that, despite their 'faith in the *principles* of Chartism', they 'do not care for the Chartism of which Feargus O'Connor is high priest'.[34]

The *Herald*'s disapproval of the reform movements and their supporters was more generalised and much stronger. In February 1841, under the heading 'Radical Loyalty!!' it referred to the 'yelping curs of Radicalism' before giving an account of a Chartist meeting at Castle Douglas, at which the local Chartist activist, Patrick M'Douall of Galloway, was due to speak. The crowd:

> we are informed that shortly before M'Douall's arrival at the room, there were in it at least seventy persons, all waiting with breathless anxiety for his appearance; when, shocking to relate, the floor gave way, and the whole mass, with a few exception who clung to the broken rafters, were precipitated headlong to the flat below. [...] Upwards of thirty individuals, however, have been more or less injured on the occasion [...] We learn that two other individuals had their legs broken; but, fortunately for them, they were wooden ones before. [...] We congratulate a friend on the loss of his silver spectacles in the affray: We trust it will be a warning to him not to hazard his nose at another Chartist meeting.[35]

The next issue of the newspaper carried a report on the injured, under the headline 'Chartist Bubble', criticising the sums paid by the National Convention to the injured 'as a mockery of human suffering' before going on to claim that 'a secret society has been formed here since the late catastrophe'.[36] A local organisation which came under the suspicion of

33   *Dumfries Times*, 6 February 1839, 4.
34   *Dumfries Times*, 3 May 1841, 2.
35   *Dumfries-shire and Galloway Herald and Advertiser*, 11 February 1841, 4.
36   *Dumfries-shire and Galloway Herald and Advertiser*, 18 February 1841, 3.

being a cover for subversive activity was the local printers' benefit society. At the beginning of February 1841, Robert M'Dowall, brother of William, was among those questioned by the Sheriff in Dumfries after the seizure of the Dumfries Typographical Society's papers and funds, apparently on the grounds that the Society was illegal. The Society, as a body, with the backing of the General Typographical Association of Scotland, of which it was a constituent member, refused to admit to that charge, or to cease its activities and after a few months, the matter was dropped.[37]

The activities of Feargus O'Connor himself were not necessarily reported with approval in the Dumfries press. In late 1841 O'Connor visited the town as part of his tour of Scotland, causing the *Times* to comment that 'after all their doubts and fears, the Chartists of the district have had their visit of the "uncaged lion", and, unless he has much changed his manners, he is not half so wild or so dangerous as he has been called'. Having travelled on the coach from Glasgow, O'Connor was met in the middle of the afternoon on the Glasgow Road, on the Maxwelltown side of the River Nith, by Andrew Wardrop and William M'Dowall and joined them in an open carriage. They joined a procession of 'men of the trades, and numbers from the other classes', which had been marshalled at the dock to the south of the town, and marched across the bridge to the Glasgow road to meet them. There was 'a deafening shout of gratulation', before the procession moved on with flags and banners 'in number numberless'. The procession moved through the streets of Dumfries, stopping at the Commercial Inn in the High Street, where 'Mr Wardrop addressed a few words to the Assembly' before announcing that O'Connor would give a speech at a 'soiree' to be held that evening. An account of the soirée follows. Following the meal, the Chairman of the proceedings, John Bell:

> sketched the lowly origin of Chartism – its progress in Dumfries, comparing the early meetings of the friends of freedom, consisting of thirteen or fourteen individuals, with the glorious display which that evening presented; and augured from this the certainty of ultimate triumph to the principles they had espoused.

37 Records of the Dumfries Typographical Society, ELD, 4 February 1841, GD25/2.

Wardrop spoke briefly, before William M'Dowall presented O'Connor with an 'address of the Chartists of Dumfries and Maxwelltown on the occasion of his visit', sitting down 'amid loud cheers'. This was followed by O'Connor's speech which lasted two hours, and was followed by one from Wardrop received with 'thunders of applause', two more speeches and 'after three cheers for O'Connor and the Charter, three for Frost, Williams, and Jones, three for the strangers, and three in acknowledgement of the excellent conduct of the Chairman [...] the O'Connor Festival terminated'.[38]

It is interesting to compare this account from the local paper with that which appeared a few days later in the newspaper edited by O'Connor himself, the *Northern Star*, published in Leeds. The *Northern Star* for 13 November 1841 covered the event using the words of the *Dumfries Times*, with some additions, notably the dramatic poem of welcome on the placard announcing his visit:

> Lo! He comes, he comes!
> Garlands for every shrine;
> Strike lyres and sound the drums,
> Bring roses, pour ye wine.
>
> Swell, swell the Dorian flute
> Through the blue triumphal sky;
> Let the cythern's tone salute,
> As the patriot passes by!

After this verse and the introductory sentence, the reports are identical, apart from a few additions in the *Northern Star*. The largest of these is the list of participants in the parade, with O'Connor's name in capitals. The procession was led by 'Two marshals on horseback', a band and the flag of the Workingmen's Association which was decorated on one side with 'the six points; and on the other an emblematical figure of Liberty, carrying on a spear the "Bonnet Rouge", with the British Lion couchant at her feet'. Irish Chartists had a prominent position and were followed by the local Incorporated Trades, such as the Curriers, Skinners and Hammermen,

---

38   *Dumfries Times*, 8 November 1841, 1.

who were all represented, other local trades organisations such as the Dumfries Typographical Society, seem to have held aloof. There was no mention of a carriage with printers working a press. The procession did, however, include 'Millar Lewis, a juvenile Chartist on a brown palfrey, with an address to Mr O'Connor, beautifully ornamented with bay leaves and holly'. This section concluded with the comment that 'It presented a spectacle such as was never before witnessed in this locality'. O'Connor, of course, had not been present at the temperance demonstration in September 1838. The rest of the article was a verbatim, but uncredited reprint from the *Times*, with the added details of the songs which interspersed the speeches, which ranged from 'Hurrah for the Charter' to 'The flowers of the forest' and M'Crimmon's lament'. The *Northern Star* followed this extended article with a small item headed: 'We copy the following account of O'Connor's visit to Dumfries from the *Dumfries Times:-*' before a paragraph giving a much reduced account of the day, using a selection of the same sentences from the article in the *Times*.[39]

After O'Connor's visit, meetings to promote the Charter and the National Petition were subsequently held in smaller towns of south-west Scotland. The *Times* for 5 December 1841 reported that Wardrop had given a 'long address' to an open air meeting in Newton Stewart on the previous Thursday evening. This meeting lasted about two hours, and had been planned to take place indoors, but permission had been refused. Wardrop urged those present to 'form an Association, and, by every peaceful means in their power, endeavour to enlighten and arouse the people'. Working Men's Associations had apparently already been established in Castle Douglas and Gatehouse and 'Steps have also been taken to form one in Stranraer'. Associations were also planned in Kirkcowan and New Galloway. The meeting broke up at ten o'clock with a vote of thanks to Wardrop after 'giving three hearty cheers for the speedy union of the middle and working classes on the principles of the People's Charter'.[40]

The meeting in Kirkcowan was held a couple of days later and reported in the same issue of the *Times*. Arrangements had been made for Wardrop

39 *Northern Star*, 13 November 1841, 1.
40 *Dumfries Times*, 5 December 1841, 1.

to address the meeting in 'Mr Milligan's ballroom' but the landlord, the 'Tory laird of Craighlaw', had signalled disapproval and Milligan had withdrawn from the arrangement, afraid of losing his licence to sell alcohol. The meeting was held instead in the street and Wardrop:

> addressed a large assemblage, including the laird of Craighlaw's footman, gamekeeper, and the rural police, who probably were sent as spies, or perhaps on the more creditable errand of preserving the peace [...] The meeting was quiet, orderly, and respectable, with the exception of this unprincipled gamekeeper, who kept up a continual mutter and growl, until severely chastised by the speaker. Mr Wardrop, in his address, went over all the points of the Charter, and concluded by urging the people to be firm and united in putting down Toryism. A vote of thanks was given to the speaker, and three cheers for the Charter, and the whole was concluded by the notable farce of a regular up-an-down fight, between the growling gamekeeper and the rural police.[41]

The following week's issue (for 13 December 1841) recorded Wardrop addressing meetings at Gatehouse and New Galloway. The issue for 3 January 1842, reported on a Chartist Ball, held in the Assembly Rooms, Dumfries on New Year's Eve, to raise funds to support the town's delegate to the National Convention, with the new year being greeted not with 'Auld lang syne' but with 'La Marseillaise'. Although he took less part in the meetings promoting the Chartist movement, William M'Dowall was also busy. The first of five projected parts of his work, *People's Charter Illustrated: being a historical introduction*, was advertised in the *Dumfries Times* for 7 February 1842, at the price of sixpence per part. It was available from the Dumfries bookseller David Halliday and at the Working Men's Reading Room in the town. Extracts were printed in the Glasgow newspaper, the *Chartist Circular*, which had earlier printed his poem 'Oh! For one hour of Wallace wight'.[42]

The *Dumfries Times* for 3 March 1842 reported that Wardrop addressed a meeting in Hawick, on the subject 'Reconciliation between the Middle and Working Classes':

41   *Dumfries Times*, 5 December 1841, 1.
42   *Chartist Circular*, 20 June 1840, 160; 30 April 1842, 559–60; 7 May 1842, 565.

It was the largest meeting for a political purpose that had been in Hawick for years; and throughout the lecturer was listened to with marked attention, and the approbation of the audience was testified at the conclusion by loud cheers. Mr Wardrop having expressed a wish to answer any questions that might be put to him in reference to his lecture, an individual rose and wished to know if the *Dumfries and Galloway Herald* were printed in Dumfries, and whether its report of a recent meeting held in the Assembly Rooms, there, were correct? To which he answered, that it was printed in Dumfries, and that, throughout, the report in question was better than some that he had seen in the same print; when taken in conjunction with the *leader* upon it, they had a tendency to convey a wrong impression of what transpired at the meeting.[43]

This report was followed by one of a meeting which had been held in Newton-Stewart on 17 February, and addressed by another local activist, Robert Somers.[44] It was also reported in that edition that local Chartist supporters had adopted the second National Petition at a public meeting in Dumfries 'to be sent to the Queen and the Commons, as expressive of their sentiments regarding the grievances of the country, and as setting forth what they conceive to be the only remedy'.[45] The *Times* complained that the editor of the *Herald* had labelled it as 'The *sneaking* Chartist Petition'.[46] This second Chartist petition was presented to Parliament and rejected in May 1842, after which local enthusiasm seemed to have waned although the institutions associated with movement, such as the 'Working Men's Reading Rooms' survived in some localities for much longer: that in Gretna, for example, continued until the 1860s.[47]

In 1839, Thomas Carlyle wrote that:

A feeling very generally exists that the condition and disposition of the Working Classes is a rather ominous matter at present; that something ought to be said, something ought to be done, in regard to it.[48]

43 *Dumfries Times*, 3 March 1842, 1.
44 *Dumfries Times*, 3 March 1842, 1.
45 *Dumfries Times*, 3 March 1842, 1.
46 *Dumfries Times*, 3 March 1842, 3.
47 *Dumfries & Galloway Standard & Advertiser*, 26 February 1862, 3.
48 Thomas Carlyle, *Selected Writings*, ed., Alan Shelston (London: Penguin, 1971), 120.

In south-west Scotland, this feeling seems to have dissipated with the failure of the second petition, and the principle local activists, Andrew Wardrop and William M'Dowall, moved on to other matters. The former became an important figure in the local co-operative movement and the latter the editor of a local newspaper, although they both retained an interest in local political life and served on the Dumfries Town Council.

PAUL WILSON

5   Hopeful Words and the Neighbourly Order of
    the World: Revealing Radical Language Practice
    through Traces of Temporary Ownership

Whilst otherwise unremarkable, the West Yorkshire town of Keighley is
notable for a particular socialised response to utopian linguistic invention:
the founding of the UK's first Esperanto society in November 1902. Like
many others at the time, this intentional community of Esperantists were
seeking a response to the emerging utopian impulses of late nineteenth- and
early twentieth-century Britain and looked to Esperanto's instrumentalisa-
tion of language as a method through which the world might be remade
through the creative elimination of a need for translation. This chapter takes
as its point of departure the seemingly unremarkable string of numbers found
on the due date slip in the lending copy of the *Esperanto-English Dictionary*
held in Keighley library. Keighley resident Joseph Rhodes (1856–1920)
was the dictionary's compiler and he played an active role in the society's
formation and upon the wider community of Esperanto speakers. In what
ways, therefore, does the dictionary provide us with a means to glimpse
Keighley's relationship with such practices of radical language on a very
local level? Through reflection on one element of one book, it is possible
to identify how one community embraced the potential of linguistic (re)
invention. Through recognition of the list as a distinct, albeit superficially
restrained, form of information storage and dissemination, it is possible to
frame it as having particular organisational and institutional uses and in
possession of certain visual and typographic characteristics. The due-date
list of loans held within the dictionary documents a fixed moment in each
individual borrower's engagement with it over a prescribed period of time
and, as such, allows us to map Keighley's neighbourly engagement with
Esperanto as a notable instance of radical language practice whilst also

allowing for a discussion of how such communities were, in part, established and sustained through a range of seemingly mundane textual artefacts.

> In Bialystok the population consisted of four different elements: Russians, Poles, Germans and Jews. Each of these elements spoke a separate language and had hostile relations with the other elements. In that city, more than anywhere, a sensitive person might feel the heavy sadness of the diversity of languages and become convinced at every step that it is the only, or at least the primary force which divides the human family into parts.[1]

For Ludwik Zamenhof (1859–1917), the creator of Esperanto, linguistic diversity was one of humanity's key sociocultural challenges. He felt it encouraged separation and, subsequently, a sense of dislocation and division between disparate language-speaking populations. As a consequence, he felt that it was only through language – and, in particular, through language innovation – that such damage might be repaired and that a positive and uniting transformation might be enacted upon the wider peoples of humankind. His method of achieving this would be the invention of a neutral, artificial language – an international language – founded upon principles of simplicity and of a functional practicality. Self-published in Russian in 1887, *Lingvo Internacia* [International Language] set out his language's sixteen grammatical rules and contained a lexicon of around 900 words. Also known as *Unua Libro* [First Book], the pamphlet was published pseudonymously with Zamenhof preferring the title of *Doctor Esperanto*, a name which explicitly positions it as intentionally utopian since within his new language the word Esperanto meant 'one who hopes' and the word would go on to become adopted as the language's name replacing Zamenhof's original title of 'International language'. Such positive aspirations were further illustrated by his wish that any growth and development for Esperanto would emerge from its users since he showed no wish to impose changes or control over the language and steadfastly refused to claim it as his own property. This open and relational approach to its propagation was

---

1   Ludwik Zamenhof in Akira Okrent, *In the Land of Invented Languages: A Celebration of Linguistic Creativity, Madness and Genius* (New York: Spiegel and Grau Trade Paperbacks, 2010), 94.

illustrated by his inclusion of eight promissory coupons with each copy of the *Lingvo Internacia* and a challenge to its readers. The coupon was to be returned to *Doctor Esperanto*, in a gesture that would demonstrate both a commitment to learning the language and a willingness to identify as a member of the emerging community of Esperantists.[2] Rather than proposing practice or study of Esperanto in a rote academic fashion, Zamenhof suggested that readers could disseminate the language to friends through a letter which would contain a text that they would translate for fun.[3] His canny focus on community formation was enthusiastically embraced and led to the publication in Esperanto in 1888 of the *Due Libro* [Second Book], together with the further publication of dictionaries (to assist in ongoing correspondence between speakers), translations of Shakespeare, the first Esperanto magazine (*La Esperantisto*, published in 1889 in Germany) and the nascent desire to establish a native, Esperanto-speaking culture and consciousness. Zamenhof would demonstrate Esperanto's value through a use of quotidian textual forms (people's letters, poetry), alongside trappings of communal identity such as a flag and the Esperantists' icon of self-identification, a five-pointed green star and a rousing anthem, 'La Espero'.

Keighley is a town and civil parish within the metropolitan borough of Bradford. With a population of just under 90,000 within the metropolitan area and approximately 51,500 in the town itself, Keighley stands largely unremarkable. There is evidence, however, of a radical impulse demonstrated within its relatively recent history. Laybourn's research into labour history in West Yorkshire positioned Keighley within the complex narrative of religious, social and cultural forces at work at the time which would lead workers to a rejection of the dominance of an 'intransigent right-wing millocracy' and to an association with the development of trade unionism, with which they had a common cause.[4] These included the gradual emergence of the Independent Labour Party (ILP) in the late nineteenth

---

2   Esther Schor, *Bridge of Words: Esperanto and the Dream of a Universal Language* (New York: Metropolitan Books, Henry Holt and Company, 2016), 72–3.

3   Okrent, *In the Land of Invented Languages*, 103–4.

4   Keith Laybourn, 'The Rising Sun of Socialism: The Growth of the Labour Movement in the Textile District of the West Riding of Yorkshire', unpublished paper delivered at

century and the growth of nonconformist Labour churches, the rapid development of the social club in and around the Bradford area, together with the emergence of the Clarion publishing brand and its associated social(ist) networks for propaganda and healthy competition.

Furthermore, Briggs argued that Keighley was active in the development of the emergent Labour movement prior to 1914, with a delegation from the town being heard at the inaugural conference of the ILP in Bradford in 1893.[5] The party's broad, popular appeal was supported by the formation and success of Labour clubs, whose activist or counter-cultural purpose was perhaps of interest due to their radical potential and their role in supporting the Labour unions.[6] The town's public library, opened in 1904, was the first Carnegie library in England and further demonstrates some zeal in the residents for education or self-betterment which was further complemented by the establishment of a Mechanics Institute in 1925. Continuing this trend for betterment, the fledgling Workers' Educational Association was active and held classes in Keighley, some of which were taught by E. P. Thompson. Keighley's first local newspaper (published monthly by the Temperance Society), the *Keighley Visitor*, came out in 1853 and the first weekly newspaper, the *Keighley News*, appeared in 1862.[7] The *Keighley Labour Journal*, first published in 1894 and which was 'for a time the longest-running local ILP newspaper',[8] was critical in supporting the town's emerging political culture and provided detailed information on local, national and international affairs together with the broader social and cultural activities of the ILP. The *Keighley Labour Journal* was also a useful means to critique corruption in local politics and so was embraced by a wider audience than just those drawn to the new Labour Party.

Huddersfield Local History Day Conference on Yorkshire Radicalism, 24 November 2012.

5   Asa Briggs, 'The Language of Class in Early Nineteenth Century England', in Asa Briggs and John Saville, eds, *Essays in Labour History* (London: Palgrave Macmillan, 1960), 43–73.

6   David James, *Class and Politics in a Northern Industrial Town* (Keele: Ryburn Publishing, 1995), 18–19.

7   Ian Dewhirst, *A History of Keighley* (Stroud: Tempus, 2006), 71–2.

8   James, *Class and Politics in a Northern Industrial Town*, 20.

When walking to the top of the stairs in Keighley library, visitors are presented with three busts and two faces (Figure 5.1). Central to this installation of three tributes, and perhaps most notable at first glance, is that of Zamenhof, Esperanto's inventor. He is flanked by two representations of the same person, Joseph Rhodes, who is described on one as a 'pioneer of Esperanto', a tribute merited by his singular contribution to the international language's development.

Figure 5.1. Busts of Joseph Rhodes and Ludwik Zamenhof, located at the entrance to Keighley Reference Library.

Rhodes was one of only five British citizens to appear on the first register of global Esperanto speakers, as number 541. Each individual on the list was assigned their number as a result of having notified Zamenhof of their commitment to his invention and this would often act as their signature when in correspondence with other speakers. By January 1902, four other Keighley residents were added to the register with another twenty-one appearing by the year's end. This apparent popularity of the language led to a socialised response – the formation of a community – and in November of the same year an Esperanto society met, the first in the UK.[9] Rhodes'

9   Peter Glover Forster, *The Esperanto Movement* (The Hague: Mouton Publishers, 1982), 269.

status as a pioneer and his contribution to Esperanto go beyond his active membership of the Keighley Esperanto Society, however. He compiled the first English-Esperanto dictionary, published in 1908, and contributed an introductory essay to the publication which outlined the opportunities and challenges that would face the language as it developed and the potential for its uptake in the wider world of non-Esperantists. For Rhodes, if Esperanto were to be successful it should be practical and simple, both in terms of its grammar and, significantly, the form of its delivery: the size and weight of the dictionary itself. Before his work compiling the dictionary Rhodes also contributed to the growing corpus of texts in Esperanto, translating both the first textbook for British students of the language and a version of Bunyan's *Pilgrim's Progress*.

At this time, Keighley seemed something of a testbed for radical language practice. Alongside the appetite of some for other, interconnected politically radical ideals and prior to the Esperanto Society's appearance, spiritualism arrived in the UK via Keighley. In 1853 a series of lectures were given by Keighley resident David Weatherhead and David Richmond (representing the American Shakers movement) in the town's Working-Men's Hall which led to the construction (by Weatherhead, at his own expense) of the Lyceum Buildings in the town's East Parade in around 1871. Following a split in the membership and a subsequent reunification (in 1885 and 1895 respectively), the Heber Street Wesleyan School was purchased and is now regarded as the 'mother church' for UK spiritualism. Unlike Zamenhof's wish for Esperanto to provide a linguistic means to repair the here-and-now, spiritualism looked towards a language which would operate beyond life and, significantly, one which acts as both channel or conduit, operating in the most universal of modes (beyond language itself). The *Yorkshire Spiritualist Telegraph* first appeared in 1855 and was the first periodical to document the flourishing Spiritualist movement. Its publisher was, perhaps coincidentally, J. Rhodes of Keighley.[10]

Perhaps the most successful – or successfully visible – period of activities for the Keighley Esperanto Society occurred during the middle of the twentieth century. Significant in sustaining the popularity of the

10   Dewhirst, *A History of Keighley*, 72.

Society in the town at the time were the married couple of Bruno and Mary Najbaro whose names appear regularly in the reports of the Society, on the pages of the *Keighley News* and in some Esperanto publications of the time. For Bruno Najbaro, Esperanto was something both to be studied and lived and, as a Polish immigrant to West Yorkshire, he saw the language as a means to carry forward an ideal of internationalism. Like Zamenhof, the Najbaros were to use a choice of naming to determine their own position in relation to Esperanto and its utopian purpose: 'Najbaro', in Esperanto, means 'neighbour' and their adoption of it looked to positively embody and enact the neighbourly practices of situation, location and association.

Such gentle, yet affecting, concepts are at the heart of Esperanto and, like the Najbaros, art historian Aby Warburg (1866–1929) held high regard for what he called the 'law of good neighbourliness'. As a bibliophile, he saw such ideas as a useful method for both organising information and the encouragement of meaningful and unintended association. While Zamenhof thought that language facilitated and reinforced damaging experiences of difference, Warburg regarded discipline (or genre) as 'a fundamental obstacle'[11] to his desire for a more 'fulfilling' library which was to be organised according to the principle of Denkraum (a space of thought).[12] For Warburg, 'intellectual research was therefore directly intertwined with, visually and spatially activated by, and made manifest in the library itself'[13] where it would become a creative curatorial space through the accidental juxtapositions, seemingly baffling associations or wonderful moments of serendipity delivered by his practice of Denkraum.

On the first floor of Keighley library, past the busts of Rhodes and Zamenhof, is its Reference library. On a shelf in this room there are two copies of the English-Esperanto Dictionary, one for lending and another for reference only (Figure 5.2). Within the reference copy handwritten annotations on the inside verso page (from 1908/1909) signal an attribution

---

11   Hammad Nasar, Anna-Sophie Springer, and Etienne Turpin, 'Intensive Geographies of the Archive', in Anna-Sophie Springer, and Etienne Turpin, eds, *Funtasies of the Library* (Cambridge, MA: MIT Press, 2016), 43.

12   Nasar, Springer, and Turpin, 'Intensive Geographies of the Archive', 44.

13   Nasar, Springer, and Turpin, 'Intensive Geographies of the Archive', 45.

of ownership: the name 'Rhodes' and a note signalling that this copy was
a gift to the library in 1911 from a friend of Rhodes, the book's compiler.

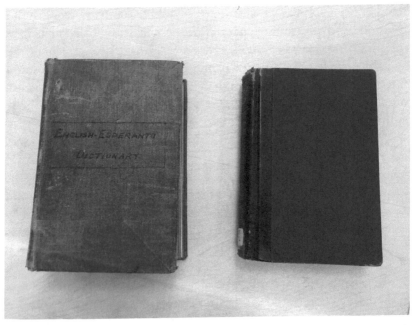

Figure 5.2. Rhodes' *English-Esperanto Dictionary* (Reference Copy and Lending Copy).

The title page of both copies bear the same declaration:

> BASED UPON THE 'FUNDAMENTO' (FOUNDATION), THE ESPERANTO
> LITERATURE, AND THE NATIONAL – ESPERANTO DICTIONARIES
> BEARING DR. ZAMENHOF'S 'APROBO' (APPROVAL).

It seems apparent, therefore, that, at the time of its publication in 1908,
there was a growing corpus of written material through which Rhodes was
able to produce this landmark for the English-speaking Esperantist and
that, while Zamenhof's wish was not to own or control his invention,
he was critical in determining or authorising the dictionary's legitimacy.
Rhodes' own credentials are given both by his 'membership' number and
his associations with professional bodies and membership of the 'language

committee', with such associative devices situating Rhodes within the community and signalling his significance to the growing number of Esperanto-speakers in England.

> The list functions curiously as a communication device, a cultural formation, a technique of administration, a storage and archival device, a poetic form and a mediator.[14]

The due-date list in the lending copy of the *English-Esperanto Dictionary* held in Keighley Reference library maps the unique history of a group of local readers whose relationship with the book was determined by an ideal which, as we have seen, looked to explore a particular set of beliefs in – and potential uses – for language itself. The traces of this one 'intentional community' of radical language practice, whose history spans the twentieth century, can be situated both materially and typographically on a slip of paper within a book located in an English provincial library. For Zamenhof, a dictionary such as that found in Keighley library (both in terms of its grammar and the words contained within it) becomes a vital instrument to fix or repair what he saw as a failure of language (or, as we have seen, of languages).

The material focus for this chapter, therefore, is that slip of paper glued to the first recto page of the dictionary: an everyday document with particular, predefined modes of operation. The list of dates written onto the surface of the slip of paper tells a story of place and people and helps to determine and visualise one kind of trace of a community. This existence has been suspended in place and time upon the surface of this document, with the list's stamped numbers operate to create a superficially abstract string of digits which functions to map and manage the public record of a radical idea. The dictionary as an object represents a notable instance of Esperanto's utopian drive, the practice of one idea of neighbourliness through a particular function for language with an intention to transform the world. The due-date list, therefore, creates a tangible instance of the

14 Liam Young, 'On Lists and Networks – An Archaeology of Form', *Amodern 2: Network Archaeology*, October 2013, available at: <http://amodern.net/article/on-lists-and-networks/>, accessed 17 July 2017.

traces of such utopian intent, documenting a network of connections that was developed over the lifetime of the book being borrowed – and returned – to Keighley library. Such a material and typographic register of the book's loans give us a clear overview of this network, allowing us to map a narrative of engagement within the town and to identify the moment in time when the town's interest in the promise of Esperanto appeared to stall or cease.

Gitelman's discussion of mundane media helps to locate and develop a critical method for the analysis of such everyday documents, allowing for a focus on institutional and everyday contexts of production, consumption and/or use. Through this, it becomes possible to identify 'patterns of expression and reception discernible amid a jumble of discourse'[15] which are themselves reinforced by methods of graphic and typographic communication utilised in their visual communication and presentation. Despite the book's superficial ordinariness, it can be seen to be in possession of a particular kind of rhetoric, 'a framework for eloquent articulation.'[16] The typographic formats employed in the list act to both visualise and concretise a series of relationships of and between the dictionary's borrowers and the Library, establishing a micro-archive that consists of each of the book's transactional loans, which are themselves codified by the numbers and letters of their date of return and which marks the point in time after which they were to be found again on the shelf. Between the first and last dates contained on the list, therefore, the reader is presented with a mosaic of moments which constitute a partial map of the network of Esperanto speakers in Keighley at this time, a device which echoes Zamenhof's numerical register of global Esperantists. It is possible to suggest, therefore, that those dates preserved on the due-date list, are the product of Esperanto's identifiable cultural impulse materialised through the object of the dictionary and its journey around Keighley and, as such, present an opportunity to reflect

15   Lisa Gitelman, *Paper Knowledge: Toward a Media History of Documents* (Durham, NC: Duke University Press, 2014), 3.
16   Robin Kinross, 'The Rhetoric of Neutrality', in Victor Margolin, ed., *Design Discourse: History/theory/criticism* (Chicago: University of Chicago Press, 1989), 133.

upon the significance of the object of the list itself, together with its constituent visible pattern of dates-as-data.

Although it is possible to speculate on how it might represent or document the dictionary's use, the list also presents the reader with something altogether more specific, a moment in time when the town's relationship with Esperanto and its utopian spirit might be seen to substantially change or perhaps end: the last due-date. Arguably the list can be seen as more than a mundane record of a series of bureaucratic transactions. Instead it tells a story about an idea being delivered to a community of readers according to a method that is unique to the system of dissemination of knowledge used within a particular organisation and indicates a town's brief and enthusiastic embrace of radical language practice whose hope was of enacting peaceful change upon the world.

> Quotidian forms like lists can tell us much about the dynamics at play between human beings and the material circumstances in which they enact thought and action.[17]

As Young argued, lists are useful tools both in terms of how (and why) they are used and what they allow us to study. However, they often reference nothing other than themselves and the systems of classification being used and so frequently resist attempts at analysis or interpretation since there is much about them and their contents which is unknown and unknowable. The names of those who have borrowed, read and made practical use of the *English-Esperanto Dictionary*, for example, together with their exact reasons for wanting to learn, read or speak the language is impossible to determine from the seemingly simple string of numbers held on the book's due-date list. Pragmatic lists such as the due-date list have no inherent literary meaning or value and so we must look to their function: their abilities to store and process information and the knowledge that is created from their contents. Within the specific context of the library, a due-date list is directly related to the management of assets of a collectively held information or knowledge resource. Such a genre of documents possess

---

17   Liam Young, 'Un-Black Boxing the List: Knowledge, Materiality, and Form', *Canadian Journal of Communication*, 38 (2013), 497.

a durational function, being produced as a blank to be completed over time. Temporary ownership of such an object – and the connection to its contents – and the subsequent circulation of knowledge are key to the function of any library. As Young stated the list is a key archival resource for such activities and its contents might actually be remarkable in what they suggest:

> The list also preserves. As a material form, the contents of a list exist in relation to one another until the list is destroyed. That is, a list preserves an account of not just the relations between its contents (how they are drawn together), but also its criteria of inclusion/exclusion, as well as the social action it facilitates.[18]

The list's material form does also make it possible to identify the characteristics of an institutional visual system for preservation via a method for marking time which documents day, month and year, together with other devices used for spatial separation and the organisation of dates as they are added to the list. Single-word headers mark out the content of each column and a method for marking the distribution or production of the blank list is registered on the bottom-left. For Eco, a list is an attempt at rendering the seemingly imperceptible or non-comprehensible into concrete form[19] and as a means to attempt interpretation of that which has been captured upon it. In a book dedicated to the discipline of naming, the list's narrative does not provides for any further identification or of any other contextual information. Such bureaucratic systems exist objectively to separate ideas of time from an individual who might be borrowing the book and who might, at some point, be identified. The list of dates in the *English-Esperanto Dictionary* might, therefore, map a chronology of engagement and indicate the book's relative 'popularity' among the populations of Keighley, in particular, those library members who are interested enough in Esperanto to require this book for extended periods of time in order to translate, study or learn. It is perhaps most likely that

18   Young, 'Un-Black Boxing the List', 498.
19   Umberto Eco, *The Infinity of Lists: From Joyce to Homer* (London: MacLehose Press, 2012), 15.

borrowing the dictionary demonstrated an active interest in the subject regardless of membership of the Esperanto Society itself, although it could be viewed as a gateway document whose use could lead to an informed engagement once the basics of the language had been grasped.

The lending copy of the *English-Esperanto Dictionary* opens to reveal a list of two sets of dates stamped upon the piece of paper that has been designed as a record of when the book must be returned. This visual device consists of three ruled columns each headed with the single word 'DATE' (Figure 5.3). The slip has, in fact, been glued on top of another – which is attached to the recto of the first spread – whose columns are far busier visually and show a list of dates which runs to the end of the last column and onto the page of the book itself (Figure 5.4). Other numbers are also inscribed onto the original due-date list: spaces exist on the slip of paper to record the library's (internal) book number and the number of volumes.

The first date(s) on the first (or bottom) list are obscured as a consequence of the top copy being glued onto it so it is impossible to be sure of the date of the dictionary's first loan (or return): only the typographic fragment of the '4th October' can be viewed and the year of issue is unclear. From what remains visible on the bottom list it is possible to record the total number of loans and their frequency with two dates in 1945, five in the 1950s and fourteen in the 1960s. The *English-Esperanto Dictionary* is book number 12,838 held in Keighley library, a statement of library inventory and stock-control presented alongside a formal declaration which outlines the terms upon which a book such as this is to be lent to a library member. Likewise, the typographic form of the due-date list is determined by the library's organisational and institutional identity and the requirement to systematically visually communicate ideas of ownership and association. There is also the necessity to document the reading public's interactions with the book in a way which makes the system of loans transparent and visible to all. As mentioned, the device of a visible grid of lines encloses the columns and constructs the cells within which the dates are to be written or stamped into. The formal visible language used within the organisational additions to the dictionary and, in particular, upon the due-date slip, denotes authority and a generic institutional identity through an application of functional, non-decorative typographic styles alongside the clear and

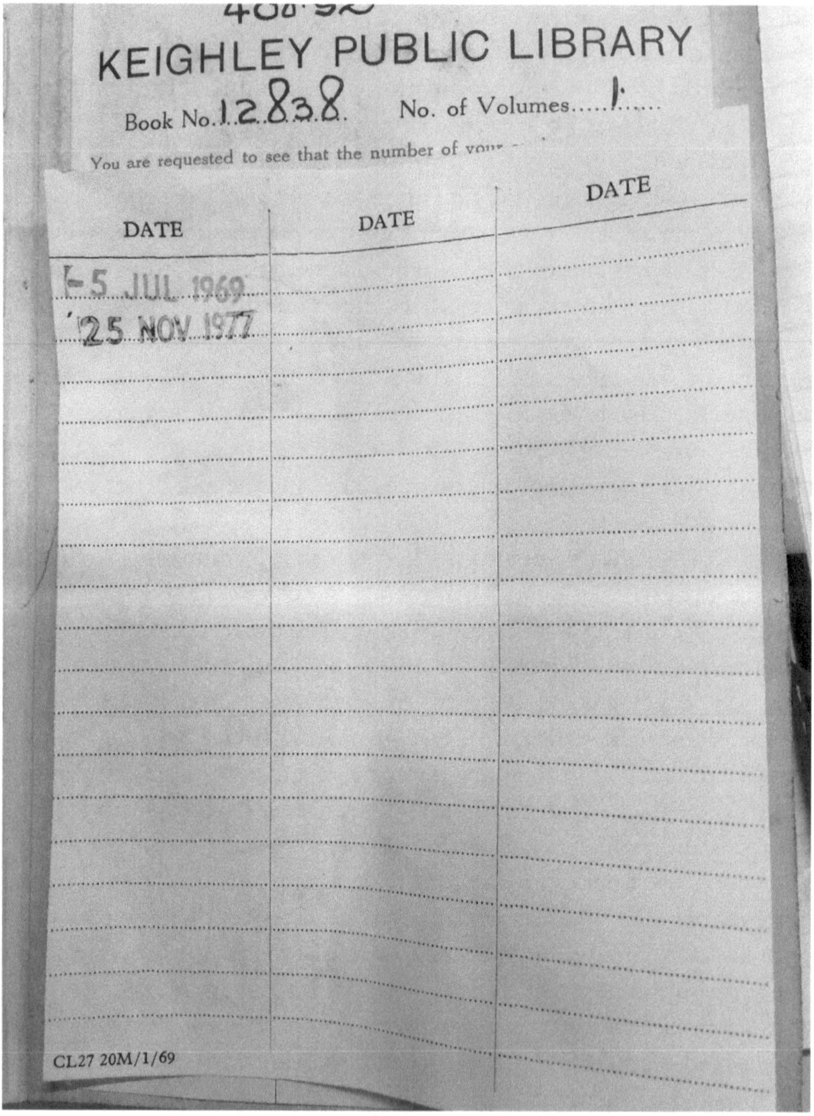

Figure 5.3. The *English-Esperanto Dictionary*'s due-date list (top copy).

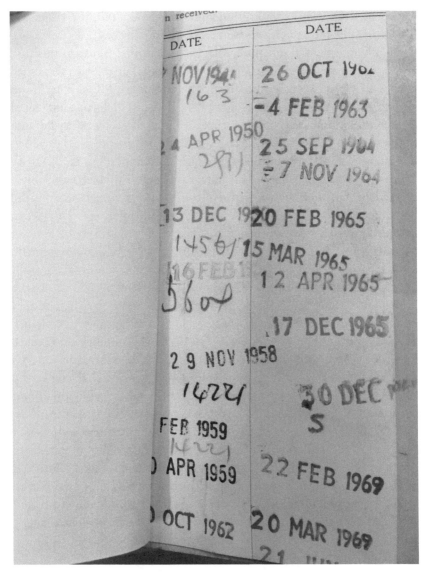

Figure 5.4. The *English-Esperanto Dictionary*'s due-date list (bottom copy).

straightforward visual composition and arrangement of those visual and typographic elements upon the surface of the slip itself.

Both in terms of their appearance and function, lists such as this are a vernacular genre of documentation[20] and are bound up in many ways with people's everyday lives where they help to determine ways of thinking in and around systems and structures of power and control. Gitelman commented that 'information has an objective, autonomous character partly because of the way it reflects the authoritative institutions and practices to which documents belong.'[21] It is possible to see such an attempt towards objectivity within the visual appearance of the library's ephemera applied to the object of the dictionary and such practices of control are extended into how the book's content is classified within a system for the ordering of knowledge itself. Using the Dewey Decimal Classification system, this book and the information contained is usefully categorised according to a systematic approach to ordering knowledge. Category 400 is 'generalities of language'; 408 is the 'treatment of language with respect to kinds of persons'; 408.9 the 'treatment of language with respect to specific racial, ethnic, national groups'. The list, therefore, acts to order and structure whatever it contains, often as a means of reinforcing certain institutional contexts and systems.

Therefore, the typographic and graphic style of the dictionary's due-date list and its accompanying ephemera suggests a character to the information being communicated and that there might be 'something persuasive about the nature of the organisation that publishes them.'[22] In the case of such quotidian visual devices as the library due-date list, such a style aims to maintain an air of objectivity, impartiality or authority which is also established by the artefact's context[23] and is subtly reinforced by the principles which underpin institutions such as lending libraries. As Gitelman reiterated, the type of everyday (blank) document which we observe the due-date list as representing exists to be evidential and is

20   Gitelman, *Paper Knowledge*, 1.
21   Gitelman, *Paper Knowledge*, 4.
22   Kinross, 'The Rhetoric of Neutrality', 134.
23   Kinross, 'The Rhetoric of Neutrality', 135.

defined by its context of production and use.[24] Adopting a formal and visually straightforward typographic style, the list sits within an assemblage of
interrelated devices whose purpose is similar: the rules of lending placed
to the left and a reminder of the operation of the library's issuing system
above it. The name of the library sits across both pages, together with the
book's number and its Dewey category classification. Each component of
the assemblage plays a part in determining the book's function and the
readers' relationships to both it and the institution of the library.

The superficially accidental string of dates captured by the due-date list
operates graphically and typographically across a number of conceptual categories. Making use of Twyman's schema for the study of graphic language
it is possible to classify the list as something whose presentation plays a part
in establishing the use of particular modes of visual rhetoric.[25] With such
a schema for interpretation, we can observe and identify within the device
of the list 'methods of configuration [...] [and] the graphic organisation
or structure of a message which influences and perhaps determines the
"searching", "reading" and "looking" strategies adopted by the user'.[26] The
due-date list operates, perhaps superficially, in a 'linear, interrupted mode'[27]
with the cells of the document visually arranged into the grid of columns and
rows through which the individual dates should flow (the bottom copy of
the list has no such cells). Each date, however, represents a 'discrete seman-
tic unit'[28] within the larger form of the table and is clearly associated with
the other dates presented within it. The method of representation of each
date – in simplified linguistic and typographic form – results in a series of
abbreviated and almost iconographic signs which represent a point in time
(of return) and whose marks are often haphazardly placed onto the slip.
The mosaic of dates presents a pattern of linked visual/typographic units

24 Gitelman, *Paper Knowledge*, 2.
25 Michael Twyman, 'A Schema for the Study of Graphic Language', in Oliver Boyd-
   Barrett, and Peter Braham, eds, *Media, Knowledge and Power* (London: Routledge,
   1987), 201–5.
26 Twyman, 'A Schema for the Study of Graphic Language', 203.
27 Twyman, 'A Schema for the Study of Graphic Language', 207–8.
28 Twyman, 'A Schema for the Study of Graphic Language', 208.

of communication, presented within a graphic device which systematically (and implicitly) orders the content it contains. There is a sense of structure and regularity to the list as a communications tool and to the linguistic units that are placed within it. Their typographic presentation, however, is less controlled and – in particular with the use of colour – gives some sense of a personalised, individual intervention.

Any form conjures up or demands a particular type of completion or 'filling' and, as Gitelman argued, forms of this type work to both 'structure knowledge and instantiate culture'.[29] They present the pattern of dates as a list, a vertical line or vector of reciprocity and, as such, have developed a particular form of typographic inscription into the empty spaces. Each date is marked by the action of an inked stamp and is composed as an abbreviation in a shortened form of two, three and four characters set in a san-serif typeface although the earliest, barely visible dates are in a serif typeface. Smudges or slips while the stamp is applied result in infrequent issues of legibility or of the date crashing into or across the ruled lines of the column or, in some cases, moving from the edge of the due-date slip and onto the page. The result of this laboured and repetitive type of visible language is a distinct form of data which captures and communicates the orbit and circulation of knowledge as an unfolding path along which the dictionary and its content is carried: a meshwork of inscribed traces which document transactions of a particular mix of experience and knowledge.[30]

> Writing is mnemonic [...] it is preservative. And so are printing and bookmaking: each [forming] a class or category of blank because each catered to the repetition of certain kinds of writing [...] [conserving] patterns of inscription and expression.[31]

As Gitelman made clear, such mundane forms of document as the due-date list begin as blank, and an emptiness in anticipation of a writing that will complete them and act to preserve their contents. As this chapter has outlined, the purpose of the category of the type of blank artefact

29   Gitelman, *Paper Knowledge*, 24.
30   Tim Ingold, *Lines: A Brief History* (Abingdon: Routledge, 2007), 28.
31   Gitelman, *Paper Knowledge*, 22.

under discussion was to record a date of return in accordance with a set of institutional rules. It would also act to preserve the particular vernacular habits of an object's loan and return, and implicitly trace a sense of movement from the library to the home or workplace of its temporary owner and back again. The due-date list is an instance of everyday mundane media which is deserving of detailed discussion. Such quotidian ephemera have a value in their production and use and how they establish the context for use for an object such as the *English-Esperanto Dictionary* held in Keighley library. The form of a list preserves information in a particular way and whilst seemingly lacking in character, both the design and content of this kind of device do reflect an organisational need and reflect a systematic approach to the management of knowledge. Is there any potential in considering such seemingly ephemeral things as lists as having some kind of radical consequence or impact? This list seems to offer a particularly poetic instance of what Eco has called the 'topos of ineffability' – some attempt to grasp at the infinite and concretise it into something relatively mundane. While notions of mobility and of movement seem to be the key characteristic of such inscriptions, what is being suggested through the pattern of dates recorded upon the slip's surface is, in fact, inertia, with the date actually describing the book's moment of return to the stability of the shelf. For all of the significance of the dates recorded upon the list in the *English-Esperanto Dictionary*, and their signification of a book in motion in and through the town's population of Esperantists and those intrigued enough to borrow it, it is also useful to reflect upon the gaps between the dates of each loan and, in particular, at the last date: the end-point for the book's circulation within Keighley. In places such as Keighley, a sense of utopian idealism seems apparent in both the practices of radical language and the emerging Labour politics that preceded it. Zamenhof established his international language via a model of distribution that seems resolutely grass-roots and non-hierarchical. He had no desire to impose a vision of practice upon Esperanto's speakers and felt it belonged to its users, encouraging a peer-to-peer sharing of it via the simple games included in the first book in order to trigger people's curiosity in an apparently meaningless text. His attitude to the language's growth was similarly open, preferring to gently manage the introduction of new words via a language committee. Perhaps contradictorily, the use of such devices as a numbered membership list acted to document, formalise and classify the growing global community of speakers. The due-date list of this dictionary – a significant publication in the history of Esperanto's global development among the English-speaking world – contributes to this short list of ephemera and printed artefacts which act as a means to measure its growth and relative popularity, in this case, a typographic representation of the trajectory of popularity among the residents of Keighley.

JAMES BRENNAN AND IAN CAWOOD

6 'We Must Get In Front of These Blighters': Political Press Culture in the West Midlands, 1918–1925

In his study of the political press in the twentieth century, Stephen Koss noted that if his work neglected provincial newspapers it was because they had 'received short shrift in reality'.[1] His implication was that political parties wished to utilise the growing national (London) press and saw little use for provincial titles. Certainly, there are several studies which have demonstrated that the sale of national newspapers, such as the *Daily Mail*, grew rapidly in the 1920s and 1930s.[2] Not only did the national press expand, the market was increasingly dominated by a small number of press groups. By the late 1930s they accounted for forty three per cent of press ownership.[3] Colin Seymour-Ure argued that the content of the provincial press became less partisan in this period and, with the growth of national newspapers, there was a decline in the abilities of political parties to express

---

1 Stephen Koss, *The Rise and Fall of the Political Press in Britain Volume Two: The Twentieth Century* (London: Hamilton, 1984), 3.

2 Jon Lawrence, *Electing Our Masters: The Hustings in British Politics from Hogarth to Blair* (Oxford: Oxford University Press, 2009), 101; Adrian Bingham, 'An Organ of Uplift?', *Journalism Studies*, 14/5 (2013), 651–62, 651.

3 Graham Murdock and Peter Goulding, 'The Structure, Ownership and Control of the Press, 1914–1976', in George Boyce, James Curran and Pauline Wingate, eds, *Newspaper History from the Seventeenth Century to the Present Day* (London: Constable,1978), 130–48, 134–5. For a more recent analysis of press amalgamations see Rachel Matthews, *The History of the Provincial Press in England* (London: Bloomsbury, 2017), 115–22.

'regional particularism'.[4] Matthew Dawson agreed that these processes, in addition to the use of the wireless, weakened the relationship between politics and the provincial press after 1918.[5]

Whilst historians agree that the sale of national newspapers increased, the extent to which they dominated has been challenged. Tom O'Malley questioned the definition of the term 'national' which he sees as being too generalised for the interwar period.[6] He referred to several issues, such as the lack of appeal to female readers, and the regional variations in national circulation figures, which prevented the 'national' press from living up to its namesake.[7] Rachel Matthews has noted that prior to the move of the *Manchester Guardian* to London in the 1950s, 'the London daily papers could hardly claim national circulation'.[8] Furthermore, there were several instances in the 1920s where the relationship between the press and political parties resembled Victorian and Edwardian practices. These included the ownership of newspapers by politicians, such as those owned by the Rowntree family and the 'Starmer group', and partisanship between competing newspapers, as in the case of the Liberal *North Devon Journal* and the Conservative/Unionist *North Devon Herald*.[9] These examples provide evidence for the continued importance of the provincial press after the First World War.

4   Colin Seymour-Ure, 'The Press and the Party System between the Wars', in Gillian Peele and Chris Cook, eds, *The Politics of Reappraisal 1918–1939* (London: Macmillan, 1975), 232–57, 238.

5   Matthew Dawson, 'Party Politics and the Provincial Press in Early Twentieth Century England: The Case of the South West', *Twentieth Century British History*, 9/2 (1998), 201–18, 217.

6   Tom O'Malley, 'Was there a National Press in the UK in the Second World War?', *Media History*, 23/3–4 (2017), 508–30, 508.

7   O'Malley, 'Was there a National Press in the UK in the Second World War?', 515.

8   Matthews, *The History of the Provincial Press in England*, 21.

9   For the Rowntree family and the 'Starmer Group' see Paul Gliddon, 'The Political Importance of Provincial Newspapers, 1903–1945: The Rowntrees and the Liberal Press', *Twentieth Century British History*, 14/1 (2003), 24–42. For the partisanship of the *North Devon Herald* and the *North Devon Journal* see Dawson, 'Party Politics and the Provincial Press', 208.

Additionally, studies have shown that the provincial press remained a crucial part of local identity. Michael Bromley and Nick Hayes argued that the commerce-driven local press in the 1920s provided *'the ubiquitous civic voice*; vital yet distanced from partisanship, or the reputed banality, of former or later years'.[10] Moreover, Rachel Matthews argued that the amalgamations of press ownership 'did not preclude an editorial stance which influenced the creation of civic identity'.[11] Hence, the provincial press became a greater part of the community in these years as it strove to provide news to its readers. Bromley and Hayes further noted that the legitimacy of the provincial press was based on five factors: the amount of local content; the degree to which the paper was locally owned and maintained; inclusiveness of its target market; circulation area; and financial standing.[12] However, the history of the medium requires more study to provide a greater understanding of its relationship to the localities it represented in the 1920s and 1930s. Indeed, there have recently been calls for more research of print culture in this period.[13] An analysis of the West Midlands press in the immediate postwar years will provide a test case as to whether there truly was a decline in the influence of the press in local and regional areas.

The vibrant press culture of the West Midlands in the late nineteenth and early twentieth century has been particularly overlooked both by local historians and historians of the press. In an article in a recent edited collection, one of the current authors sought to correct this oversight by investigating the fecundity of the satirical press in the later Victorian period in Birmingham and its impact on the public perception of Joseph Chamberlain both regionally and nationally.[14] Further investigation has

---

10   Matthew Bromley and Nick Hayes, 'Campaigner, Watchdog, or Municipal Lackey? Reflections on the Inter-War Provincial Press, Local Identity and Civic Welfarism', *Media History*, 8/2 (2002), 197–212, 197.

11   Matthews, *The History of the Provincial Press in England*, 135.

12   Bromley and Hayes, 'Campaigner, Watchdog, or Municipal Lackey?', 199.

13   See Annemarie McAllister and Andrew Hobbs, 'Introduction', *The International Journal of Regional and Local Studies*, 5/1 (2009), 5–15, 10.

14   Ian Cawood and Chris Upton, 'Joseph Chamberlain and the Birmingham Satirical Press', in Ian Cawood and Chris Upton, eds, *Joseph Chamberlain: International Statesman, National Leader and Local Icon* (London: Palgrave, 2016), pp. 176–210.

revealed that the Labour party, often regarded as unusually under-developed in the city at the turn of the century, actually attempted to use this well-established tradition of satirical periodicals to enhance its identity in the city. In June 1902, the Birmingham Socialist Centre's (BSC) executive committee approved the proposal by 'a number of members of the Centre [...] to purchase the *Town Crier*'.[15] This was undertaken as part of the local Labour party's attempt to prevent the privatisation of the new Birmingham tram service by the British Electrical Traction company. The *Town Crier* was the most venerable (and, by then, the least popular) of the Birmingham satirical periodicals having been founded by a collective of civic-minded Liberals, including George Dawson, in 1861, but it had been quickly supplanted in the city's affections by more scurrilous, more visual and less respectful papers, such as the *Dart* and the *Owl* (which were Unionist and Liberal respectively by 1902).[16]

The move was a bold one for an inexperienced and relatively poorly funded body such as the BSC, as previous experiments with a newspaper entitled the *Labour Standard* had failed earlier in 1902 after only four months of publication.[17] Such was the popularity of the satirical journal as a means of political engagement in Birmingham that perhaps the BSC felt that this was a more promising venture. The first edition of the journal under the editorship of J. D. Shallard, the BSC secretary, appeared on 12 July 1902 and was, at first sight, barely distinguishable from the previous

15   Archives and Collections, Library of Birmingham, Birmingham Socialist Centre minutes 1902–1912, 'Executive meeting', 20 June 1902, XC 9/2/1.

16   Despite the formation of the 'Conservative and Unionist Party' in May 1912, parts of the West Midlands remained distinctly 'Unionist'. This reflected the popularity of Joseph Chamberlain in Birmingham and other parts of the region. After 1918, the term was still employed in the region's press with 'Unionist' also becoming increasingly employed by the national party in the inter-war years. See Stuart Ball, *Portrait of a Party: The Conservative Party in Britain: 1918–1945* (Oxford: Oxford University Press, 2013), 68.

17   Peter Drake, 'The *Town Crier*: Birmingham's Labour Weekly, 1919–1951', in Anthony Wright and Richard Shackleton, eds, *Worlds of Labour: Essays in Birmingham Labour History* (Birmingham: University of Birmingham, 1983), 103–27, 104.

week's edition. However, a prominent advert for the *Clarion* newspaper and an overt attack on the British Electrical Traction company marked a change in editorial tone in a magazine that had trumpeted the benefits of privatisation only a few months earlier.[18] Sadly, the only immediate response to this change of tone appears to have been by the *Town Crier*'s advertisers and, in the following months, companies such as Mitchells and Butlers, whisky distillers, spirit sellers, gun manufacturers, banks and cigar salesmen ceased to market their wares in the magazine. By early 1903 only cocoa sellers, bicycle companies, Beecham's pills and patent medicine peddlers were advertising, though it is not certain if ethical objections by Quaker supporters of Labour may have resulted in a refusal of the paper to carry adverts from gunsmiths, brewers and spirit-dealers. The paper briefly rallied following Joseph Chamberlain's dramatic adoption of Tariff Reform and resignation from the Unionist Cabinet in 1903, as it lambasted the former mayor for adopting a policy of 'Zollverein', associated with the cartels and authoritarian regime of the 'Kaiserreich' in Germany.[19] This was not sufficient to halt the decline, however, and the last number of the pre-war *Town Crier* was published on 10 July 1903, almost exactly a year since the first issued published by the BSC. Although the Centre's minutes only obliquely refer to the progress of the paper, it is clear that the scale of the challenge of operating a weekly magazine had been underestimated and that Shallard's attempt to run both the *Town Crier* and the BSC had proved unsustainable.[20] W. J. Chamberlain, who revived the paper in 1919 claimed then that defeat of the privatisers and the municipalisation of Birmingham's trams 'was regarded as the completion of the work of the *Town Crier*',[21] but the *Town Crier*'s long-standing rival the *Dart* noted 'it

18   *Town Crier*, 12 July 1902; *Town Crier*, 1 March 1902.
19   *Town Crier*, 19 June 1903.
20   Birmingham Socialist Centre minutes 1902–1912; 1 December 1902; 29 January 1903; 7 September 1903.
21   *Town Crier*, no. 1, 3 October 1919.

ought not to have been started as a weekly' by its new owners.[22] The problem of combining the editing of a weekly newspaper and carrying out political duties as a party officer would prove equally challenging to the editors of successive political papers in the inter-war years.

The post-war politics of the West Midlands were marked by press battles rather than by the physical electoral confrontations which had survived into the Edwardian polity.[23] The *Birmingham Daily Post* (which became merely the *Birmingham Post* on 21 May 1918) had been a long-standing supporter of the Chamberlain family, having shifted from radical to Unionist with Joseph Chamberlain in 1886 and then adopting Tariff Reform two years after Chamberlain announced his conversion to the cause in 1903.[24] The *Post*, with an estimated circulation of 40,000, was hugely influential when it adopted a hostile tone towards the Labour movement from the moment the war ended, with an editorial at the time of the 1918 'Coupon' election in which it was stated that Labour 'is being run by an extreme pacifist, Bolshevik group'.[25] The sister paper of the *Post*, the *Birmingham Mail*, was equally fervent in its Unionism, however, as it was largely a working-class paper with an even higher circulation than the *Post*, it attempted to disguise this through a more balanced approach towards the Liberals and Labour. But, just as Laura Beers has recently explored in her studies of the national press in this period, the *Mail* became more partisan as the 1920s progressed and industrial tension and domestic division over Soviet Russia rose.[26] The general manager of the *Post* and *Mail*, Charles Hyde, personally

22   *Dart*, 26 October 1903.
23   Ian Cawood, 'Life after Joe: Politics and War in the West Midlands, 1914–1918', *Midland History*, 42/1 (2017), 92–117.
24   Harold Richard Grant Whates, *The Birmingham Post 1857: 1957: a Centenary Retrospect* (Birmingham: Birmingham Post and Mail, 1957), 178–9; Henry Miller, 'Print, Politics and Public Opinion: Newspapers in the Nineteenth Century', *History West Midlands*, 3 (2013), 26–8.
25   *Birmingham Post*, 14 December 1918.
26   Laura Beers, 'Education or Manipulation? Labour Democracy and the Popular Press in Interwar Britain', *Journal of British Studies*, 48/1 (2009), 129–52, 131; Laura Beers, *Your Britain: Media and the Labour Party* (Cambridge MA: Harvard University Press, 2010), 50–68. Following the collapse of the Triple Alliance, the *Mail* printed a cartoon showing an impoverished working-class family. 'Why don't you go back

supported an accommodation with the Labour movement, but he was soon disillusioned by the actions of the 1924 MacDonald government and the General Strike and his papers became implacable opponents of the Labour party, and he personally donated funds to the local Unionist Association.[27] However, the shifting position of the *Post* and *Mail* may simply have reflected the fluctuating mood of public opinion towards the Labour Party in the fluid first half of the 1920s. As Matthews concluded, the provincial press was primarily a profit-focused industry which only adopted a public service role to legitimise its financial interests.[28]

The only non-Unionist voice in the city by 1918 was the weekly *Birmingham Gazette*, owned by close allies of the Rowntree family, J. B. Morrell and Charles Starmer, who had converted it from an arch-Tory to a Liberal paper in November 1912, to join the rest of the Westminster Press Group.[29] By the end of the war, it supported the Asquithian Liberal party but had backed Labour in Birmingham since the split in the Liberal Party in 1916 and the virtual collapse of the Birmingham Liberal organisation.[30] The city's Labour party had itself split over conscription and the pacifist element had taken control. In the December 1918 'Coupon election', the Birmingham Labour Party had put up sympathetic fellow pacifists as candidates, many of whom were also outspoken socialists. The result was

---

to work?' asks the wife holding an infant. 'Because the trade union leaders won't let me', replies the husband. *Birmingham Mail*, 17 April 1921.

27 Whates, *The Birmingham Post 1857: 1957*, 190–7; Neville Chamberlain to Ida Chamberlain, 29 May 1920, Neville Chamberlain Papers, Cadbury Research Library, University of Birmingham, NC18/1/258; Walter Barrow to Neville Chamberlain, 5 October 1938, NC5/8/68.

28 Matthews, *The History of the Provincial Press in England*, x.

29 M. T. Gammage, 'The *Birmingham Daily Gazette*: A Case Study in the History of the Conservative Provincial Press 1862–1914' *West Midland Studies*, 13 (1980), 29–33, 30; Ian Packer, ed., *The Letters of Arnold Stephenson Rowntree to Mary Katherina Rowntree, 1910–1918* (Cambridge: Cambridge University Press, 2002), 10; Ian Packer, 'A Curious Exception? The Lincolnshire Chronicle and the "Starmer group"', *Journalism Studies* 7/3 (2006), 415–26, 417.

30 Archives and Collections, Library of Birmingham, Birmingham Central Labour Party minute book, 1918–1919, 14 August 1919, 329.94249 LAB; *Town Crier*, 3 October 1919; Drake, 'The *Town Crier*', 104–8.

catastrophic with no Labour candidates elected and some failing to gain even 20 per cent of the vote. This was in marked contrast to the success of more moderate Labour figures in the Black Country and Staffordshire and a very creditable showing in unlikely targets for Labour such as Shrewsbury and Oswestry. As in 1902, the timing of the re-launch of the *Town Crier* in October 1919 was, therefore, no accident. The Birmingham Labour party realised that they needed to build a local following and the paper was launched with W. J. Chamberlain as editor and chief copy-writer, chiefly to ensure a good result in the Birmingham municipal elections of November 1919. As Mike Savage and Chris Cook have established, after 1918 the Labour party prioritised progress in municipal elections fought on issues of local services and for this they needed a voice in the city.[31]

W. J. Chamberlain had come to Birmingham in 1918 as he had been imprisoned in Winchester gaol as a conscientious objector during the war. Chamberlain had worked on the *Daily Citizen* and was keen to continue his career as a journalist. He managed to persuade Fred Rudland, the secretary of the Birmingham Trades Council and a printer by trade, that the local party needed to start a paper. The £150 required to fund the venture was provided by the chief financiers of the pacifist Labour movement, the Quaker shopkeepers Harrison Barrow and Joseph Southall. In his initial editorial (under the pseudonym 'The Watchman'), Chamberlain confessed (in the third person) that he struggled for a name for the new paper,

> He was rather tired of the usual 'Pioneer', 'Forward', 'Worker', and so on through the range of stereotyped titles, and spent many sleepless nights searching for something new under the sun [...] Mr Harrison Barrow came along to that meeting with the offer of the copyright of 'The Town Crier' and the Committee jumped at it. And here we are![32]

---

31   Mike Savage, 'Urban Politics and the Rise of the Labour Party, 1919–1939', in Lynn Jamieson and Helen Corr, eds, *State, Private Life and Political Change* (Basingstoke: Macmillan, 1990), 204–23; Chris Cook, 'Liberals, Labour and Local Elections', in Gillian Peele and Chris Cook, eds, *The Politics of Reappraisal, 1918–1939* (Basingstoke: Macmillan, 1975), 166–88.

32   *Town Crier*, 3 October 1919; Drake, 'The *Town Crier*', 106–7. Barrow had been one of the members of the Birmingham Socialist Centre who had paid for the purchase of the original *Town Crier* in 1902.

The Birmingham Labour Party realised that a focus on 'housing, our Municipal Services [...] Gas and Tram charges and the elimination of a narrow, selfish policy' would appeal very effectively to the municipal electorate.[33] In its first issue on 3 October 1919, the *Town Crier* published 'a manifesto of the Birmingham Labour Party' with a focus on the issues of housing, the rating system, a demand for more municipal services, expansion of education and open access to Birmingham's markets (Figure 6.1).[34]

Chamberlain was also determined to avoid accusations of left-wing extremism, criticising striking railway workers at a mass meeting at Smithfield market for their hostility towards representatives of the *Birmingham Mail* and *Birmingham Post*, as a result of their newspapers having printed anti-strike cartoons. Chamberlain also praised the *Birmingham Gazette*'s 'sympathetic' reporting of the strike, even though he admitted 'I loathe the politics of the *Gazette*'.[35] The paper also wittily debunked one of the more extreme right-wing attacks on Labour, as it bemoaned the financial pressures on the party, 'Bolshie gold not having come to hand'.[36] Although the influence of the *Town Crier* is impossible to determine, there was a significant increase in the Labour vote in November 1919 and the party won twelve of the twenty municipal seats contested in Birmingham (as well as a third of the seats in Coventry municipal elections).[37] The significance of the municipal elections remained a crucial feature in the political press war in the city in the 1920s.

33 Birmingham Central Labour Party minute book, 1918–1919, 27 June 1919.

34 *Town Crier*, 3 October 1919.

35 *Town Crier*, 10 October 1919. Chamberlain later explained that, as a pacifist, imprisoned during the war, he resented 'the silence of Mr Asquith while papers were being suppressed and our prisons were packed with honest men'. The *Town Crier*, 17 October 1919.

36 *Town Crier*, 3 October 1919.

37 *Town Crier*, 7 November 1919; Library of Birmingham, Archives and Heritage Service, Birmingham Unionist Association (hereafter BUA) Executive Committee minutes, 21 November 1919, 329.94249 Con; Peter Walters, *Great War Britain: Coventry, Remembering 1914–1918* (Stroud: The History Press, 2016), 136.

Figure 6.1. The *Town Crier*, new series, no. 1, 3 October 1919. Reproduced with permission of Archives and Collections, Library of Birmingham.

As David Thackeray has commented, little of the Unionist response to this challenge has been studied.[38] Neville Chamberlain had emerged as the leading figure in Birmingham Unionism during the war and he was not satisfied by the support given by the *Post* and the *Mail* in the 1919 municipal campaign. He consequently met with Hubbard and Harvey (the respective editors) before the 1920 election.[39] The minutes of the Birmingham Unionist Association (BUA) Management Committee revealed the true relations between the Unionist press and Chamberlain as both editors assured him that 'they were quite anxious to do better this year'.[40] The Management Committee, worried by the impact of the *Town Crier* in the city, went further and announced the 'urgent need for the issue of a Unionist paper in the Division' in March 1920, to rival the *Town Crier*.[41] The Publication Sub-committee duly discussed the 'need for a local Unionist publication of some kind to counter-act the Socialistic propaganda which was, at the moment, the only form of political literature which was finding its way into the houses of the people'. The question of whether this was to be a party newsletter or a full newspaper (in the style of the *Town Crier*) revealed the limited ambitions of the Sub-committee, for it was decided that 'it should be as local as possible, giving reports of as to all the local doings of the Party'. The title suggested was one issued by Joseph Chamberlain's local association in West Birmingham as a four-page broadsheet before the war: *Straightforward*.[42] The Unionists also suffered from a lack of newspaper

38   David Thackeray, *Conservatism for the Democratic Age: Conservative Cultures and the Challenge of Mass Politics in Early Twentieth-Century England* (Manchester: Manchester University Press, 2013), 4.

39   Chamberlain met with Hubbard on 11 January 1920, Neville Chamberlain to Hilda and Ida Chamberlain, NC18/1/239. Charles Hyde, the owner of the *Post*, visited Chamberlain in May 1920. Neville Chamberlain to Ida Chamberlain, NC18/1/258, 29 May 1920.

40   BUA Management Committee minutes, 8 October 1920.

41   BUA Management Committee minutes, 15 March 1920.

42   BUA Publication Sub-committee minutes, 31 March 1920. This name was confirmed by the BUA Management Committee in May 1920. BUA Management Committee minutes, 28 May 1920.

experience, with the chairman of the Sub-committee, John Bedford Burman, having to explain the process of distribution of newspapers to his colleagues and the Committee unable to identify the necessary print run to cover the city other than as somewhere between 50,000 and 100,000 copies.[43] The Sub-committee were also astonished at the cost of running a paper and realised that a run of twelve monthly issues would require £1,000 from the Management Committee.[44] When they drafted their report to the Committee in May 1920, the Publication Sub-committee also realised that it would 'be necessary to engage some person of [journalistic] experience' to write the paper. They also blithely assumed, seemingly on the basis of no market research, that companies would wish to advertise in the paper.[45] Trevor Jones, of the *Birmingham Mail*, was proposed as 'sub'-editor, but was unable to be named as full editor as his employment at the *Mail* prevented his involvement with a partisan publication and Burman, who had trained and worked as a journalist in Birmingham and had inherited his father's printing company since the 1880s, was named as editor instead.[46] The Management Committee responded that they were worried by 'the extraordinarily heavy cost of printing' and would only advance the funds if a small limited company, comprised of the senior

43   BUA Publication Sub-committee minutes, 31 March 1920; 12 April 1920. In the event, only 10,000 copies of the first issue were printed. BUA Publication Sub-committee minutes, 16 April 1920. The pre-war title was *Straightforward* and the post-war title was *Straight Forward*.

44   BUA Publication Sub-committee minutes, 16 April 1920. W. J. Chamberlain appeared to have a spy in the Unionist camp as he gleefully reported later in the year that 'seven true-blue Tories of Birmingham formed themselves into the 'Straight Forward Publishing Company, Ltd.', with a capital of £1,000, and set about producing an anti-Labour monthly, which was to essay the task of counteracting the pernicious influence of the *Town Crier*', *Town Crier*, 10 September 1920.

45   BUA Publication Sub-committee draft report, 19 May 1920.

46   BUA Publication Sub-committee minutes, 25 June 1920; *Straight Forward*, April 1921; Burman's irrelevance to the editing of the magazine was illustrated in early 1922, when the Management Committee confessed that he had been 'abroad for some time, but during his absence, the paper had been carried on with its usual "go"'. BUA Central Committee minutes, 17 March 1922.

members of the Publication Sub-committee was formed.[47] Nevertheless, the first issue, costing one penny, was printed by Percival Jones Ltd and sold in September 1920 with a mission statement 'to expose false prophets who seek to delude ignorant people' and a cartoon showing a Unionist car attempting to overtake a Labour charabanc with the caption 'We must get in front these Blighters' (Figure 6.2).[48]

The Management Committee noted their approval and even overlooked the tiny number of subscriptions (220) that had been taken up by the time of the second issue in October 1920.[49] The Liberal *Birmingham Gazette* was not impressed, however, commenting wryly, 'if *Straight Forward* is a measure of Unionist intelligence in Birmingham, then the progressive forces, Liberal or Labour, ought to soon break that thirty-five year political monopoly'.[50]

This activity appeared to bear political fruit, however, as the Unionists improved their performance in the 1920 municipal elections in which they won six seats from Labour and only lost two (both in Aston), a performance that the *Birmingham Gazette* described as a 'surprise result'.[51] Neville Chamberlain duly recorded his satisfaction with the 'very material assistance' that the *Post* and *Mail* had been given to Unionist candidates.[52] To further underline the significance of political print culture in the first days of a democratic polity, the Unionist Association then established a full Propaganda Committee in 1921 to promote a nuanced message suited to the working men and women of the city.[53]

As many studies of press history reveal, however, commencing a newspaper is an easier challenge than sustaining one. As early as January 1921, Burman was warning that *Straight Forward* was losing £20 on every issue and that within the paper's first four months, advertisement revenue 'had

47   BUA Management Committee minutes, 15 October 1920.
48   *Straight Forward*, September 1920.
49   BUA Management Committee report to the Central Committee, 15 October 1920
50   *Birmingham Gazette*, 3 September 1920.
51   *Birmingham Gazette*, 2 November 1920.
52   BUA Management Committee minutes, 12 November 1920
53   BUA Executive Committee minutes, 21 November 1921.

Figure 6.2. *Straight Forward*, no. 1. September 1920. Reproduced with permission of Archives and Collections, Library of Birmingham.

fallen to the value of £36 on the last issue', but the Management Committee felt that the political benefits were worth the financial burden and Burman was ordered to 'proceed with its publication'.[54] Burman did manage to persuade the city's public libraries to agree to take copies of the journal and, as a reward, he and the other directors of *Straight Forward* were appointed to a new 'Press Sub-committee' whose task it was to keep the editors of the *Post* and *Mail* 'in touch with matters connected with Municipal and Parliamentary organisation'.[55] When, in September 1921, Burman reported an overall cost to the Association of £226 for the publication of twelve issues of the newspaper, he was authorised to continue publication for another twelve months.[56] The loss of four council seats (three to Labour and one to the Liberals) in the 1921 municipal elections as the effects of the post-war downturn were felt in the city, meant that the Unionist propaganda effort had to be maintained.[57] The BUA was also perturbed by the publication of a national Unionist newspaper, the *Popular View*, which first appeared in May 1921. It was intended that local branches would adapt the *Popular View* and 'localise' it with the addition of their own inserts, but the directors of *Straight Forward* proposed that the *Popular View* should merely be an insert in their publication.[58] The decision was taken, however, to maintain Birmingham's traditionally independent position within the Unionist movement and to continue to publish *Straight Forward* 'in its present form and to preserve its Birmingham identity'.[59] Judging from the minutes of the BUA, however, the paper was somewhat neglected in 1922, with Burman first abroad for several months and then co-opted onto the Demonstration Sub-committee as well as chairing the Press Sub-committee. By July 1922, Burman had to admit that the advertising revenue had dropped further and that the paper was running at a loss of £25 per issue. He was, however, instructed to continue to publish the journal and was granted a further £250

54   BUA Management Committee minutes, 14 January 1921.
55   BUA Management Committee minutes, 8 April 1921.
56   BUA Management Committee minutes, 9 September 1921.
57   *Birmingham Gazette*, 2 November 1921.
58   BUA Central Committee minutes, 10 June 1921.
59   BUA Central Committee minutes, 17 March 1922.

to finance *Straight Forward* for another year.[60] The Press Sub-committee appeared to have neglected *Straight Forward* in favour of producing a series of leaflets and a printed manifesto for that year's municipal elections.[61] The consequence of this was a financial crisis, revealed in the minutes of a special meeting of the Management Committee in December when Neville Chamberlain pointed out that the Association was spending £7,000 per year, but only raising £4,000 by subscriptions and through funds raised at Demonstrations and other social events.[62]

As a consequence, the future *of Straight Forward* was discussed in depth at a meeting of the Management Committee in February 1923, with Neville Chamberlain present. Burman pointed out that Percival Jones Ltd had lost the contract to publish the paper and a lower offer had been accepted (by none other than Burman's own company, Burman, Cooper and Co.). The £250 allocated by the Management Committee six months earlier had been spent. Burman blamed the crisis on the poor circulation of the paper and the refusal of local Associations to pay for their copies. Neville's wife, Annie Chamberlain, suggested that a 'page for women' (rather than about women's political activities) should be added (in emulation of the *Town Crier*), and the Management Committee agreed that as their 'opponents had a paper circulating very widely' and that the alternative was to rely on leaflets, they would advance a further £100.[63] Sadly, however, the BUA had not anticipated that the election of November 1922 would be followed by a further two general elections within the next two years. The effort to prevent a Labour breakthrough in the city would eventually fatally weaken the BUA's ability to maintain a monthly newspaper.

In April 1923, the Management Committee was forced to report to the Central Committee that the production of 'three special editions of *Straight Forward*' for the general and municipal elections had resulted in the failure to produce issues in December 1922 and February 1923. Although the Committee announced its intention to resume monthly publication,

60   BUA Management Committee minutes, 14 July 1922.
61   BUA Press Sub-committee minutes, 22 September 1922; 29 September 1922.
62   BUA Management Committee minutes, 29 December 1929.
63   BUA Management Committee minutes, 9 February 1923.

it was noted that there was 'a healthy rivalry' for BUA resources between the Carnival (as the annual Demonstration had been re-titled) and the newspaper and that the finances of the newspaper still remained fragile.[64] These were further strained by the need for a further special edition for the municipal elections in October 1923 and then a further special edition, hurriedly printed for the snap general election in December. In November 1923, Burman was forced to admit to the Management Committee that 'the publication had no funds left'. The Committee chairman did point out that the Management Committee had actually authorised £1,000 to be spent on the paper in its first year and that only £804 had been spent in the whole three years of the paper's existence. A further £200 was advanced to the limited company and the directors of the paper were thanked profusely for their 'excellent election number'.[65] The expense paid off and, against the national trend, the Unionists of Birmingham, as in 1906, withstood the national party's defeat and held all the Birmingham seats (although Herbert Austin's majority in King's Norton was reduced to 1,554). The BUA was forced to find a further £250 to keep the paper afloat as early as March 1924 and admitted in September that it was costing £300 a year to publish the paper.[66] Burman now voiced the opinion to the Management Committee that the paper's 'most necessary functions had now to some extent gone' now that the support of the *Mail* and the *Post* was stronger than it had been in 1919 and that 'in his opinion *Straight Forward* would [...] have to cease'. He proposed a further edition 'once or twice a year, when found necessary'. Some others suggested making use of a local insert in either *The Man in the Street* (which had replaced the *Popular View* in May 1924) or the women's Unionist paper, *Home and Politics*, but Burman was not keen, noting that 'it was not the first of [Central Office's] adventures in this direction and it did not seem to him in any way to compete with the daily newspapers.'[67]

64   BUA Central Committee minutes, 13 April 1923.
65   BUA Management Committee minutes, 9 November 1923.
66   BUA Finance Sub-committee minutes, 14 March 1924.
67   BUA Management Committee minutes, 12 September 1924.

As Burman planned, the paper continued every month until October 1924, happily lambasting MacDonald's Labour government, but it was clearly over-stretched by the combination of general and municipal elections on 29 October and 1 November respectively. Although there was a call for a special General Election edition, Burman's death knell had reduced enthusiasm for the project and 'it was decided that coverage for October be confined to the Municipal number'.[68] The October 1924 edition of *Straight Forward* duly only included three references to the General Election, above the mast head and in the editorial column. There were no profiles of the general election candidates, in contrast to the vibrant election edition of the *Town Crier*. The result was Labour's first general election breakthrough in the city, taking King's Norton from Austin in 1924 with a majority of 133 and coming within seventy-eight votes of unseating Neville Chamberlain in Ladywood. This was in contrast to the Unionists' triumph in the municipal elections when the party won twenty of the twenty-five seats being contested. The decision to end the regular appearance of *Straight Forward* as a monthly was not rescinded, however, and the next edition of the publication after October 1924 was not until April 1925. Money was spent instead on the organisation of new central party offices (in a building named Empire House), funding of the annual Empire Carnival/Demonstration and the highly popular women's organisation's 'socials, dances, whist drives and children's parties'. Burman became distracted with the organisation of a football league for the junior branches.[69] *Straight Forward* only appeared as election issues for the rest of the inter-war period, the only exception being a twelve-page special edition in July 1936 to mark the centenary of the birth of Joseph Chamberlain. Into the gap left by *Straight Forward*, local Associations launched their own papers to challenge the *Town Crier*, such as Yardley which launched *Progress* in 1925.[70] These fared equally poorly and most lasted less than a year. There was a brief discussion in 1926 as to reviving *Straight Forward* as a monthly, but Burman was adamant that such a paper was not merely

---

68   BUA Management Committee minutes, 12 September 1924.
69   BUA Central Council minutes, 1 May 1925; 6 November 1925.
70   Yardley Division Unionist Association report, 12 February 1926.

redundant but actually a financial drain.[71] Despite Burman's pessimism, *The Man in the Street*, with its strong use of cartoons and satire and *Home and Politics*, with its portraits of unlikely Unionist pin-ups (Figure 6.3), cookery and gardening pages, proved far more enduring, lasting until 1929 (when they amalgamated into *Home and Empire*) and helped to fill the gap that *Straight Forward* had left. The *Birmingham Post* and the *Birmingham Mail* remained steadfast supporters of the Unionist cause and exploited the growing popular disillusion with the Labour Party after 1924 very effectively. On the national stage, this was the age of Beaverbrook's *Daily Express*, which effectively claimed to be impartial and avoided the extreme anti-socialism of the *Daily Mail* (and even *The Times*) whilst endorsing Baldwin's leadership.[72] It was not as if the Unionist voter was short of alternative reading material, once *Straight Forward* ceased to be published regularly. As Geraint Thomas suggests, *Straight Forward*'s launch can be read as an attempt by the Birmingham Unionists 'to augment the local as the site of political competition' but its decline demonstrated the weakness of an overtly party political publication, no matter how well designed, in an age of weakening public identification with party labels.[73]

Ironically, while the Labour party finally achieved a significant break-through in Birmingham in 1924, the party itself was bitterly divided and the *Town Crier* had inadvertently revealed this throughout its publica-tion history. As early as September 1920, W. J. Chamberlain had turned against his previous radical allies and attacked them for 'wild and mean-ingless outbursts that merely provide the anti-Labour forces with excel-lent propaganda material'.[74] In the same month, he criticised trade

---

71   BUA Management Committee minutes, 11 June 1926.
72   Beers, *Your Britain: Media and the Labour Party*, 76–7.
73   Thomas, 'Political Modernity and 'Government' in the Construction of Inter-War
      Democracy: Local and National Encounters', in Laura Beers and Geraint Thomas,
      eds, *Brave New World: Imperial and Democratic Nation Building in Britain between
      the Wars* (London: Institute of Historical Research, 2011), 44. Thomas, in common
      with most commentators, incorrectly refers to the Birmingham Unionist Association
      as 'Conservatives'.
74   *Town Crier*, 10 September 1920.

Figure 6.3.   Front cover of *Home and Politics*, no. 28, August 1923. Reproduced with
permission of Conservative Party Archive, Bodleian Library.

unions for resorting too quickly to 'the clumsy weapon of the strike'.[75] Chamberlain began to promote a far more emollient image for Labour, printing an article which claimed that 'the Labour party programme comes nearer to expressing the Christian ideals than any other'[76] and welcoming the decision of Ramsay MacDonald to form a minority government in January 1924.[77] This latter decision opened a rift with Joseph Southall, a key funder of the Birmingham Labour Movement, who wrote to the paper claiming that 'in the long run [...] a semi-Labour government [will] be found to be worse than no Labour government at all'. Chamberlain responded that 'semi-criticism may be found in the long run to be worse than no criticism at all'.[78] Finally, in 1924, the decision of the Birmingham Labour party, of which W. J. Chamberlain was by this point the president, to invite Oswald Mosley to contest Neville Chamberlain's seat in Ladywood proved too much for some.[79] The hard-left journal, the *Worker*, acerbically commented 'the game was to find some stupid, devoted old worker who had worked up to within sight of victory and then push the mug out by getting a tame ILP branch to nominate Mosley'.[80] Chamberlain angrily responded by calling this article 'a tissue of falsehoods from beginning to end'.[81] Chamberlain's move away from hard left socialism appeared to be justified in 1924, following Robert Dennison's victory in King's Norton, and the headline 'Birmingham Labour breaks through!' was accompanied

75   *Town Crier*, 17 September 1920.
76   H. Dunnico, 'The Churches and Labour', *Town Crier*, 7 December 1923.
77   *Town Crier*, 25 January 1924.
78   *Town Crier*, 5 September 1924.
79   The influence of the *Town Crier* was clearly felt by Neville Chamberlain as his papers contain the 25 July 1924 edition of the *Town Crier* in which Mosley was announced as 'New Labour Champion for Ladywood' and, most threateningly, 'His Challenge to Neville Chamberlain'. NC5/10/29. Neville Chamberlain also discussed the *Town Crier* with his wife. Neville Chamberlain to Annie Chamberlain, 8 August 1924, NC1/26/334.
80   Quoted in *Birmingham Gazette*, 13 August 1924. Mosley was in fact, nominated by none other than Ramsay MacDonald. R. MacDonald to Oswald Mosley, 23 October 1924, Cadbury Research Library, OMD1/1/6.
81   *Birmingham Gazette*, 14 August 1924.

by an angry editorial attacking the tactics of the *Birmingham Mail*, commenting that 'of one thing I am sure and that is that the putrid stuff put out by the *Mail* during the campaign was so bad that it stank even in the nostrils of many of those who have hitherto supported the Unionist Party'.[82]

Part of Labour's success was that the *Town Crier* had become a far less overtly party political publication than *Straight Forward*, continuing the vibrant print culture of pre-war Birmingham by including book and theatre reviews, a children's page, a gardening column, a serial story and items on socialist history. As Thackeray has commented, this was 'emblematic of its vigorous attempts to engage with the daily life of working families'.[83] By contrast, *Straight Forward* failed to print anything more than encomiums of party leaders, details of Unionist events and endless exhortations for 'armchair Unionists' to rouse themselves.[84] Even with the backing of local Unionist businesses such as Mitchells and Butlers, Bird's of Wolverhampton and Birmingham Small Arms, *Straight Forward* was only ever a monthly publication, often with more illustrations than editorial material, while *Town Crier* survived as a weekly until after the Second World War, despite only carrying adverts from Westwood's (kitchenware) and the S. M. Company ('shirts and overalls [...] made by trade union labour') in its early editions and only achieving an estimated circulation of 1,500 copies.[85] Unlike readers of *Straight Forward*, however, which faced many political alternatives in its market, as the *Town Crier* was the only Birmingham Labour paper, perhaps the readership of each issue was far higher than these

82   *Town Crier*, 31 October 1924.
83   Thackeray, *Conservatism for the Democratic Age*, 133.
84   See for example, 'Wake Up, Men! Curse and Danger of Apathy', *Straight Forward*, June 1923.
85   *Town Crier*, 10 October 1919; Drake, 'The *Town Crier*', 103–26. The editor of the *Town Crier*, W. J. Chamberlain, sought 'immediate financial assistance' for his paper from the Birmingham Borough Labour Party within six months of its launch; Archives and Collections, Library of Birmingham, Birmingham Borough Labour Party Minutes of Meetings Vol. 1, 1919–1921, 12 February 1920, 329.94249. In September 1923, Mitchells and Butlers ceased to advertise in *Straight Forward* and, from 30 November 1923, advertised in *Town Crier* instead.

figures suggest.[86] Adrian Bingham has described the state of the national Labour press in the 1920s as too party-political and out of touch with its working-class audience, a problem of left-wing papers that Chamberlain clearly avoided with his range of popular features that an editor such as George Lansbury would have deprecated.[87] The survival of the *Town Crier* was also due to the response to regular appeals for financial support (in a similar fashion to those which kept the *Daily Herald* afloat)[88] such as that issued to local trade unionists in November 1920.[89] W. J. Chamberlain swiftly became a powerful figure in West Midlands Labour politics, being elected to the Labour Joint Executive Committee in September 1922.[90] It was Chamberlain's support for Mosley that led to the Birmingham Labour Party inviting him to contest Ladywood in 1924 and Smethwick in 1926. This alienated influential figures within the Labour Movement such as Southall and Robert Dunstan, who had contested Ladywood in 1922 and 1923 and led to the Independent Labour Party (ILP) refusing to invite *Town Crier* reporters to their meetings.[91] Chamberlain's strategy was, however vindicated, as the Birmingham Labour party finally took more than a single seat in the 1929 election, winning half of Birmingham's seats, unseating Arthur Steel-Maitland in Erdington and capturing Ladywood (although Neville Chamberlain had retreated to Edgbaston).

Among the Labour activists, the moderate 'Labour Church' movement which had been particularly powerful in pre-war Birmingham, was revived by the Birmingham branch of the ILP, but, although there is no indication from the pages of the *Town Crier* that this movement reached

86   John Boughton suggested that the *Town Crier*'s importance was as 'mouthpiece, informant and source of identity' for the Birmingham Labour movement. John Boughton, 'Working Class Politics in Birmingham and Sheffield, 1918–1931', PhD thesis, University of Warwick, 1985, 168.

87   Adrian Bingham, 'Representing the People? The *Daily Mirror*, Class and Political Culture in Inter-War Britain', in Beers and Thomas, eds, *Brave New World*, 109–28, 113–16.

88   Beers, *Your Britain: Media and the Labour Party*, 77.

89   Birmingham Borough Labour Party minute book, i, 1919–1921.

90   Birmingham Borough Labour Party minute book, i, 1919–1921, 21 September 1922.

91   Drake, 'The *Town Crier*', 112.

an audience beyond existing ILP members, other Labour publications give the impression of genuinely religious-focused meetings.[92] It seems from the evidence, however, that the Labour churches arose both from the genuine religious convictions of many of the Birmingham Labour figures, such as the Quaker, Joseph Southall, but also as a means of disproving Unionist press attacks on Labour as supporters or fellow-travellers of the 'godless Bolsheviks'. The use of 'Bolshevism' as a synonym for Labour, was not fully supported by the Birmingham Unionist press, however, despite its frequent employment by right wing Unionist politicians (and impassioned Unionist journalists at election time).[93] The *Birmingham Mail* was quite content to refer to the Labour party without qualification, even though it referred to the *Daily Herald* as 'the Bolshevik Organ',[94] while the *Birmingham Post* used the term 'Labour' in inverted commas until 1921 (as did the national Unionist newsletter, *Gleanings and Memoranda*).[95] *Straight Forward* preferred to refer to its chief opponents in the city as 'the socialists'. As an editorial explained in November 1924:

> The candidates in opposition to those of the Unionist party are, almost without exception, described as 'Labour'. There is no greater misnomer than this. The word 'Labour' is used because at election times it is more attractive than 'Socialism' – mere party expediency suggests its use. Of course a 'Labour' candidate has a right to be a Socialist if he believes in Socialism. But if he is a Socialist he should call himself a Socialist so that persons may know what they are voting for.[96]

---

92   Minutes of the Birmingham city branch of the Independent Labour Party 1915–1921, 3 March 1917; George John Barnsby, *Socialism in Birmingham and the Black Country 1850–1939* (Wolverhampton: Integrated Publishing Services, 1998), 353–6. See also: Jacqueline Turner, 'Labour's Lost Soul? Recovering the Labour Church', in Matthew Worley, ed., *The Foundations of the British Labour Party: Identities, Cultures and Perspectives, 1900–1939* (Farnham: Ashgate, 2009), 153–69.

93   G. W. Hubbard reported that Lloyd George referred to the Labour press as 'Bolshevist and ILP agents' when he met Neville Chamberlain in January 1920. Neville Chamberlain to Hilda Chamberlain, 11 January 1920, NC18/1/239.

94   *Birmingham Mail*, 16 April 1921.

95   *Gleanings and Memoranda*, January 1924, Conservative Party archive, Bodleian library, Oxford, XFilms 64/5.

96   '"Labour" means Socialism', *Straight Forward*, November 1924.

Although Laura Beers appears to suggest that this was a successful strategy, we would argue that this lack of consistency in the Unionist propaganda was a weakness which Labour in Birmingham was clearly able to exploit, especially in the 1919 and 1921 municipal elections.[97] The *Birmingham Gazette* mocked Chamberlain's attempt to 'waggle' 'the Bolshevik bogey' in the first issue *of Straight Forward*.[98] *Straight Forward* continued with this strategy until 1921 with little success, if the municipal election results of that year are any indication.[99] The Liberals also used the claim to ridicule their Unionist opponents, noting in a pamphlet in 1919: 'some people think that every member of the Labour party is a Revolutionist or a Bolshevist. But that is absurd.'[100] In March 1922, Neville Chamberlain opined to his sister that 'to go to the country purely on economy and anti-Socialism seems bad tactics to me'[101] and he was supported in this by Leo Amery, the MP for Sparkbrook.[102] It is noticeable that after this date, the Unionist press promoted a more 'constructive approach' with the *Birmingham Post*'s 1922 municipal election coverage beginning with a report of the Unionist slogan 'Cheaper Houses, Small Houses, Many Houses.'[103] The result was startling, with Labour losing such working-class wards as Balsall Heath, Small Heath, Soho and Sparkbrook. The *Birmingham Post* could confidently state that 'the Labour assault has been firmly met.'[104] Although the anti-socialist message never disappeared from the Birmingham Unionist press, especially once Labour formed a minority government in 1924, the use of 'Bolshevism' as a term of abuse for Labour

---

97 Beers, *Your Britain: Media and the Labour Party*, 56–7.

98 *Birmingham Gazette*, 3 September 1920.

99 See for example, *Straight Forward*, October 1921.

100 *The Real Aims of the Labour Party*, Liberal Party pamphlet 1919/14, National Liberal Club Library, London.

101 Neville Chamberlain to Hilda Chamberlain, 26 March 1922, quoted in Robert Self, ed., *Neville Chamberlain Diary Letters Vol Two: The Reform Years, 1921–1927* (Aldershot: Ashgate, 2000), 104.

102 Notes for Unionist Workers and Speakers, December 1921 Leo Amery Papers, Churchill College, Cambridge, AMEL 4/9.

103 *Birmingham Post*, 27 October 1922.

104 *Birmingham Post*, 2 November 1922.

seems to have subsided after this point. Baldwin's inter-war success was to incorporate the Labour party into the national polity and so he was reluctant to endorse such over-exaggerated and insulting behaviour towards his fellow-Parliamentarians once he became leader, even in 1924 at the height of the 'Red Scare'. Neville Chamberlain may not always have been as scrupulous, but he too ensured that public discourse became more substantive and less abusive after 1923.[105] The *Birmingham Mail* launched a charitable fund, similar to work carried out by Annie Chamberlain and Smedley Crooke, MP for Deritend.[106] In this way, the Birmingham Unionist press became increasingly moderate under Neville Chamberlain's influence, just as W. J. Chamberlain was achieving the same for the Labour press.

In the national and municipal elections between 1918 and 1924, the lack of a clear denominational divide between the parties was consistently noted by the whole spectrum of the local press and the attempts of long-serving Liberals to appeal to nonconformist consciences had very limited effect as Robert Outhwaite, David Mason, John Wilson and Richard Fairbairn all soon discovered.[107] As Thackeray noted, 'many of the issues which had rallied the Nonconformist conscience carried little weight in politics after the First World War'.[108] Stanley Baldwin and Neville Chamberlain both continued the tradition, begun by Joseph Chamberlain in the 1880s, of appealing to the nonconformist tradition as part of British civic identity rather than as a separate entity and then delivering the votes of this community to the Unionist cause.[109] In addition, Peter Catterall has demonstrated

105 Phillip Williamson, *Stanley Baldwin: Conservative Leadership and National Values* (Cambridge: Cambridge University Press, 1999), 222–3.

106 BUA minutes, 12 December 1924; The *Town Crier* complained that the *Birmingham Mail* fund was used for unfair political advantage in the city. *Town Crier*, 13 January 1922.

107 Outhwaite came a poor third in Hanley in 1918. Mason came last in the poll of six candidates in Coventry in December 1918 and Wilson lost the seat which he had held for twenty-seven years in 1922 – the first time he had faced a Unionist candidate. Fairbairn lost three of the four elections he contested in Worcester in the period, in 1918, 1923 and 1924.

108 Thackeray, *Conservatism for the Democratic Age*, 180.

109 Stephen Koss, *Nonconformity in British Politics* (London: Batsford, 1975), 174–7; Williamson, *Stanley Baldwin: Conservative Leadership and National Values*, 354–5.

that nonconformity continued to inform the views of many within the Labour Party after 1918.[110] The only religious group clearly excluded from the national collective was 'the Jew', who was frequently associated with Bolshevism in both Germany and Russia in Unionist publications and was the butt of jokes regarding his assumed untrustworthiness and 'cosmopolitan' identity.[111] As Stuart Ball has noted, 'there certainly was an under-current of anti-Semitism in Conservative [and Unionist] circles' especially in the febrile atmosphere of post-war Europe.'[112]

In the place of religious festivals and events, Labour and Unionist publications sought to develop their own calendar of cultural activities as an attempt to replace the denominational ceremonies and events which had dominated many people's social lives in the years before 1914, thereby taking their political rivalry into the public behaviour of the city. For the Labour Party, this meant the celebration of the socialist May Day. The event had a long pedigree, but was revived in 1920 as a means of protesting against the Trade Union Bill, with a procession through central London to Hyde Park.[113] That organised by the Birmingham Labour Party in 1920 was relatively modest, but, with W. J. Chamberlain co-opted onto the Sub-committee in 1922, the event expanded into a public display of floats on lorries, depicting 'Labour marching (of all ranks) under Labour's banner.'[114]

---

110   See, for example, Peter Catterall, *Labour and the Free Churches, 1918–1939: Radicalism, Righteousness and Religion* (London: Bloomsbury, 2016); Peter Catterall, 'The Distinctiveness of British Socialism? Religion and the Rise of Labour, c. 1900–1939', in Matthew Worley, ed., *The Foundations of the British Labour Party: Identities, Cultures and Perspectives, 1900–1939* (London: Routledge, 2009), 131–52.

111   See *Straight Forward*, especially September 1920 and September 1921.

112   Ball, *Portrait of a Party*, 65; Geoffrey Russell Searle, *Corruption in British Politics, 1895–1930* (Oxford:, 1987), 328–37. It must be noted that there was evidence of racial prejudice within the Birmingham Labour Party as well, as a meeting of the party in 1920 unanimously approved a motion which protested against 'the invasion of Germany by black troops' and called on the government 'to secure the withdrawal of this menace from Europe'. Birmingham Borough Labour Party minute book, i, 1919–1921, 15 April 1920.

113   The *Sphere*, 8 May 1920.

114   Minutes of Labour Party meeting, Birmingham Borough Labour Party Minutes of Meetings i, 1919–1921, 15 January 1920; Minutes of Labour Party May Day

Straight Forward therefore championed the existing 'Empire Day' as a rival day of celebration and its growing scale appears to have developed as a response to the success of the May Day celebrations, especially once a Labour government was in office and able to channel the resources of the state towards their feast day. The Unionist 'Demonstration' was first held in 1920 and according to Neville Chamberlain, 'there was a great crowd'.[115] The Empire Day celebrations grew out of this event, adapting an event that had been largely only celebrated by scouting organisations and schools in the Midlands hitherto.[116] The first mention of Empire Day in *Straight Forward* was in the June 1924 edition. However, unlike the pre-war celebrations which dated back to Lord Meath's establishment of Queen Victoria's birthday (24 May) as a day of celebration of Britain's 'glorious Empire', in Birmingham, as elsewhere, the post-war emphasis was on the contribution of the Empire in the Great War.[117] The increased scale of the event was stimulated by the British Empire Exhibition at Wembley which had opened in April and by a preceding 'Empire Shopping Week' in which the Birmingham Chamber of Commerce attempted to 'reproduce the Wembley atmosphere'.[118] The timing of holding such an overtly patriotic event with a Labour government in office was clearly influential in stimulating the Unionists to such heights of activity. The event itself was substantial, with tableaux, pageants, parades, motor car processions, decorated lorries, musical entertainments and speeches.[119] Spurred into a response, the Birmingham Labour Party organised a similar event on their 'feast day' on 3 May 1925, with, as the *Birmingham Gazette* reported, a procession to Calthorpe Park of trade unions, Labour parties, the co-operative

---

Sub-committee meeting, 27 April 1923, Birmingham Borough Labour Party Minutes of Meetings ii, 1921–1924.

115   Neville Chamberlain to Ida Chamberlain, 19 September 1920, NC18/1/272.

116   Jim English, 'Empire Day in Britain, 1904–1958', *Historical Journal*, 49/1 (2006), 247–76; Neville Chamberlain to Ida Chamberlain, 18 September 1920, NC18/1/272; *Birmingham Gazette*, 25 May 1921.

117   English, 'Empire Day in Britain, 1904–1958', 261–2; Neville Chamberlain to Hilda Chamberlain, 23 May 1924, NC18/1/437.

118   *Birmingham Gazette*, 19 May 1924.

119   *Straight Forward*, June 1924.

movement, guild socialists, young socialists' leaguers and girls' labour clubs – 15,000 people in total.[120] With a Unionist government in power, however, the scale of Empire Day diminished in 1925 and it once again became an event involving 'school children, Boy Scouts, Girl Guides and Grammar School Cadets' (marred by a typical English spring downpour).[121]

David Thackeray has already identified that the local Conservative party organisations in the West Midlands were very effective at directing their message towards the newly enfranchised female voters.[122] J. B. Burman, the head of the Publication Sub-committee which had founded *Straight Forward* in 1920, had also been the first, in the same year, to suggest the appointment of 'a lady organiser, to organise the Women's Associations throughout the City'.[123] Burman's wife served on the Women's Section of the city's Unionist Management Committee alongside Annie Chamberlain, which may explain the prominence given to women's meetings in the early years of the newspaper. This strong female involvement in the activities of the party in the West Midlands was also reflected in the national Unionist publication, *Home and Politics*. Both Lucy Baldwin and Annie Chamberlain appeared on the front cover of the magazine and contributed to the publication. The Birmingham women's organisation, like its male counter-parts, preferred its autonomy from national direction, however. There are no references to Birmingham activities in the regular column 'Our work in the constituencies' until after the demise of *Straight Forward* in 1924 – it was clearly accepted that Birmingham needed no assistance from outside the city. The Unionist newspapers proved much better at appealing to women, as well. The *Birmingham Mail* featured a prominent woman's page entitled 'Everywoman: Dress, the Home, Women's Work and Play' with a variety of issues covered. The page from 3 November 1919, for example, covered 'Paris Fashions', 'Should Women Smoke?' and 'Duties of a War Pensions Secretary' with an illustration of the latest Paris

---

120   *Birmingham Gazette*, 4 May 1925.
121   *Birmingham Gazette*, 16 May 1925.
122   Thackeray, *Conservatism for the Democratic Age*, 140–8.
123   BUA, Management Committee minutes, 8 October 1920. A Miss Alice Pratt was eventually appointed at a salary of £200 p.a. in March 1922. BUA, Management Committee minutes, 10 February 1922.

fashions (Figure 6.4). The Lib-Lab *Birmingham Gazette* which had hitherto largely focused on sporting news (with a whole page given to football every week), was forced to respond, producing its own illustrated 'Gazette Home Page for Woman Readers' with fashion advice, film news, society gossip, household tips and a serial from November 1922.[124] The *Birmingham Post*, though clearly aimed at a masculine, business audience, eventually attempted to widen its appeal with a 'Women's Correspondent' column (but only on the penultimate page) from 1921. Perhaps more significantly, it also halved its price to 1d in 1921.[125] Laura Beers has noted that although such stereotypical topics as fashion, consumerism and society gossip may have upheld gender divisions in the inter-war period, they may reflect 'a broader restructuring of the relationship between politicians and the democratic nation' and that by employing such approaches, Unionist publications may have made their message more understandable and made it easier for a non-partisan voter to endorse it at election time.[126]

For the Labour party, the situation was reversed. The national party produced a journal called *Labour Woman* as early as 1913 which was distributed by the local party after the war.[127] W. J. Chamberlain did his best with limited resources, announcing in September 1920 that a women's page with 'social questions, housekeeping, home dressmaking, and other topics will be introduced'.[128] Although it is difficult to be conclusive, given the limited circulation of the *Town Crier*, it is possible to see the seeds of Labour's breakthrough in Birmingham and across the country in the 1929 general election, in the ability of Labour newspapers to appeal to a female audience.[129]

---

124 *Birmingham Gazette*, 8 November 1922.
125 Whates, *The Birmingham Post 1857: 1957: a Centenary Retrospect*, 190–1.
126 Laura Beers, '"A Timid Disbelief in the Equality to which Lip Service is Constantly Paid": Gender, Politics and the Press between the Wars', in Beers and Thomas, eds, *Brave New World*, 129–48, 148.
127 Minutes of Labour Party meeting, 15 January 1920, Birmingham Borough Labour Party Minutes, i 1919–1921.
128 *Town Crier*, 25 September 1924.
129 Beers, *Your Britain: Media and the Labour Party*, 130–1.

Figure 6.4. 'Everywoman: Dress, the Home, Women's Work and Play', *Birmingham Mail*, 3 November 1919.

Finally, one must consider the position of the Liberals, never a strong party in Birmingham since the split of 1886 and the Birmingham Liberal Association's decision to adopt Unionism in 1887. The limited attempts of the national party to adapt to the new political print culture and the failure to provide local newspapers with sufficient material stymied the party's attempt to stage a revival. The *Birmingham Gazette* increasingly supported Labour candidates (as 'Progressives')[130] and carried adverts for the *Town Crier* and national publications such as the *Liberal Flashlight* (only four pages long and with insufficient circulation) proved inadequate (Figure 6.5).

George Cadbury jnr, who had already switched his financial support to the ILP before the war, finally resigned from his local association in Selly Oak and announced that he was severing his long connection with the party. He subsequently joined the Birmingham Central Labour Party.[131] However, the example of Richard Fairbairn in Worcester provides a convincing case that Liberalism was by no means dead in the West Midlands. Fairbairn had taken advantage of the support of a local newspaper company, the Worcestershire Newspapers and General Printing Company, and his own reputation in the city as a local councillor and Food Transport Officer for the Midlands, to fight back against the power of the Conservative Association, which had bought its way to power in the pre-war years and which controlled the *Berrow's Worcester Journal* and the *Worcestershire Times*.[132] Despite the exaggerated claims of the strongly right-wing Worcester Conservative press,[133] the editor of the *Worcestershire Echo*, W. G. R. Stone, and Fairbairn refused to block the growth of the local Labour party and encouraged fellow Liberals to copy their hard work, in much the same way that that *Daily News* supported the Poplar

---

130   For example see *Birmingham Gazette*, 1 November 1920.

131   *Birmingham Gazette*, 24 January 1920; 15 October 1920. Later that year, Cadbury wrote to the *Daily News* urging Liberal and Labour organisations to form a progressive coalition. *Daily News*, 6 October 1920.

132   Denise Mylechreest, 'A Singular Liberal: Richard Robert Fairbairn and Worcester Politics, 1899–1941', MPhil thesis, University of Worcester, 2007, 51–76.

133   For example see *Berrow's Worcester Journal*, 21 May 1921.

THE BEST THING OF ALL.

THE best thing of all, is to be SURE.

You are not asking for great riches, nor for a life of idleness. And you are not afraid of work.

The thing that gets you down is the fear that next week, or next month, or perhaps next year, you may be *out of work*. To be out of work is like being lost and forgotten by the world. The fear of it is a nightmare.

Then what do you want? You want to know *for certain* that any willing worker who is out of work will have the right to draw a wage which will properly carry him and his family through the bad time.

There is no reason at all why every willing worker should not have this SECURITY. Security comes by *insurance*. It was the Liberals who invented Unemployment Insurance. And the time has now come to carry it further, to make it *complete*, to make it *certain*, and to make it belong to the worker *as a right*.

The Liberal Party is set upon doing this piece of work—upon giving Security, which is the best thing of all.

THIS IS
THE LIBERAL WATCHWORD
SECURITY FOR THE WORKER.

Figure 6.5. The *Liberal Flashlight*, no. 25, January 1924. Reproduced with permission of the National Liberal Club Library, London.

councillors in 1920.[134] In addition, they defended Labour politicians from Conservative attacks. In response to the accusation that Labour councillors were increasing rates, the *Worcestershire Echo* noted how 'Labour members are less to blame than any half-dozen Tory councillors'.[135] However, whilst providing support to a fledgling Labour Party in Worcester, the Liberal press recognised the potential impact they posed to Liberal election successes. In 1924, the *Worcestershire Echo* reported that a vote for Labour would result in a victory for the Conservatives.[136] The newspaper was certainly a platform for Fairbairn who remarked in 1921 that the *Worcestershire Echo* 'was where his views were represented'.[137] Whilst Labour had the potential to split the Liberal vote, a key oversight of the Worcestershire Liberal press (and the area's press culture in general) was its neglect of the female electorate. In contrast to Birmingham, where the Labour and Unionist press reported the activities of women in politics, the press in Worcestershire did little to interact with female voters. In July 1924, for instance, the *Worcestershire Echo* contained a small column, 'Woman's World', which discussed Lady Frances Balfour's views on women's fashion, and featured another small paragraph entitled 'Bottling Fruit'.[138]

The lack of attention given to the role of women in political matters by the Worcestershire press, however, did not prevent Liberal election successes. In 1922, their tenacity paid off when Fairbairn finally won the Worcester seat. It was a pyrrhic victory however, for he held it for little over a year and was defeated in December 1923 as the farming vote forcefully backed Baldwin's protectionist manifesto and a Labour candidate spilt the anti-Tory vote. Despite the dominance of Baldwin in Worcestershire politics from that point onwards, Fairbairn remained at the centre of politics in Worcester, with the backing of a strong local Liberal Association and the *Worcestershire Echo* and he stood, albeit unsuccessfully, in the

134   *Worcestershire Echo*, 1 November 1920; 3 November 1920; *Birmingham Post*, 3 April 1939.
135   *Worcestershire Echo*, 30 October 1920.
136   *Worcestershire Echo*, 21 October 1924.
137   *Worcestershire Echo*, 2 November 1921.
138   *Worcestershire Echo*, 1 July 1924.

parliamentary elections of 1924, 1929, 1931 and 1935.[139] The Liberals in Worcester managed to fight off the Labour challenge for the parliamentary seat, with the *Echo* claiming that they were 'working together [with the Tories] for the continuance of the Conservative misrepresentation of the city'.[140] Fairbairn eventually became Mayor of Worcester.[141] The support of the independent Worcestershire Newspaper Company which, until 1930, ran the pro-Liberal *Worcestershire Echo, Worcester Herald*, and *Worcestershire Chronicle*,[142] was crucial in resisting the apparently inevitable decline of the Liberal party in the 1920s.[143]

The debate on the concept of 'modernity' in British political culture has, in recent years shifted its focus away from the late nineteenth to the First World War and the post-war years.[144] Although the term 'modernity' remains ill-defined and elusive, the features of political modernity have been assumed to include the growth of a 'national politics' – one in which issues such as international affairs and class and gender issues in political debate replaced the focus on local issues such as municipal government,

139   Andrew J. Taylor, 'Stanley Baldwin, Heresthetics and the Realignment of British politics', *British Journal of Political Science*, 35/3 (2005), 429–63.

140   *Worcestershire Echo*, 21 October 1924. Labour only overtook the Liberal vote in one parliamentary election in Worcester, in 1929, for the whole of the interwar period.

141   Mylechreest, 'A Singular Liberal: Richard Robert Fairbairn and Worcester Politics, 1899–1941', 180.

142   *Dundee Evening Telegraph*, 6 January 1930.

143   Recent research has demonstrated that Liberal ideas continued to inform British politics after the First World War. See for example: Ewen Green and Duncan Tanner, eds, *The Strange Survival of Liberal England: Political Leaders, Moral Values and the Reception of Economic Debate* (Cambridge: Cambridge University Press, 2007); Robert F. Haggard, *The Persistence of Victorian Liberalism: The Politics of Social Reform in Britain, 1870–1900* (Westport, CT: Greenwood Press, 2001).

144   Martin Daunton and Bernhard Rieger, eds, *Meaning of Modernity: Britain from the Late-Victorian Era to World War II* (Oxford: Oxford University Press, 2001); Simon Gunn and James Vernon, eds, *The Peculiarities of Liberal Modernity in Imperial Britain* (Berkeley: University of California Press, 2011); Jon Lawrence, 'The Transformation of British Public Politics after the First World War', *Past & Present*, 190 (2006), 185–216; Thomas, 'Political Modernity and 'government' in the Construction of Inter-War Democracy', in Beers and Thomas, eds, *Brave New World*, 39–66.

the personalities of individual regional MPs and the denominational character of the regions of Britain.[145] As the *Birmingham Gazette* noted as
early as October 1920, the growing significance of national political events,
such as country-wide strikes, did challenge interest in local politics, such
as the municipal elections.[146] This study has sought to confirm that the
West Midlands still retained a prized distinctive political character after
the war and that the focus of the provincial political press remained to
refract national issues to suit the interests and concerns of the citizens
of Birmingham and Worcestershire. As the failure of *Straight Forward*,
the financial woes of the *Town Crier* and the partisan nature of political
discourse in the provincial press demonstrate, however, this distinctiveness was increasingly under assault by the post-war tendency to centralise
political organisation, to focus on issues of industrial conflict and foreign
policy and the influence of the national press, typified by Beaverbrook and
Rothermere's newspapers. Charles Hyde may have fought off the attempt
by the Rothermere press to break his near-monopoly of the Birmingham
press, but he admitted that he never recovered from the bitterness of the
General Strike which pitted printers against journalists and managers.[147] The
Worcestershire Echo may have been the most innovative newspaper in the
cathedral city in the inter-war years, but the Liberal Party never won 30 per
cent of the vote after 1923. The *Town Crier* was able to mobilise a moderate
message that won six Birmingham seats for Labour in 1929, but these were
swept away in the 'Doctors' Mandate' election of 1931. Between 1920 and
1924, provincial journalists in the West Midlands struggled to articulate
and defend a distinctive provincial political culture, but, if the pattern of
West Midland politics survived to any extent after the General Strike, it was
largely due to the influence of Stanley Baldwin and Neville Chamberlain
at Westminster. It was these two Midland politicians, ill at ease with the
metropolitan politics and the culture of the St James clubs and networks,
who practised an inclusive and 'constructive' form of Unionism with great

---

145   James Vernon, *Distant Strangers: How Britain became Modern* (Berkeley: University
        of California Press, 2014), 1–17.
146   *Birmingham Gazette*, 25 October 1920.
147   Whates, *The Birmingham Post 1857: 1957*, 192–3, 196.

success between 1923 and 1937. The development for a 'national politics', albeit in a Midlands mould, was, despite the best efforts of the Starmer press, W. J. Chamberlain, G. W. Hubbard, J. B. Burman and countless others in Birmingham and the wider West Midlands, already well underway before the National Government was born in 1931.

7 'We Defy Mr Watkin Williams to Point to a Single Instance ... Where His Personal Character Has Been Assailed': The *Wrexham Guardian* v Watkin Williams, MP

The year 1868 was an 'annus mirabilis' in the electoral history of Wales – for the first time ever Wales returned a majority of Liberal MPs, twenty-three to ten Conservatives.[1] Although historians have debated the extent to which those elected to Parliament in 1868 demonstrated a move away from political representation by an aristocratic, Anglicised, and Church of England class towards a closer reflection of Welsh-speaking, nonconformist Wales,[2] 1868 did mark a turning point in Wales' political history. One significant consequence of this defeat was a Conservative investment in both party organisation and propaganda as the party sought new means of engaging with voters; one method of such engagement being the creation of supportive newspapers, three of which were established in Wales shortly after the election. One of these newly established, Conservative-supporting newspapers was the *Wrexham Guardian*, based in the north Wales border town. As to be expected, the *Guardian* was a staunch opponent of the local

---

1   Jane Morgan, 'Denbighshire's Annus Mirabilis: The Borough and County Elections of 1868', *Welsh History Review*, 7 (1974), 63–87; 63.

2   Morgan argued that this change in the make-up of Welsh MPs was only a partial transformation as the vast majority were either gentry or aristocracy with Liberal MPs tending to be of the Whig persuasion. Kenneth O. Morgan, *Rebirth of a Nation: A History of Modern Wales* (Oxford: Oxford University Press/University of Wales Press, 1981), 12. For a more positive view see Matthew Cragoe, 'George Osborne Morgan, Henry Richard, and the Politics of Religion in Wales, 1868–1874', *Parliamentary History*, 19/1 (2000), 118–30.

Liberal MPs – Watkin Williams and George Osborne Morgan; Williams in particular. However, Williams was to discover that the *Guardian*'s attacks on him encompassed a personal rivalry with a local Conservative politician, beyond party politics. The story of Williams and the *Guardian* reveals the complexities of a Conservative-supporting newspaper in Victorian Wales and the difficulties of balancing party support against commercial realities.

Politicians had long recognised the value of a supportive newspaper and in the nineteenth century it was common for newspapers to be 'overtly' aligned to political parties, both in London and throughout the country.[3] Even before the 1868 election, the Conservative party had recognised that it needed a press that appealed to the urban voters newly enfranchised by the 1867 Reform Act.[4] At the same time, the party recognised deficiencies in its organisation and, therefore, in November 1867, the first conference of the National Union of Conservative and Constitutional Associations took place. The National Union, described by Blake as a 'propagandist body',[5] aimed 'to increase and multiply the influence of the Conservative press throughout the United Kingdom' to counter the overwhelmingly Liberal-supporting London and provincial press.[6] Unfortunately, the National Union lacked influence within the party and amongst the leadership at this stage but its recognition of the potentially crucial role of a supportive

3   Rachel Matthews, *The History of the Provincial Press in England* (London: Bloomsbury, 2017), 59. Chapter 3 of Matthews discusses the press and political patronage. For a discussion of the relationship between London-based ('national') newspapers and politics see Hannah Barker, *Newspapers, Politics and English Society 1695–1855* (Harlow: Pearson, 2000) and Stephen Koss, *The Rise and Fall of the Political Press in Britain*, 2 vols (London: Hamish Hamilton, 1981–1984).
4   Lucy Brown, *Victorian News and Newspapers* (Oxford: Clarendon, 1985), 63; E. J. Feuchtwanger, *Disraeli, Democracy and the Tory Party: Conservative Leadership and Organization after the Second Reform Bill* (Oxford: Clarendon, 1968), x.
5   Robert Blake, *The Conservative Party from Peel to Thatcher* (London: Fontana, 1985), 151.
6   National Union Minutes, 12 November 1867. Quoted in Koss, *The Rise and Fall of the Political Press in Britain*, I, 184.

press, amongst a growing an increasingly literate electorate, was to be acted upon in Wales.[7]

Having recognised the need for sympathetic newspapers throughout the country, the Conservatives now had to develop them, either by establishing new titles or through changing the political allegiance of existing newspapers. The provincial Liberal press could claim a number of MPs amongst newspaper owners or editors, notably Edward Baines (1800–1890) of the *Leeds Mercury*, J. C. Stevenson (1825–1905) of the *North & South Shields Gazette* and John Candlish (1816–1874) of the *Sunderland Beacon and the Sunderland News*. In contrast, the aristocrats and gentry who dominated the ranks of the Conservative MPs shied away from any acknowledged engagement with the press trade. Conservatives who wished to keep their involvement with the press hidden, benefitted from the Companies Acts of 1856 and 1862 which introduced the concept of limited liability and led to an increase in company ownership of newspapers, instead of the traditional model of either a single owner or family ownership.[8] Being a shareholder in a newspaper company was a way by which local Conservatives could financially support a local Conservative newspaper with minimal involvement and leave the public unaware of their connection with it. For example, Matthews wrote that in 1865 the *Carlisle Patriot* was purchased by the Carlisle Conservative Newspaper Company and that one of the company's founding shareholders was an MP but the failure to mention this MP's name suggests that his identity was deliberately hidden from the public.[9]

The years after 1868 saw three Conservative newspapers established in Wales, all of which, initially at least, survived due to financial support from aristocratic supporters, as was common for political newspapers.[10] In south Wales, the daily *Western Mail* first appeared on 1 May 1869, having been established by the 3rd Marquess of Bute. The Bute family were well-known throughout the south, especially in Cardiff with Bute docks being named

7   Feuchtwanger, *Disraeli, Democracy and the Tory Party*, 105.
8   Matthews, *The History of the Provincial Press in England*, 115.
9   Matthews, *The History of the Provincial Press in England*, 71.
10   Brown, *Victorian News and Newspapers*, 70.

for the family. The *Western Mail* was not the Bute family's first attempt at newspaper ownership. In 1832, the 3rd Marquess's father had established the first Conservative supporting newspaper in Glamorgan – the *Glamorgan, Monmouth, Brecon Gazette and Merthyr Guardian* – but did not advertise his ownership with his involvement known only to a small number of close political allies.[11] Its lack of success and debts did not, however, dissuade his son from founding another newspaper. The Conservatives also recognised the importance of establishing a Welsh-language newspaper as Welsh was spoken by the majority of the population. *Y Dywysogaeth* [*The Principality*] first appeared on 5 February 1870 and was financially supported for three years by the 2nd Earl Cawdor, a former Conservative MP for Pembrokeshire.[12] A letter to the *Western Mail* set out *Y Dwysogaeth*'s priorities as promoting constitutional principles and providing a mouthpiece for the Conservative party and the Church of England to combat the 'many squeakish, one-sided, discordant, melodiless hurdy-gurdies of Dissent', such as the Liberation Society and the campaign to disestablish the Church of England in Wales.[13] *Y Dywysogaeth* mustered a circulation of 3,300–3,500 weekly, but, according to the *Western Mail*, its supporters grew tired of financially subsiding it and it was merged with the Welsh-language Church of England newspaper, *Y Llan* [*The Church*], to create *Y Llan a'r Dywysogaeth*.[14]

The second Conservative newspaper to be established after 1868 was the *Wrexham Guardian*, which first appeared on 4 September 1869. Its arrival some ten months after the 1868 election result could suggest that it took some time for local Conservatives to arrange the necessary financial support. The 1868 general election delivered two dramatic results in north-east Wales: in the Denbigh Boroughs[15] the sitting Conservative

11   R. D. Rees, 'South Wales and Monmouthshire Newspapers under the Stamp Act', *Welsh History Review*, 1 (1960), 301–24, 313.
12   Letter from T. Mousley to J. J. Ffoulkes, 27 August 1870, Carmarthen Record Office, Cawdor MS 2/149.
13   'The New Welsh Paper "Y Dywysogaeth"', *Western Mail*, 16 May 1870, 3.
14   'The Conservative Press in Wales', *Western Mail*, 13 March 1874, 6.
15   The Denbigh Boroughs consisted of four boroughs – Wrexham, Denbigh, Ruthin, and Holt. Wrexham was the largest with a population of 18,561 in 1866.

MP, Townshend Mainwaring, was defeated by 'genuine radical' Watkin Williams and in the two-member county seat of Denbighshire one of the sitting MPs, the 'Adullamite' Whig Col. Myddelton-Biddulph, was replaced by another radical Liberal MP, George Osborne Morgan.[16] This replacement in political representation of two traditional landowners by radical, nonconformist-supporting, Liberal MPs would have concerned local Conservatives greatly, especially coupled with other poor election results across Wales. North Wales already had a Conservative-supporting newspaper – the *North Wales Chronicle* – but this newspaper was published in Bangor in north-west Wales and therefore Denbighshire Conservatives clearly felt that there was a need for a supportive newspaper in their own county.

Unlike most of the Welsh MPs at this time, Watkin Williams hailed from the middle class, rather than the gentry or the aristocracy. He was the eldest son of Peter Williams, the rector of Llansannan in Denbighshire and was educated at Ruthin Grammar School before leaving to study medicine at University College Hospital. He soon gave up medicine and turned to the law and was called to the bar.[17] Williams' election in 1868 was a noticeable break from the previous representatives of the constituency, both in his political beliefs and his social class.

The hope for the Conservatives lay in the Denbighshire's sole remaining Conservative MP – Sir Watkin Williams-Wynn, the 6th Baronet of Wynnstay, who had represented the constituency since 1841 (and his family had sat for Denbighshire since 1708). He was Wales's largest landowner with 28,721 acres in Denbighshire, 70,559 acres in Montgomeryshire, 42,044 acres in Merionethshire, and he also owned land in Flintshire and Cardiganshire.[18] In addition to the 6th baronet representing Denbighshire, his cousin, Charles Williams-Wynn, and

16   Morgan, 'Denbighshire's *Annus Mirabilis*,' 75.
17   Gerald Le G. Norgate, rev. by Eric Metcalfe, 'Williams, Sir Charles James Watkin', *Oxford Dictionary of National Biography* <https://doi.org/10.1093/ref:odnb/29490>, accessed 1 July 2018.
18   John Bateman, *The Great Landowners of Great Britain and Ireland* (Leicester: Leicester University Press, 1971), 491.

Figure 7.1. 'Aelodau Seneddol Cymru' [Members of Parliament for Wales] XII –
Watkin Williams, *Trysorfa y Plant* [*The Children's Treasury*], Rhagfyr 1876
[December 1876], rhif. 180 [no. 180].

his son had represented Montgomeryshire since 1799. So powerful and
influential was Sir Watkin that he was known as 'the Prince in Wales'.
Unfortunately for local Conservatives, Sir Watkin was not as rich as the
Marquess of Bute (despite owning more land, it was in the more rural,

less industrialised areas of Wales), nor was he a particularly impressive politician. Well regarded locally as a just and fair landlord, his involvement in the House of Commons and national politics was minimal and it appears as if his MP status was something he had inherited and was a family tradition, rather than any burning political desire on the part of Sir Watkin. Nevertheless it was to him that the local Conservatives looked to for leadership.

The *Guardian* appeared, without any apparent notice of its arrival. There was no promotional advertising in any of Wales's other Conservative newspapers, nor any promotional circulators. The newspaper's first printer and publisher was John Ramsden, printer and publisher of the *Chester Courant*. Ramsden, a native of Birmingham, was a 'Tory of the old school'[19] and, as publisher of the *Courant* since 1851, would have been familiar with Wrexham and north Wales as only eleven miles separated Wrexham from Chester and, like many border newspapers, the *Courant* bore the sub-title *and Advertiser for North Wales* to indicate that it circulated beyond the city. In the absence of a Conservative-supporting newspaper in Wrexham, Conservatives in north-east Wales may have looked to the *Courant* as their nearest sympathetic newspaper. It is unclear whether Ramsden owned the *Guardian* or whether, as with the *Courant*, he was merely the publisher and printer. If Ramsden was not the *Guardian*'s owner, then who was? Ramsden remained printer and publisher of the *Courant*, which could suggest that the *Courant* and its owner, Randle Wilbraham, a prominent Cheshire Conservative, were involved in the establishment of the *Guardian*. The two newspapers, the *Courant* and the *Guardian*, made no reference to each other, although the *Guardian* may have been printed at the *Courant*'s office in Northgate Street in Chester.[20] The exact circumstances surrounding the establishment of the *Guardian* remain unclear.[21]

---

19   'Death of Mr John Ramsden', *Chester Courant*, 7 June 1905, 8.

20   The *Guardian*'s imprint stated 'printed by John Ramsden, and published by him at the *Guardian* Office, Bank Place, Wrexham', which suggests that it was printed elsewhere, possibly at the *Courant*'s office.

21   A printed circular sent to local Conservatives in 1869 stated a company was formed and the *Wrexham Guardian* commenced publication. However, with the NWCPCo

The *Guardian* proudly admitted its support for Conservatism in its first issue.[22] Whatever Ramsden's involvement in the establishment of the *Guardian*, it was over in less than a year as the newspaper announced new management in July 1870.[23] The new owners were the North Wales Constitutional Press Company Limited (NWCPCo). The company was incorporated under the Companies Act that month, with its memorandum of association dated 28 June 1870.[24] The first aim of the NWCPCo was 'the establishing, carry on, printing and publishing, in Wrexham and elsewhere in North Wales, of a Constitutional newspaper', with 'Constitutional' in reality meaning Conservative.[25] As the company aimed to 'establish' a Conservative newspaper, this may suggest that it was formed earlier and, whilst the legalities were finalised, Ramsden ran the newspaper on a temporary basis. The twelve named directors of the NWCPCo included some of the wealthiest Conservatives in north Wales, not only Sir Watkin Williams-Wynn, but also the Hon. George Kenyon, son of the 3rd Baron Kenyon; Edmund Peel, owner of 5,779 acres in Flintshire, Denbighshire and Montgomeryshire; Thomas Lloyd Fitzhugh, a mine owner who also owned 3,362 acres in Denbighshire and Flintshire; and Peter Walker, a Wrexham brewer and brother of Sir Andrew Barclay Walker (future Lord Mayor of Liverpool and builder of the Walker Art Gallery).

---

not being incorporated until ten months after the *Guardian* was first published, did the NWCPCo take over ten months to become incorporated or was there another (unknown) company running the *Guardian* until NWCPCo took over?

22   Editorial, *Wrexham Guardian*, 4 September 1869, 4.
23   'Notice to our Readers', *Wrexham Guardian*, 30 July 1870, 4.
24   For more information on the North Wales Constitutional Press Company Limited see Lisa Peters, 'The Troubled History of a Welsh Newspaper Publishing Company: The North Wales Constitutional Newspapers Company Limited, 1869–1878', in Peter Issac and Barry McKay, eds, *The Moving Market: Continuity and Change in the Book Trade* (New Castle, DE: Oak Knoll Press, 2001), 117–25.
25   Company No: 4989; North Wales Constitutional Press Company, Ltd. Incorporated in 1870. Dissolved before 1916, The National Archives (TNA), BT31/1552/4989.

Table 7.1. Occupation of North Wales Constitutional Press Company
shareholders, 1871.

Occupation	Number of shareholders
None	27 (45.8%)
Legal	7 (11.9%)
Religious	5 (8.5%)
Medical	4 (6.8%)
Alcohol Trade	4 (6.8%)
Army	3 (5.1%)
Miller	2 (3.4%)
Other	7 (11.9%)[26]

Like its southern counterpart, the *Western Mail*, the *Guardian* adopted
a tactic of unrelenting criticism of the Liberal government, the Prime
Minister, William Gladstone, and Denbighshire's two Liberal MPs.
However, the *Guardian's* criticism bordered on the obnoxious and, had
Williams been of a litigious disposition, the *Guardian* may well have faced
more than one libel case.[27] In its second issue, the *Guardian* described
Williams as 'a man of essentially mediocre abilities and attainments',[28]
as it criticised his campaign for Welsh disestablishment. Despite being a
son of an Anglican vicar, Williams was a committed supporter of Wales'
nonconformist majority and the campaign to disestablish the Church of
England as the state Church. In August 1869, he introduced a motion in
the House of Commons to disestablish the Church of England in Wales,
a motion seconded by Denbighshire's other Liberal MP, George Osborne
Morgan – a direct attack on the Church of England at a time when the
Conservative party felt threatened by the tide of change and was determined
to protect the status quo of the monarchy, the Church, and the Empire –[29]

26 'Other' included 'MP' Lord Edmund Hill-Trevor (son of the 3rd Marquess of
    Downshire) and 'baronet' (Sir Watkin).
27 Although, as a barrister, Williams would have been more aware than most MPs, of
    the dangers and complexities of suing a newspaper for libel.
28 Editorial, *Wrexham Guardian*, 11 September 1869, 4
29 Martin Pugh, *The Tories and the People 1880–1935* (Oxford: Basil Blackwell, 1985), 4.

which would have horrified local Conservatives and hardened their resolve against Williams. Unfortunately for Williams his motion failed, indeed it drew so little support from his fellow Welsh Liberal MPs that Morgan described it as an ignominious failure.[30] In addition, Williams was allegedly difficult to work with and this gave the *Guardian* several personal failings, as well as his politics, to criticise.[31]

Guardian editorials on Williams were uncommon until July 1871 when the Hon. George Kenyon, aged thirty-one, announced that he would be standing as the Conservative candidate in the Denbigh Boroughs in the next election. In a predominantly working-class constituency that had seen a significant rise in its electorate since the 1867 Reform Act, Kenyon was not a natural choice. The Kenyon estate was at Gredlington in Flintshire, but Kenyon had been born in London and educated at Harrow and Oxford, arguably giving him fewer links with the constituency than Williams, who had been born in and educated in Denbighshire.[32] Kenyon was a director and a shareholder in the NWCPCo, so it is unsurprising that the *Guardian* welcomed this announcement. An editorial described Kenyon as 'an excellent Parliamentary candidate ... young, active and energetic ... an able, eloquent and thoughtful speaker' whose sole aim would be the serve the people of the Denbigh Boroughs.[33] A week later, an editorial on Williams condemned him as a London lawyer who, due to his absences in the capital, had no interest in the constituency and its people.[34] The *Guardian* conveniently failed to mention that, unlike his land-owning Conservative rival, he needed to earn a living as a lawyer in London as MPs

---

30 Morgan, *Rebirth of a Nation*, 12.

31 Morgan described him as a 'difficult colleague' and see Kenneth O. Morgan, *Wales in British Politics, 1868–1922* (Cardiff: University of Wales Press, 1970), 30–1, for a commentary on how the Liberal party responded to Williams's unexpected disestablishment motion.

32 John E. Lloyd, rev. by H. C.G Matthew, 'Kenyon, George Thomas, *Oxford Dictionary of National Biography* <https://doi.org/10.1093/ref:odnb/34293>, accessed 1 July 2018.

33 'The Representation of the Denbighshire Boroughs', *Wrexham Guardian*, 29 July 1871, 4.

34 'Is Denbighshire Represented?', *Wrexham Guardian*, 5 August 1871, 4.

were not paid, and it seemingly condemned him for being a professional man rather than a local landlord.

From July 1871 onwards, editorials attacking Gladstone, the Liberal party, Williams, or Osborne Morgan were a regular occurrence. Not satisfied with its own editorials, the *Guardian* also extracted editorials from other Conservative newspapers, the *Liverpool Courier* and the *Western Mail*, attacking Williams, thereby informing the voters of the Denbigh Boroughs that the failings of the their local representative were known outside the county.[35]

Whilst the *Guardian* was promoting Kenyon and pointing out the supposed failings of Williams to its readers, it was suffering financial difficulties. In 1873, the NWCPCo required a loan of £1,000 from Kenyon's election agent[36] and, in an effort to raise more funds, the company's capital was raised to £8,000 by issuing an additional 5,000 shares,[37] which were not purchased.[38] The *Guardian* also suffered from low circulation, selling an average of 1,855 per issue for the last quarter of 1873.[39] In comparison, its Liberal-supporting rival, the *Wrexham Advertiser*, had reached a circulation of over 3,000 per issue a decade earlier and had been established nearly twenty years longer than its rival. Despite these financial difficulties, the *Guardian* needed to continue until the next election to support Kenyon's campaign, otherwise its existence would have been for naught.

Having assured support from the *Guardian* for his candidature, Kenyon was given the opportunity to purchase support from another Conservative-supporting newspaper in north Wales, the *North Wales Chronicle*. In October 1873 William Lee Brookes, Kenyon's election agent,

---

35   *Wrexham Guardian*, 29 November 1873, 5.

36   Letter from William Lee Brookes referring to a loan of £1000 from himself to the Company on 13 July 1873, 6 August 1874. Flintshire Record Office, (FRO) D/KT/22. This loan was later repaid by Kenyon.

37   'Special Resolution of the North Wales Constitutional Press Company Ltd. Passed on 9 August 1873'. TNA, BT31/1552/4989.

38   'Summary of Capital and Shares of the North Wales Constitutional Press Company Limited made up to the seventh day of December 1876', TNA, BT31/1552/4989.

39   Dr Granville in a/c with the Constitutional Association (the *Wrexham Guardian*), from October 13 to December 1873, FRO, D/KT/22.

received a letter from a Mr Wynne Evans, reporting that he had been visited by Mr Douglas, the owner of the *Chronicle*, who had offered to publish the weekly *Chronicle* as a daily newspaper during the election if Kenyon would 'assist him in some form'.[40] The nature of this assistance becomes clearer in a letter written shortly afterwards from Douglas to Kenyon where he sets out the cost of his support: Kenyon must advertise his election address in the *Chronicle* and agree to purchase 500 copies of each issue of the newspaper at election time.[41] In exchange then, the *Chronicle* would hire a reporter exclusively for the Denbigh Boroughs who would promote Kenyon's candidature.[42] Whether Kenyon accepted the *Chronicle*'s offer is unknown, although the *Chronicle*'s continuation as a weekly newspaper throughout the election suggests it was not.

In January 1874, Parliament was dissolved and the country went to the polls. This was the *Guardian*'s moment; this is what it had been created for – to fight for the Conservative cause in Denbighshire's elections. The Liberal party decided not to put up a second candidate in the county seat, therefore Osborne Morgan and Sir Watkin were returned unopposed. With the status quo being maintained in Denbighshire, the *Guardian* focused its attention on the campaign in the Denbigh Boroughs. The *Guardian* arranged for 'two gentlemen from London' to assist in reporting the election campaign, thereby increasing the newspaper's reporting costs by £30 for the first three months of 1874.[43] Election news in its issue of 31 January, the first after the election was called, was almost universally devoted to reporting Kenyon's meetings throughout the constituency. In Wrexham, the *Guardian*

---

40   Letter from Wynne Evans to W. L. Brookes, 29 October 1873, FRO, D/KT/21,
41   This request to purchase additional copies to distribute to supporters at election was relatively common. Connell comments that the Conservatives bought 1,000 extra copies of special election editions of the *Westmorland Gazette* in 1880 to support the Conservative candidate. A. N. Connell, '"Ice in the Centre of a Glowing Fire": The Westmorland Election of 1880', *Transactions of the Cumberland & Westmorland Antiquarian & Archaeological Society*, 3rd series, VIII (2008), 219–39, 228.
42   Letter from Mr Douglas, 31 October 1873, FRO, D/KT/21.
43   Dr Granville in a/c with the Constitutional Association (the *Wrexham Guardian*), from October 13 to December 1873 and Granville in a/c with the North Wales Constitutional Association, from 1 January to 28 March 1874, FRO, D/KT/22.

reported that the working men lined the street to welcome him to the town;[44] at Denbigh he delivered an excellent speech that even impressed Liberal supporters;[45] and in Ruthin he enjoyed a 'hearty reception', leaving traditionally Conservative-supporting Holt as the only borough of the constituency that he did not visit.[46] In the same issue, the *Guardian* reported gossip that Dr Evan Pierce, a former mayor of Denbigh and well-known for his work during the 1832 cholera epidemic, had withdrawn his support from Williams and speculated that other voters would follow Dr Pierce's example.[47] The *Guardian*'s enthusiastic praise for Kenyon even went so far as publishing a poem about him written by a supporter with the (perhaps inappropriately) chosen nom-de-plume of 'Storm Cloud'.[48] In contrast, the *Guardian* reported Williams as being poorly received by the voters.[49]

The *Guardian* concluded its first issue of election coverage by commenting on the respective merits and failings of the two candidates. Naturally, Kenyon enjoyed all the merits and Williams all the failings. Whilst Kenyon was an 'English gentleman making personal sacrifices for the cause he believes to be just', who already enjoyed a high social position, the *Guardian* failed to list any of Kenyon's qualities, beyond his social status, or what he would do for the largely working-class constituency should he be elected, arguably a mistake considering that the working-class support for Williams had turned the election in his favour in 1868. The *Guardian* preferred attacking Williams to promoting Kenyon's policies, describing him as 'an adventurous lawyer ... [who] has more than once deceived large bodies of his late constituents'.[50]

44 'The Denbigh Boroughs – Enthusiastic Reception of the Hon. Geo. T. Kenyon – Great Conservative Demonstration in Wrexham', *Wrexham Guardian*, 31 January 1874, 2.

45 'Mr Kenyon at Denbigh – Great Meeting Wednesday Night – Enthusiastic Proceedings', *Wrexham Guardian*, 31 January 1874, 3.

46 'Mr Kenyon at Ruthin – Hearty Reception by the Electors', *Wrexham Guardian*, 31 January 1874, 5.

47 'A Split Amongst the Liberals', *Wrexham Guardian*, 31 January 1874, 3.

48 'For Kenyon and Honour', *Wrexham Guardian*, 31 January 1874, 5.

49 'Mr Watkin Williams Unable to Obtain a Hearing', *Wrexham Guardian*, 31 January 1874, 3.

50 'The Two Candidates', *Wrexham Guardian*, 31 January 1874, 6.

The next issue of 7 February continued the attacks upon Williams. Upon reporting a Liberal meeting at Wrexham Public Hall, the *Guardian* claimed that the audience consisted of 'schoolboys, females, country people, colliers from Brymbo district, non-electors, and gentlemen residing out of the boroughs' – of the people who turned out to hear Williams speak, there was not an eligible voter amongst them![51] Additionally, the *Guardian* alleged underhand practice from the Liberals in persuading the promoters of a temperance conference to postpone the event to allow the Liberals to use the Public Hall instead. The report alleged that Williams had told the voters that a promise made during a canvas was not binding on him, therefore supporting their earlier claims of his untrustworthiness.[52] Unsurprisingly, the *Guardian* predicted victory for its candidate, but a 'Latest news – by telegraph' item on the last page declared that Williams had won the Denbigh Boroughs.[53]

The result in the Denbigh Boroughs was close, with Williams securing 1,238 votes against Kenyon's 1,208 – a Liberal majority of only thirty. The *Guardian* confessed itself to be astonished at the result and reported rumours that the Liberals had engaged in bribery[54] and that they had brought 'questionable influences' to bear upon those who had pledged to vote for Kenyon.[55] These are serious allegations for the newspaper to have made, although nothing seems to have come of them, as they were not reported in other newspapers, nor did Kenyon petition against the result. The *Wrexham Advertiser* commented acidly that the increase in the Conservative vote of 264 was due to voters it described 'tak[ing] no interest in politics, who will only vote when almost dragged to the booth, and who think one party is as good as another',[56] demonstrating that the *Guardian* was not the only newspaper critical of voters who failed to support their preferred candidate.

51   'Mr Watkin Williams in Wrexham', *Wrexham Guardian*, 7 February 1874, 3.
52   'Mr Watkin Williams in Wrexham', *Wrexham Guardian*, 7 February 1874, 3.
53   'Latest News – by Telegraph', *Wrexham Guardian*, 7 February 1874, 8.
54   'The Denbigh Boroughs', *Wrexham Guardian*, 14 February 1874, 4.
55   'Notes of the Week', *Wrexham Guardian*, 14 February 1874, 4.
56   'The Denbigh Boroughs Election – The Liberal Victory', *Wrexham Advertiser*, 14 February 1874, 5.

The *Guardian*'s vitriol against Williams did not go unnoticed. Thomas Gee, owner of the Denbigh-based *Baner ac Amserau Cymru*, Wales' leading Welsh language newspaper and a keen supporter of Williams, was reported to have described the *Guardian* as 'the Wrexham Tory journal [which] was a disgrace to the newspaper press of this country'. The *Guardian* responded by describing Gee, one of the most important political figures in Wales, as insolent and ill-educated.[57] Having published the newspaper throughout the election campaign, by April the NWCPCo owed the bank £1,830[58] and the owner of the *North Wales Chronicle* had made an offer for the newspaper.[59] A meeting was held in July to consider winding up the company and selling the newspaper,[60] but William Lee Brookes loaned the company £1,000 (with interest at 5 per cent a year) which secured its short-term survival.[61]

Kenyon's defeat in the 1874 election did not end the *Guardian*'s regular attacks on his rival, however. In July 1874, an editorial again cast aspersions on the legitimacy of his election win and accused Williams of being a man of no conviction who had broken the promises that he had made to the electors.[62] With Kenyon planning to contest the Denbigh Boroughs seat at the next election and no doubt buoyed by the narrowness of Williams' majority, the *Guardian*'s attacks on him continued and arguably became more intense. An 1876 editorial with the descriptive headline 'MR WATKIN WILLIAMS ON THE RAMPAGE' contained a litany of complaints about Williams and the Liberals. The *Guardian* commenced its commentary by referencing Williams's legal career and argued that when he lacked evidence to support his case, he was reduced to abusing his opponents.

57 'Misrepresentation', *Wrexham Guardian*, 7 February 1874, 4.
58 Letter from Wm. Trevor Parkins to George Kenyon, 20 April 1874, FRO, D/KT/22.
59 Letter from Evan Morris to John Jones, 29 May 1874, FRO, D/KT/22.
60 Letter from Evan Morris to Shareholders, 2 July 1874, FRO, D/KT/22.
61 Agreement between North Wales Constitutional Press Company Ltd and William Lee Brookes, 30 July 1874, FRO, D/KT/22.
62 *Wrexham Guardian*, 11 July 1874, 4. In particular, Williams was accused of having pledged to support Irish Home Rule but absenting himself from a parliamentary vote on the issue.

Though he does not practise in the Old Bailey, Mr Watkin Williams, Q. C., is familiar with the legal doctrine – 'No case, abuse the other side'. He follows it faithfully. He hurls ugly epithets at the enemy, pelts them with false accusations, and holds them accountable for misdeeds with which they have no more association than the man in the moon.

Having attacked Williams, the *Guardian* then moved onto criticising the Liberal party for their supposed foolishness in supporting Williams.

When we listen to such a perversion of reason and fact, we ask are the Liberals ignorant and irrational beyond their fellows? Have they no knowledge of passing events, no power of discrimination between fact and fiction, no gift of reasonable understanding? Mr Williams must think so, else he would not presume so far on their credulity, or allow his audacity to carry him to lengths which in any other constituency would make him the butt of common ridicule.

The *Guardian* concluded its attack on Williams with a number of personal insults and denigrated him for his comments on the action of the Conservative government.

There is an arrogance of tone in his criticisms, which, coming from so small a hero, is more likely to provoke laughter than wrath. There is something comical in a man who has never done a single deed of fame, passing abrupt and dogmatic judgment on the men and measures of the Government.

In early 1878 Williams announced to the voters of the Denbigh Boroughs, courtesy of a notice in the *Wrexham Advertiser*, that he would not contest the Denbigh Boroughs seat at the next election. Williams cited the difficulties of the role of MP alongside his continuing legal work and family life as the reason behind his decision, but did intriguingly hint that he felt that he had lost the confidence of many of the Liberals in the constituency due to his political views.[63] This suggests that Williams had fallen out with the local Liberal party and feared that they were seeking to replace him with another candidate for the next election. The *Guardian* greeted the news

---

63   'To the Electors of Denbigh, and the Contributory Boroughs of Holt, Ruthin, and
       Wrexham', *Wrexham Advertiser*, 13 April 1878, 1.

by suggesting that his political career had been a failure both in Parliament and in the Denbigh Boroughs and, as usual, offered strong criticism of his political judgements.[64]

In fact, the *Guardian* claimed credit for doing what Kenyon had failed to do through the ballot box in 1874; namely to oust Williams from the constituency. It argued that:

> At the outset he had an easy course to parade his platitudes, and without fear of journalist opposition for the local press was all on his side. The establishment of a Conservative newspaper in the county considerably altered matters and may reasonably deduce from Mr Williams's furious attack against this journal that we have contributed in no inconsistent degree to reduce the Liberal majority ... and to have hastened his contemplated retreat from a Welsh constituency ... We defy Mr Watkin Williams to point out a single instance since his election where his personal character has been assailed in this journal.

The *Guardian* stated that it had always behaved in a courteous manner towards Williams, a sentiment it is difficult to support, considering some of the comments directed again him and the *Guardian*'s allegations of bribery and misrepresentation during the 1874 election campaign. Indeed, the *Guardian* stated, with undisguised pride, that if it had contributed in any way to Williams' decision not to seek re-election in the Denbigh Boroughs, then it had done its duty as a Conservative party newspaper.[65]

Once Williams' replacement as Liberal candidate at the next election for the Denbigh Boroughs was announced, it became clear that the *Guardian*'s objections were not restricted to Williams, but also to any candidate the Liberals put up against Kenyon. The new Liberal candidate was local aristocrat, Sir Robert Cunliffe, 5th Baronet, who had lost his Flint Boroughs seat in 1874. Sir Robert was described by the *Guardian* as a 'Radical', however the *Guardian* described practically every Liberal in the country as a radical in order to paint their rivals as dangerous subversives. Sir Robert's main failing (in the eyes of the *Guardian* at least) was that he

64   'A Welsh Member's Vagaries', *Wrexham Guardian*, 16 February 1878, 4 and 'Mr Watkin Williams' Retreat', *Wrexham Guardian*, 13 April 1878, 4.
65   'Notes of the Week', *Wrexham Guardian*, 27 April 1878, 4.

was a candidate who would promise to support any cause in his quest for votes,[66] a characteristic which the *Guardian*'s readers would recognise as displaying inconsistency and a lack of judgement and making Sir Robert manifestly unsuitable as the parliamentary representative of the Denbigh Boroughs.[67]

Williams was to enjoy a final victory over the *Guardian* and the Conservative party in Denbighshire, however. In his farewell speech to his constituents, he criticised the Conservative party for its role in establishing local newspapers for the purpose of insulting and attacking local and national politicians. Williams pointed out that these Conservative newspapers could not support themselves through circulation and advertising sales, so relied on the financial support of local Conservatives to survive. Williams made reference to a local newspaper that was in this situation and claimed to have gained evidence that it was financially supported by local Conservatives. Should the reader of his speech, as reported in the *Wrexham Advertiser*, still be unaware which newspaper he was referring to, the *Advertiser* report helpfully added that, at this moment, a Mr John Owen shouted 'Wrexham Guardian'. Williams named Kenyon as a financial supporter of this newspaper and urged the voters not to allow themselves to be influenced by it, for if they did, they would, he announced dramatically, be a disgrace to Wales.[68] These were passionate words spoken by a man who clearly felt that he had been mistreated by the *Guardian*.

In response, the *Guardian* scoffed at Williams' criticism of itself, claiming that it had merely been guilty of exposing the MP's inconsistency on issues. It did not deny that it was financially supported, but argued that its readers were capable of judging its arguments for themselves. It pointed

---

66   'Mr Watkin Williams, MP and his Farewell Address', *Wrexham Guardian*, 27 April 1878, 5.

67   Tosh described the ideal character of a Victorian man as 'rationality against emotionality ... constancy instead of variability ... taciturn rather than talkativeness'. John Tosh, *Manliness and Masculinities in Nineteenth Century Britain: Essays on Gender, Family and Empire* (Harlow: Pearson Longman, 2005), 69.

68   'The Representation of the Denbigh Boroughs – Mr Watkin Williams and his Constituents – Speech of the New Candidate', *Wrexham Advertiser*, 27 April 1878, 3.

to the hypocrisy of Williams' criticism of local Conservatives for supporting the *Guardian*, whilst he had been asked to put his name forward for
a seat in Newcastle, where the Liberal MP owned the local newspaper.[69]
As far as the *Guardian* was concerned, this attack merely summed up the
'spiteful littleness of [Williams'] character'.[70]

Nevertheless, now that he was free of the need to fight another campaign in the Denbigh Boroughs, Williams was determined to tell the
voters that the newspaper that had insulted him for the past eight years
was in the hands of his political rivals. He obtained a circular written by
Kenyon, soliciting contributions towards paying off the *Guardian*'s debts
and providing the newspaper with a regular financial subsidy. The circular
revealed that the newspaper had been set up by local Conservatives and
had received a regular financial subsidy from them, with the newspaper
being entirely supported by Sir Watkin and Kenyon for the past few years,
with Sir Watkin providing a subsidy of £2,870 and Kenyon one of £600.[71]
Williams promptly forwarded this circular to the *Wrexham Advertiser*,
together with a letter pointing out that he had been 'showered' with scurrilous and vulgar abuse by the *Guardian* for years and it turned out to
be a newspaper funded by his political opponents that could not survive
without a subsidy from them. He finished his letter by asking his constituents if they wished to be represented by a wealthy aristocrat who used
his wealth to establish a newspaper as a clandestine front for publishing
abusive attacks on his rival.[72]

69   The *Guardian* was referring to James Cochran Stevenson, owner of the *North &*
     South Shields Gazette and Liberal MP for South Shields since 1868. However, unlike
     the *Guardian*, Stevenson openly stated his ownership of the newspaper of the *North*
     & South Shields Gazette from 7 January 1874, but not for the six years he was MP
     before that.
70   'Mr Watkin Williams, MP and his Farewell Address', *Wrexham Guardian*, 27 April
     1878, 5.
71   This regular subsidy, coupled with the £1,579 12 6 that Kenyon spent on the 1874
     election campaign, indicates the extent of Kenyon's ambition to be elected to the
     Denbigh Boroughs. Brookes and Lee in accounts with the Hon. G. T. Kenyon
     (Denbigh Borough election), FRO, D/KT/22.
72   'The Hon. George Kenyon and the Press', *Wrexham Advertiser*, 25 May 1878, 4.

Unlike the *Western Mail*, its Conservative counterpart in the south, which was known to be financially supported by the Marquess of Bute shortly after it was first published,[73] it appears that the finances behind the *Guardian* were unknown to the public until their exposure by Williams. The *Guardian*'s response came in editorial a week later, arguing that Liberals established supportive newspapers so why should the Conservatives be condemned for doing the same? In seeking to address the issue of its financial backers being party members and its second largest backer being Williams' electoral opponent, the *Guardian* argued the public should judge a newspaper by the content it published, not its ownership and denied that its financial backers had any say in the printed copy of the *Guardian*. The *Guardian* concluded defiantly that, if Williams believed himself libelled by it, then he was welcomed to sue.[74] It also published, in the same issue, an anonymous letter claiming that Caernarvonshire's Liberals were financially supporting the *North Wales Express* and hoping that any private and confidential circulars issued by this newspaper would not fall into the hands of Williams, as he might end up passing them to another newspaper for publication.[75]

Kenyon's circular failed to generate sufficient financial support, however, and NWCPCo found itself unable to pay its debts. William Lee Brookes took control of the company and sold it, at a loss, to Evan Morris (later Sir Evan Morris), a local lawyer and Conservative party member. Morris then sold the newspaper in August 1878 to Frederick Roe, a journalist from Dover. This change of ownership was announced in the newspaper in an editorial acknowledging the financial support it had previously received from local Conservatives, but stating that it would no longer require such support.[76] However, this statement is refuted by a note in Kenyon's personal papers, stating that a subsidy of £450 had been promised to Roe for three years.[77]

---

73   'Upsetting of Lord Bute's *Mail*', *Cardiff Times*, 31 July 1869, 4.
74   'Party Politics and the Press', *Wrexham Guardian*, 1 June 1878, 4.
75   Anti-Humbug, 'Mr Watkin Williams, MP, and the Press', *Wrexham Guardian*, 1 June 1878, 7.
76   'To our Readers', *Wrexham Guardian*, 7 September 1878, 4.
77   Untitled paper, 19 August 1878, FRO, D/KT/22.

Roe continued to uphold the *Guardian*'s support for the Conservative party, Sir Watkin, Kenyon, and the tradition of regular abuse of the Liberals continued. Kenyon fought the Denbigh Boroughs constituency again in 1880, losing this time by fifteen votes before winning the seat in 1885, fourteen years after he first announced his intention to stand for the constituency. After leaving the Denbigh Boroughs, Williams stood in the Caernarvonshire seat for the Liberals in the 1880 election, when he came up against the other Conservative-supporting newspaper in north Wales, the *North Wales Chronicle*, who, unsurprisingly, condemned him as an interloper with no interest in the constituency, beyond promoting himself and having no knowledge of the issues facing Caernarvonshire's inhabitants.[78] Although he faced yet another hostile Conservative newspaper in his new constituency, the *Chronicle* never fell to the level of personal abuse that the *Guardian* had inflicted upon Williams, with its comment that Williams was the 'cast-off member for Denbigh', reflecting its general attitude towards him.[79] However, Williams' electoral luck held and he spectacularly overturned a Conservative majority of over 400 and won the seat by over 1,000 votes, defeating the sitting MP, the Hon. George Douglas-Pennant of Penryhn Castle. When the *Guardian* claimed victory in 1878, in forcing Williams out of the Denbigh Boroughs, little could it have realised that its action would result in not only the Liberals holding the Denbigh Boroughs seat in 1880, but also in the Conservatives losing the Caernarvonshire seat to their arch-enemy!

Williams resigned as a MP only months after his victory in Caernarvonshire to become a High Court judge and died in July 1884 in Nottingham whilst holding the assizes in that city. However, Williams evoked scandal, even in death, as *Reynold's Newspaper* published the *Nottingham Journal*'s account of the inquest into Williams' death, at which it was discovered that Williams died in the local brothel. The *Guardian* did not comment on this, but had Williams still been the Denbigh Borough's MP when he died, the *Guardian* would not doubt have echoed

---

78 'Mr Watkin Williams', *North Wales Chronicle*, 20 March 1880, 4.
79 'Cownselor o Lundain – Sassiwn yn Nghymru', *North Wales Chronicle*, 20 March 1880, 4.

Reynold's Newspaper's comment that he was a 'thorough-paced hypocrite and filthy debauchee.'[80]

In conclusion, like the *Western Mail*, the *Wrexham Guardian* was a failure for the Conservative party. It was a financial failure, although it cost Sir Watkin and Kenyon significantly less than the £50,000 the Marquess of Bute spent on the *Western Mail* before selling it in 1877.[81] Politicians did have their 'mouthpieces' in the press, but helping to fund a newspaper solely to viciously attack your electoral rival, arguably took the *Guardian*'s role beyond that of a mere mouthpiece for Kenyon's views.[82] The sorry history of the *Guardian* and the NWCPCo also demonstrates that party newspapers needed to be financially viable, with a good circulation and guaranteed advertising revenue, if they were to fulfil successfully their role as a political organ.[83] The *Guardian*'s tactic of vitriolic abuse of a hated Liberal, whose policies and views stood in stark opposition to their own, ultimately backfired. Williams enjoyed revenge against the *Guardian*, not only in exposing it as the personally financed mouthpiece of his rival, but also in winning the seat of Caernarvonshire for the Liberals. The story of the *Wrexham Guardian* shows that, regardless of political support, newspapers needed subscribers and readers to survive.[84] Ongoing efforts to digitise Britain and Ireland's provincial newspapers provides press historians with the opportunity to research Conservative- and Liberal-supported newspapers over several centuries, to discover more about the delicate balance these newspapers trod between party loyalty and the need to be commercially viable.

---

80   'Discreditable and Dreadful Death of a Judge', *Reynold's Newspaper*, 27 July 1884, 5.
81   Joanne Mary Cayford, 'The *Western Mail* 1869–1914: A Study in the Politics and Management of a Provincial Newspaper', PhD thesis, University of Wales, 1992, 54.
82   Brown, *Victorian News and Newspapers*, 54.
83   Matthews, *The History of the Provincial Press in England*, 60.
84   A point also made by Baker, *Newspapers, Politics and English Society*, 86, in relation to London newspapers in the early nineteenth century.

VICTORIA CLARKE

8 Identifying the Readers and Correspondents of the *Northern Star*, 1837–1847

One of the most famous early Victorian provincial newspapers was the *Northern Star* (1837–1852), whose fifteen years of publication has made it a valuable source for all those studying Chartism. While many historians of Chartism have relied on the *Star* as a means of explaining the narrative of the movement, this chapter argues that its place in media history is worthy of an alternative cultural analysis. The *Northern Star* occupied several liminal spaces: based in Leeds and then London, it was both a local and a national newspaper. It contained a mix of local news, births, deaths, and marriages, reports of various trade union and labour society meetings and essays by figureheads of the movement, from Bronterre O'Brien to Richard Oastler to Friedrich Engels in its last years. For one week in 1838, it even outsold *The Times*, making it the best-selling newspaper in the country, with *The Times*' 2,666 stamp duty sales paling in comparison to the *Star*'s 9,822.[1]

This unparalleled success was down to many factors, not least that it was shaped for and by the Chartist movement. The *Star* enjoyed a readership approximately seven times its sales figures due to its popularity as a kind of social event, bought in groups by those too poor to afford their own individual issue and read communally in the domestic hearth, the pub, or the workshop.[2] Thus, the *Star* was a tool for communication. Chase writes that 'several national industrial unions used the paper as their main

---

1   James Mussell, 'The *Northern Star*', Nineteenth-Century Serials Edition (NCSE) (2009), <http://www.ncse.ac.uk/headnotes/nss.html>, accessed 1 March 2018.

2   Stephen Roberts, 'Who Wrote to the *Northern Star*?', *The Duty of Discontent: Essays for Dorothy Thompson*, eds, Owen Ashton, Robert Fyson and Stephen Roberts (London: Mansell, 1995), 64.

medium of communication', including those who had their own trade papers.[3] It was in the Readers' and Correspondents' column in particular that this symbiotic relationship between the *Star* and its readers was most clearly demonstrated. Corresponding societies were still illegal following several laws passed by the British government in the panic of the French Revolution in the 1790s and known Chartists' letters were opened and inspected in transit.[4] Consequently, radicals had to think outside the post-box. By writing to the paper, they could not guarantee their letter would be published, but it was as good a plan as any for communication, even used as a loophole by proprietor Feargus O'Connor's during his imprisonment for libel and ban on writing for publication.

Table 8.1. Length of R&C column in total words, then average by month and year.

Year	1837[5]	1838	1839	1840	1841	1842	1843	1844	1845	1846	1847
Total no. words	344	19,267	30,979	37,564	60,060	71,184	77,902	52,503	98,895	53,327	87,404
Average words per month	173.5	1,604.75	2,566.4	3,130.3	5,000.5	5,932	6,491.8	4,375.2	8,241.2	4,443.9	7,283.6

Stephen Roberts, in his study of the *Star*'s correspondence, describes the Readers and Correspondents column as 'the greatest distraction of all' when mining the paper for unrelated projects.[6] His essay describes the variety of material found in the column, from legal advice to general advice, poetry submissions, reports of branch meetings, charity appeals for imprisoned Chartists and their now destitute wives and children, as well as suggestions for the organisation of the movement and everyday

---

3   Malcolm Chase, *Early Trade Unionism: Fraternity, Skills and the Politics of Labour* (Aldershot: Ashgate, 2000), 185.

4   Dorothy Thompson, *The Chartists* (New York: Random House, 1984), 47.

5   Only two issues survive from 1837, which explains the relative absence of matter in the Readers and Correspondents column at this time.

6   Roberts, 'Who Wrote to the *Northern Star*?', 55.

activism. While this offers a brief snapshot of the contents of the column, it is possible to argue that its sheer wealth of material (see Table 8.1) can provide more than descriptive colour to the study of Chartist history. An analysis of the column can provide a deeper exploration of *who* wrote to the paper and how they saw themselves, in addition to *what* they wrote. This chapter will examine these letters to discover what the *Star* can tell us about the identities of its many readers, and the identities of everyday Chartist folk.

The 'Readers and Correspondents' made up the community of the movement. While many individuals wrote to the *Star* under their own name (and were sometimes rebuked by William Hill for the 'childish anxiety [...] to see his name in print'),[7] and thus were able to proclaim that they had been published, full transparency was not an option for all due to the risks of dismissal, at a time of few workers' rights and considerable elite fear of Chartism. While many correspondents circumvented this through use of initials, a great many chose instead to write under a pen name, which offered the working classes an opportunity to define themselves and have some creative agency in their *nom de plume*, to choose what aspects to foreground in presenting their own identities to the world. Due to the anonymous nature of these letters, this chapter will use a gender-neutral pronoun when describing examples. And, given that no correspondence from the offices for the R&C column survives, it will use the editors' replies to such letters in order to infer the names which they published under. These would have needed to be recognisable to the writer and distinct from others to avoid confusion. While other papers were able to brand Chartism and the Chartists as whatever they liked, the *Northern Star* offered an opportunity for self-expression on a public scale. This chapter is therefore divided into two sections: individual identities and collective identities. By analysing the relationships between their pseudonyms and messages, it hopes to show the ways in which everyday Chartists sought to make an impression.

One can infer that the correspondents' and readers' pen names were not pseudonyms assigned to particular letters by the editor in response,

7   'The Ramsbottom Subscription for Mr M'Douall', *Northern Star*, 8 August 1840.

partly because of the brevity of so many answers. The following, rather abrupt example, was not uncommon at particularly busy points of the year, including parliamentary sessions:

> A CONSTANT READER, MANCHESTER, J. W. Clarke, A Chartist of the Old School, Richard Workman, Barraclough – No room.[8]

With 'no room' as the editors' response to several correspondence at once, here one can see a variety of the names adopted by correspondents. Thus, one can appreciate the ways in which the readers clearly identified themselves as addressees in the paper; 'A Chartist of the Old School' need not be confused with 'An Old Chartist', or similar. By choosing their pseudonyms, correspondents demonstrated agency in their active engagement with the self-identified 'Chartist' paper, with the editorial team and the community of fellow readers. Through an examination of these pseudonyms, this section will explore how readers of the *Star* saw themselves and what they considered was important to them, in the construction of their individual identities.

The *Star* being a literary document, in the sense that it was literally written down, several correspondents explicitly self-identified using literary markers: a 'poet', a 'writer', a 'correspondent' demonstrated clear identification with the act of literacy in writing to the paper, a concrete assimilation of authorship as their identity. What is particularly interesting in the *Star*'s Correspondence column, as opposed to the poetry column, is the use of Greek and Latin pseudonyms: Calvinus, Gracchus, Phliantropus, Pharisee, Medicus, Viscimus, Animus, Hericus, Publius, Fidus, Junius Rusticus, Democritus, Clericus, Brutus, Charterus, and Misticus Secretus are just a selection of pseudonyms used in the column. These take a specifically Latin name form, indicating knowledge of classic history and an ability to read Latin, not usually taught to working-class children at this time. Given that, even by 1867, only one in seven children had attended any kind of school,[9] the creative literacy displayed in the column seems

---

8   *Northern Star*, 30 July 1842.
9   John Doheny, 'Bureaucracy and Education of the Poor in Nineteenth Century Britain', *British Journal of Educational Studies*, 39.3 (1991), 338.

all the more striking. Classically inspired pseudonyms in correspondence were not unique to the *Star*: its contemporary, the *Leeds Times* informed a correspondent named 'Vindex' (which translates to 'Champion', as well as referring to the Roman ruler of Gaul)[10] that they 'ought also to furnish us with his real name',[11] as in a paper such as the *Leeds Times* anonymity was not strictly necessary. While grammar schools, established in the Tudor period, still held strong across the country and focused on classical grammar, local private or Church schools for the children of tradesmen tended to neglect this, particularly in the north of England, with parents seeing it as superfluous, given that their children were unlikely to enter universities.[12] Though many 'gentlemen' were involved in the movement, one striking example being John Watkins, alias 'Brutus' and 'Junius Rusticus',[13] the use of classical pseudonyms did not always necessarily indicate a class division. There were many examples of autodidact pride, as encouraged by the *Star*, in actively co-opting knowledge and skill restricted to and by the upper and middle classes' educational and corresponding practices, which was a tradition of eighteenth-century broadsheets, into working-class reading practices.

Furthermore, there is evidence of direct engagement with these topics: 'Calvinus', and 'Brutus' clearly borrowed their names from the Ancient Roman generals, assuming oneself to be a powerful figure, another example of 'rank' in the Chartist 'army', more commonly demonstrated by proclamation of age and experience. Likewise, 'Gracchus' borrowed from the two brothers, Tiberius and Caius Gracchus, populist politicians in Ancient Rome,[14] engaging with the political teachings of the classics and re-imag-

10   Brian Campbell, 'Gaius Iulius Vindex', *Oxford Classical Dictionary* (2016). Website [DOI: 10.1093/acrefore/9780199381135.013.3434], accessed 10 March 2018.

11   *Leeds Times*, 4 March 1843, 4.

12   Martin Lowther Clarke, *Classical Education in Britain 1500–1900* (Cambridge: Cambridge University Press, 2014), 74–6; 86–7.

13   Malcolm Chase, 'Watkins, John (1808–1858)', *Dictionary of Labour Biography*, Vol. X, eds, J. Bellamy and J. Saville (Basingstoke: Palgrave Macmillan, 2000), p. 299.

14   Ernst Badian, 'Sempronius Gracchus, Gaius', *Oxford Classical Dictionary* (2015), website [DOI 10.1093/acrefore/9780199381135.013.5812], accessed 10 March 2018.

ining themselves as part of it; a contribution to what Robert Hall refers to as the 'myth' of 'People's History'.[15]

By co-opting these names, the writers aligned their contemporary political values by borrowing classical expressions. 'Democritus' modelled themself on the Ancient Greek philosopher and scientist, but co-opted the more commonly used label, 'Democrat', to demonstrate their support and identification with the Chartist ideal of democracy. 'Amicus' has several possible meanings: it is a technical term in law for an impartial advisor, a friend, as well as a synonym for 'purpose' or 'courage', and, furthermore, a direct translation from the English 'heart', evoking principles of kindness, love, and strength. Other 'classical' writers had fun with the Latin form and generated their own pseudonym, based on ideas they have; while 'Medicus', which translates into English as 'physician', simply warned their fellow readers against quack medicines on sale in publications,[16] others made up their own words. 'Philantropus' would indicate something to do with goodwill or philanthropy, while 'Charterus' takes the Latin form to incorporate the People's Charter, demonstrating a more specific engagement with politics old and new. 'Misticus Secretus', on the other hand, would translate to 'mysterious secret'. Sadly, they 'must excuse [the editors] – [they] have no room',[17] so any potential mysterious secrets divulged in their only letter (as far as the archive suggests) have been lost to the *Star*'s office fire.[18] Without any further clues, or anything of the utmost importance for publication, one can infer the writer just to be having fun with the form of the pseudonym, obscuring their real name. These examples, although not nearly as common as English language pseudonyms or even initials, were prevalent throughout the *Star*'s print run. By actively engaging

15   Robert G. Hall, *Voices of the People: Democracy and Chartist Political Identity, 1830–1870* (London: Merlin Press, 2007), Chapters 1 & 2.
16   *Northern Star*, 4 November 1843.
17   *Northern Star*, 27 August 1842.
18   The editors replied to many 'blackguard' letters by stating that their correspondence had gone in the office fire: whether this economical practice was reserved only for poison pens or for all rejected or previous correspondence cannot, obviously, be proved. *Northern Star*, 30 April 1842.

and co-opting classical language and ideals, these writers introduced themselves as not only literate but as learned readers, creating their own identities based on their own ideas and engagement with a long history of philosophy and political thought.

In addition to these demonstrations of literary engagement, many correspondents aimed to showcase their loyalty to the paper. Many a 'Constant Reader' and 'Subscriber' wrote in to share their feedback or comment on matter of previous weeks, both flattering the editorial team and demonstrating their experience with the paper and its ethos. These were individual 'constant readers' and 'subscribers', as they were differentiated by location in the editors' replies to them. Throughout the ten years covered by this study, there were no fewer than forty self-identified 'subscriber' from locations all over the country, from Ashton[19] to York[20], and even as far abroad as Copenhagen.[21] In many cases these aged Radicals, who boasted of their years of service, showed off their period of loyalty to the *Star:* for example, one correspondent, writing in 1842, signed themself, 'A Subscriber from the Commencement'.[22] Others who proclaimed their subscription could have this loyalty used against them, as below:

> A CONSTANT SUBSCRIBER, AND LOVER OF '*STAR*'- LIGHT, TYLDSLEY, is informed, and ought to have known, that no notice of a forthcoming meeting is inserted in the *Star* unless it bears the signature of the sub-Secretary of the locality where it purports to come from, or is sent by one of our own appointed Correspondents, who is expected to make himself acquainted that 'all is right' before he transmits it. We know of no 'General Lee' of Ashton-under-Lyne; and think his notice a very suspicious one.[23]

This 'Constant Subscriber' perhaps overstepped the mark, not only advertising their loyalty in subscribing to the paper, but additionally proclaiming to be a 'lover of *Star*-light', using the *Star*'s own joke about its

19   *Northern Star*, 15 February 1845.
20   *Northern Star*, 29 January 1842.
21   *Northern Star*, 6 May 1843.
22   *Northern Star*, 8 October 1842.
23   *Northern Star*, 29 July 1843.

importance in an attempt to engage them. Perhaps this was too flattering a pseudonym to be trusted, as the suspicions about having 'ought' to have had authority from the area's branch officials when sending notices, meetings and introducing themself with their real name (even if this real name was not to be published) to the editors. Given that Ashton-under-Lyne was a hotspot for Chartist activity, the editors were furthermore demonstrating their strong bond with the community there in questioning this 'suspicious' correspondent. The use of flattery in the pseudonym seems designed to encourage the editors to comply with their request and print their notice. Likewise, 'A Six Years' Subscriber' was one of several examples of 'X Years Subscribers' who wrote with questions and requests that were complied with; their legal question received a detailed answer.[24] Meanwhile, several 'Constant Reader's, more unusual or impractical requests became the subject of mockery, questioning the validity of the assertion of 'constant' readership, as in one example from 1844:

> CONSTANT READER, BOWLING, must surely have mistaken the nature of our avocation. Our business is to make newspapers; not to ferret out genealogies, or make out titles to property.[25]

This 'Constant Reader' mistook the variety of noticeboard content within the column and was thus rebuked. In doing so, the editors did not chide them directly but sarcastically, while also underlying the use of the column as public correspondence and a part of the newspaper they were in the business of making. These humorous responses challenged the writers to defend their claim of 'Constant' readership and tested those other readers in their close engagement with the paper. Like those who asserted their status as 'writers', 'poets' and autodidacts, 'constant readers' asserted themselves as loyal to the *Star* and had to be prepared for this claim to identity to be challenged.

The final category identified for individual self-identification in the column is that of value alignment. Unlike demonstrations of literacy and

24   *Northern Star*, 1 February 1845.
25   *Northern Star*, 10 August 1844.

readership, many correspondents used their pseudonyms to align themselves with what they (and the *Star*) valued. These followed some newspaper correspondence traditions, not unlike the *Leeds Times*' various responses to 'A Lover of Information',[26] an 'Enemy to War'[27] and, most touchingly, 'A Friend to True Love'.[28] The five quantifiers: 'Lover', 'admirer', 'hater' of such and such a quality, or 'friend' and 'enemy' to whatever detestable quality, made an ideological statement from the first: they were introduced to the *Star* and its readers, not as a reader, man or woman, veteran or youth, member of a trade, but as a holder of specific principles. Like their classical column-fellows, in choosing these pseudonyms they made a statement. However, by doing so in English, they put themselves in relation to something, rather than likening themselves not only as educated, but as a leader, physician, philanthropist, etc.

A simple search within the corpus for the term 'a lover' yields around thirty results, with correspondents proclaiming to be lovers of Truth, Justice, Fair-Play, Freedom, among others. In the majority of cases, these principled pseudonyms were used to introduce a suggestion for agitation, or to support a case previously discussed by the *Star*. For the following examples, one can infer the nature of their letters:

> A LOVER OF TRUTH, JUSTICE, AND EQUALITY – We have no room for his 'Letter to the aristocracy of all Nations'.[29]

> A LOVER OF GOD AND ALL MANKIND. – An operative in Wakefield – We have read his letter carefully and admire the spirit in which it is written. We perfectly agree with all its positions, but cannot find room for his letter.[30]

These pseudonyms were showcased by the published responses: although the editors said that they cannot 'find room' for the whole letters, their self-identified labels and the tone of the letter were published,

---

26   *Leeds Times*, 16 September 1843.
27   *Leeds Times*, 17 January 1846.
28   *Leeds Times*, 4 January 1840.
29   *Northern Star*, 23 October 1841.
30   *Northern Star*, 29 June 1839.

demonstrating the existence of such individuals who 'love truth' and
'mankind'. The 'Lover of Truth [etc.]' furthermore referenced the French
and American Revolutions in their pen name, recalling the United States'
founding father, Thomas Jefferson's advice to 'follow truth, justice, and
plain dealing',[31] as well as the new proclamation of the French state for
'liberté, egalité, fraternité' in their own 1789 Declaration, a Charter-like
document.[32] Likewise, 'A Lover of God and all Mankind' evoked principles
of Christianity, a strategy used often by Chartists to argue that the movement was part of God's will, giving them a kind of moral high ground over
their 'oppressive' upper and middle-class foes.[33]

By contrast, the more negative names, such as the 'Enemies' of 'Tyranny',
'Oppression', etc., tended to be associated more with direct action within
the movement, particularly with labour rights and practices, as the following examples indicate:

A HATER OF TYRANNY. – It depends on the 'rates' of the mill. The millowner
has the power if any such rules are hung up in the working room, stating that such
are the terms on which those whom he employs must be content to labour.[34]

AN ENEMY TO WHIG AND TORY TYRANNY sends us the following: –

Some of the men employed in the Glasgow Pottery are in the habit of reading the
Star; and the articles which appear therein necessarily give rise to some remarks
from those who read them. Some way or other, the master received information
of this, and he immediately gave orders to the effect – that all who were known to
be Chartists, or readers of that pernicious journal, (the Star,) would be turned off
from their employment. [...] To the workmen I would say, cease not to read those

---

31   Thomas Jefferson, *The Essential Jefferson*, ed. John Dewey (Mineola, NY: Dover
     Publications, 2008), 81.
32   Jack R. Censer and Lynn Hunt, *Liberty, Equality, Fraternity: Exploring the French
     Revolution* (University Park, PA: Penn State University Press, 2001), 45.
33   For more on Chartism and Christianity, see Jutta Schwartzkopf, *Women in the
     Chartist Movement* (London: Palgrave, 1991), 105–14.
34   *Northern Star*, 2 December 1843.

newspapers which you think will give you the most information, and advocate those principles which will prove most beneficial to you.[35]

These particular adages, specifically opposing oneself to the Whigs and/or Tories, framing oneself as 'lover' or 'hater', used a binary system to candidly align the reader with specific values: those values defined both by themselves, as readers, and within the community of readers of the *Star*. The 'Enemy to Whig and Tory Tyranny' specifically thought that the practice of being sacked for reading the *Star* was not only 'downright tyranny', but they defended the paper as one which was most 'informative' and 'beneficial'. They identified the communal reading practices of radical texts in the workroom and demonstrated the importance of the *Star* to their identity: so important that they risked losing their employment for it. By identifying themselves as 'lovers of truth' and 'haters of tyranny' they endorsed the *Star*'s values. In periods of strife and scandal for the paper and the movement in particular, these defiant pseudonyms made a statement to other readers and invited further engagement with the philosophy and practice of the paper and the movement.

What was seen in these varied uses of individual names in the *Star* was an exploration of different components of individual identity, much of which is multifaceted. Limited space and anonymisation required the correspondents to make their introductions clear and concise; they had to decide what they wanted to be known for, to the *Star* and to other readers, and to lead with this. This was all the more difficult knowing that unpopular opinions in the Chartist readership would not be welcomed. Adjectives and multiple categories were used to differentiate between individual correspondents and to build identities. 'An Old Radical', for example, signified not only old age and their political views, but demonstrated a level of maturity to it, built over time; while 'A Brother Democrat, Rochdale'[36] aligned his masculinity as part of a group, using fraternity to forge extra links with his fellow 'democrats' in the readership. Though several of these labels: 'brother', 'democrat', 'radical' were generic, the various combinations

35   *Northern Star*, 21 October 1843.
36   *Northern Star*, 23 January 1847.

of them could be explored and exploited for a specific, distinctive effect. These demonstrate how individual readers saw themselves and wanted to be seen, distinctly, by others.

In addition to the varied individual names or pseudonyms that formed the 'Readers and Correspondents' of the *Northern Star*, there were groups of several people writing under one name, linked through region, interest, or some other common purpose. These self-proclaimed collective identities built on the format of individual identities and served a linked, but very different function: unifying several distinct individuals. Throughout the years of the *Star*, the frequency of appearances of these groups ebbed and flowed, but reflected the unifying point of the collective, falling into three broad categories: labour or occupational groups, regional groups, or interest groups. It was the trade, the locality, or dedication to a cause such as teetotalism that was the unifying and defining feature of these groups. This section will explore the motives behind these collective identities and analyse the ways in which these small communities represented themselves to the wider audience of the *Star* and, indeed, the nation.

Given the *Star*'s obvious audience of working-class men (and the editorial team were specific about the 'working' aspect), it is no surprise that occupation was taken as a label for many correspondents. While the use of occupation or trade as a distinguishing feature of individual correspondents' pseudonyms does occur, many letters from trade unions and associations appeared in the paper to campaign for labour rights. There is also clear evidence of a hierarchy of working-class trades: those who were 'operatives' or 'labourers' versus 'makers' and 'artisans'. These occupational labels are significant: to do a job for ten hours a day, six days a week would naturally have become part of an individual's identity; more than that, many trades carried traditions and were part of a region's heritage. It is to this intrinsic identifying factor which scholars including Robert G. Hall and Sonya Rose attribute the 'rage against the machine' of the Luddite revolutions, that by mechanising many of these trades, the society suffered the loss of an inherently masculine skill-set, thus the agency, identity, and status of the workmen.[37] A

---

37   Sonya Rose, 'Gender Antagonism and Class Conflict: Exclusionary Strategies of Male Trade Unionists in Nineteenth Century Britain', *Social History*, 13:2 (1988), 193; Hall, *Voices of the People*, Chapter 2.

search through the corpus of the column shows no fewer than twenty-seven types of self-identified 'maker', confirming that most worked within the manufacturing industries. More specific job titles appeared as well, including 'woolcombers', 'flax-dressers', 'cloth-dressers', as well as skilled titles including 'carpenter', 'milliner', and 'tailor'.

The industry of manufacture was ingrained with the history of the 'noble artisan' whose work formed the backbone of British capitalism and on whom everyone relied; just as the 'noble' agricultural labourers fed the country, the weavers, spinners, and tailors clothed the country. Indeed, as Schwartzkopf identifies in her study of women in the movement, the working classes were conscious that they were the 'producers of wealth' of Britain and the world and that the emerging materialism of the burgeoning middle classes relied on the labour of the working classes in manufacture.[38] In self-identifying with their work, the writers of letters in the *Northern Star* acted as representatives of the trade. These varied greatly, between singular workers and collectives, as this example from 1844 demonstrates:

> LONDON JOURNEYMEN SHOEMAKERS. – We are sorry that we cannot find room for their excellent petition.

> A FACTORY WORKER. – The subject of his letter to Lord Brougham has already been disposed of in the speeches of Mr Oastler and Mr Harney, reported in the *Star* of last week.[39]

The above examples appeared side by side (or one atop the other) in the same column of the same issue of the *Star* and one can glean an idea of the content of their unpublished letters: the group of shoemakers sharing a petition, most likely concerning a labour dispute. Whereas the singular 'Factory Worker' used this as their distinguishing feature for a separate letter, albeit connected with factories, but subsumed by another feature. The 'London Journeymen Shoemakers', having a petition for their specific cause, got a personal apology for want of room. The individual's letter was personal; although they publicly self-identified with their job, it was one voice subsumed by others; as opposed to the many represented by the group

38 Schwartzkopf, *Women in the Chartist Movement*, 264.
39 *Northern Star*, 20 April 1844.

voice of the London Journeymen Shoemakers, a shared opinion put forward
s strongly. The Shoemakers' self-identification as such furthermore allowed
them to be seen by other trade groups, opening the potential for solidarity and
correspondence between branches of trades, an alternative social network to
that of the aristocracy. Perhaps the best illustration of this was trade groups
approach to fundraising, the attribution to the recipients of such funds:

> THE INDOMITABLE MINERS – We are glad to learn that the 'West End Men's
> Men' shoemakers have determined to send £20 to the heroic and brave men of the
> north. Let every Trade, and every section of a Trade follow the generous example,
> and the cause of Labour will soon be triumphant.[40]

This notice, addressed to a group of miners, appeared at the time of unrest
for the miners of Northumberland, whose strike action and public letters
appeared frequently in the *Star* in 1844. What made this notice significant,
however, was that not only are the 'West End Men's Men' shoemakers
fundraising to support the miners (a totally unrelated and geographically
distant trade group to themselves), but had praise heaped upon them in
the form of editorial commentary. The 'generous example' was printed
for all to read, while the miners, in their struggle for labour rights, were
'indomitable', 'heroic and brave men'. The 'West End Men's Men' shoemakers were an established trade group, but also had some fun with their pen
name, as noted by the quotation marks around them: 'men's men' not only
rhymes with 'West End', but specifies that they were male artisans who made
shoes for male customers. Furthermore, the 'men's men' suggests the idea
of brotherhood, exemplified by their support for the miners. Local and
regional trades groups who wrote to the paper to air disputes were enabled
to gain cross-country support from their fellow tradespeople. Tailors and
shoemakers, being a feature of every town and region, made up an enormous
proportion of manufacturing occupational mentions (see Figure 8.1) and
claimed a unique place within radical politics.

In practical terms, tailoring and shoemaking were social working
environments: workers were public-facing in a shop, as well as having the
space and quiet to chat in a workshop (unlike the factory, mill, mine, or

40   *Northern Star*, 10 August 1844.

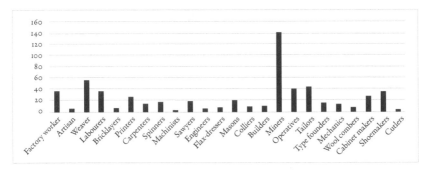

Figure 8.1. Self-identified occupations in the *Northern Star* readers
and correspondents column, 1837–1848.

metalshop, where noise and heat rendered conversation impossible); as well as a tradition of radical activity. E. J. Hobsbawm and Joan Wallach Scott, in their history of 'Political Shoemakers', wrote that such radicalism was proverbial. They reported Robert Peel, at the height of the Chartist activity, confronting a group of shoemakers in a labour dispute and asking in exasperation 'how is it ... that you people are foremost in every movement? ... If there is a conspiracy or political movement, I always find one of you is in it.'[41] For a trades group to advertise in the *Northern Star* or make an appeal, they were able to count on others of their ilk all over the country, as per the following example:

> THE MANCHESTER TAILORS are informed that we have received a letter from the Burslem and Tunstall Tailors' Protection Society (Potteries), signed by John Billington, Dale Hall, near Longport, Potteries, wishing to know whether the Manchester Tailors are still on strike. [...] The above Society would be willing to contribute their aid to the Manchester Tailors, if still on strike; they therefore desire information on the subject.[42]

This example was one of several from various trades appearing in the *Star*, from tailors through sailors to miners. While trade papers such as the

41   Eric J. Hobsbawm and Joan Wallach Scott, 'Political Shoemakers', *Past and Present*, 89 (1980), 86–114; 93.

42   *Northern Star*, 24 August 1844.

Tailors' Advocate were in existence, the decision to air labour disputes in the *Northern Star* spoke to the ethos of the *Star* and the Chartist movement: a movement of working-class men. [43] This demonstrated the success of O'Connor's aims for the newspaper to facilitate national discussion, the ways it was used, in addition to private correspondence between groups. By publishing this notice, the 'Manchester Tailors' could be held accountable and manage their aid and relationship with the tailors of the Potteries. The editors sought to represent the operatives and hirelings of the nation's industries and, by amplifying the voices of unions and trades groups at a time when paper was expensive and small newsletters scarce, it demonstrated this commitment in a practical manner.

Just as with occupational or trade groups writing, and indeed alongside it, examples of regional identity also feature in the Readers and Correspondents' column. For the letters of individuals, locations were given in order to differentiate similar writers, as was (and indeed, remains) standard editorial practice in this context. For collectives, locality and regional identities were again used specifically to differentiate groups as well as unify those members of a region and, in the case of trade disputes, to give context.

While the 'Tailors' are an example of cross-regional dialogue in the *Star* and acts of solidarity between localities, one may also conclude that regionalism was integral to self-identity and the *Northern Star's* portrayal of people's history. Just as the London Working Men's Association consciously evoked Magna Carta in the creation of the Charter,[44] regional history was intrinsically linked to regional identities. Manchester and Lancashire had cotton-spinning, Yorkshire had the woollen industry and Northumberland and the North East had mining: just as industrialisation and loss of worker agency within some trades[45] led to a loss of masculine status and identity for the tradesmen during

---

43 Referenced in *Northern Star*, 11 April 1846.
44 London Working Men's Association, 'The People's Charter' (London, 1838), British Library website <https://www.bl.uk/collection-items/the-peoples-charter>, accessed 12 March 2018.
45 Mining was not yet mechanised at this time, nor many 'artisan trades' such as tailoring, tanning, or shoemaking. It was, however, still undergoing many changes with regards to increased management hierarchy in collieries.

the Industrial Revolution,[46] so it altered the regional identity of these areas and the rural/urban makeup of a place. These local identities and affiliation with trades remained strong and were infused with a type of revolutionary masculinity, the opposite of the mainstream propaganda in praise of the British Empire. Questions of local and national pride were configured in these letters in terms of their activism and devotion to the Charter. David Powell has suggested that the creation of the British state as a national identity was a move by the establishment to quell any radical ideas inspired by the French Revolution from the end of the eighteenth century. In reality, many ordinary people felt more patriotic towards their hometown, towards being Welsh, or Scottish or English, or even in terms of region such as Cornish identity.[47] Historians have established that Chartism had its strongholds in parts of Wales, Scotland and industrial regions of England such as Yorkshire, Lancashire, and Leicestershire. That said, localities were clearly driven to demonstrate their devotion and display in a type of regional patriotism: just as women Chartists redefined 'abroad' as outside the local vicinity, 'outside the domestic' rather than 'overseas';[48] 'patriotic' was defined by the anti-establishment Chartists as their home region, as below:

> STARS TO IRELAND. – What are the Sheffield friends about? We know that the circulation of the *Star* is rapidly increasing in their town, why not give their Irish brethren the benefit of it? Let them use the list sent them by the Irish Universal Suffrage Association. The little trouble of so doing will be amply repaid by the great and lasting good that will be effected.

> THE COVENTRY CHARTISTS appeal to their townsmen to come forward and join the new organisation: especially the avowed Chartists, who will prove their sincerity by responding to the appeal. We hope they will do so. 'England expects every man to do his duty'.[49]

---

46   Hall, *Voices of the People*, 14.
47   David Powell, *Nationhood and Identity: The British State Since 1800* (London: I. B. Tauris, 2002), 12.
48   Schwartzkopf, *Women in the Chartist Movement*, 103.
49   *Northern Star*, 4 November 1843.

In 'Stars to Ireland', the Sheffield Chartists and readers were appealed to as 'friends', before having their devotion to the cause questioned and encouraging the development of cross-national community in this case. The 'Irish brethren' had specifically fraternal, familial ties drawn between themselves and the Sheffield 'friends' and it was this familial framework that was used to unite the two communities and to call upon the Sheffield residents to demonstrate their local pride. In both examples, the effort was minimal: the 'avowed Chartists' had to prove their worth by joining the new group, while the Sheffield readers were obliged to take a 'little trouble' to help their Chartist brethren over the Irish sea in an act of charity. The editors of the *Star* strategically played on the idea of regional rivalries to create a sense of friendly competition between Chartists across the country. By turning one's neighbourhood into a Chartist hotspot, one demonstrated their commitment to the cause and furthered their political agency. Likewise, the Coventry Chartists appealed to 'their townsmen', reinforcing the idea of smaller groups becoming larger collectives with England's 'expectations': this appeal was a 'duty', not an option. What is interesting about these examples is that they focused on larger areas. Katrina Navickas identifies Ashton-under-Lyne as one of the most consistently active Chartist communities,[50] while it was the larger towns like Coventry and industrial proto-cities such as Sheffield which were identified by the *Star* as lacking in their efforts.

Table 8.2. Adult populations of Radical townships, towns, and proto-cities according to 1841 census data.[51]

Town	Adult male population	Adult female population	Total adult population
Ashton-under-Lyne	5,562	5162	10,674
Coventry	7,898	8,883	16,781
Sheffield	28,798	30,041	58,839

50   Katrina Navickas, *Protest and the Politics of Space and Place, 1789–1848* (Manchester: Manchester University Press, 2016), 106.

51   Data taken from the 1841 Census, held at the National Archives. 'Adult population' in this case refers to those aged twenty years and over.

Perhaps they identified these regions, due to their larger population size, as areas of greatest potential for mass radicalisation. This regional kind of patriotism was defined by activism as demonstrated through the joining of a Chartist collective, mutually publicised and defined through the Coventry Chartists and the *Northern Star*. The correspondents' collective identities drew upon shared qualities with their townsmen to create a kind of performance and literal 'in' and 'out' groups within their imagined communities.

Self-identification of unions, societies and associations were present in a variety of causes, from local party fundraising to small trades groups, temperance societies, co-operatives and, of course, Feargus O'Connor's great land scheme. 'Membership' of such groups was a term that appeared frequently in the column and it is through examining this turn of phrase that one can examine how collective identities were created and used for propaganda in the *Northern Star*. Examples of the use of the term 'membership' indicate that participants in these groups literally became card-carrying members of the group, with these cards and ephemera (such as medals) acting as proof of participation. Given the *Star*'s ethos of democracy and inclusivity, it is interesting the group membership was cemented by awarding exclusive tokens. The following example demonstrates the ceremony and materiality of such membership:

> Mr O'Connor has the honour to acknowledge his card of admission to the Leeds Working Men's Association, conferring all the privileges of membership; Mr O'Connor feels honoured by the compliment, and begs, in return, to assure his brother members, that no exertion upon his part shall be wanting to make the Association a rallying point for the industrious, a terror to tyrants, and a credit to the town of Leeds.[52]

> EDWARD BEEDLE must write to Mr Heywood privately. There is no other expence [*sic*] in joining the National Charter Association than that of the card of membership.[53]

O'Connor's flattery at receiving his 'card of admission' to the Leeds WMA sounds insincere to modern ears, but it does show the value and symbolism

---

52   *Northern Star*, 10 March 1838.
53   *Northern Star*, 19 March 1842.

of such a card: to have the card was to have the 'privileges of membership'. Given that many of the Leeds WMA did not see themselves having much social privilege, the 'privilege' of membership gave an air of exclusivity, something special literally to hold onto was symbolised in the card. O'Connor's 'honour' in joining the association and publishing this notice in the paper, acted as advertising for the group, raising awareness of their work. The Leeds Working Men's Association, as a name, joined together its social class as a group of self-identified working men and Leeds; to which O'Connor built on the sense of regional patriotism by stating that it will be 'a credit to the town of Leeds' and a 'rallying point for the industrious', foregrounding the 'working' identity marker and identifying the group as something to unite like-minded people. The National Charter Associaton (NCA), by contrast, united those who believe in the Charter to a National body, transcending regional divides. The placement of these two notices is also interesting: the 'minimal expence [*sic*]' in joining the NCA pales in comparison to 'all the privileges of membership' of a similar group, as promoted by O'Connor earlier. This was a unique part of these types of 'interest' or activist groups: in order to name oneself as a member there was a joining fee, however small; whether it was a small fee to cover the cost of stationery, as for the NCA, or the larger contributions necessary to join the Land Plan scheme. Even to become a recognised member of a trade union, you would be demonstrating your membership, firstly, by your labour and, secondly, by a subscription: something had to act as proof of membership. This joining fee signified a commitment to the cause of the organisation and by self-identifying as part of such in the Readers and Correspondents' column, the writer became propagandist. One example of this came from a recurring correspondence maintained between Ernest Jones and 'A Member of the Land Plan, Plymouth', in his Legal Questions subsection in 1847. Perhaps it was an editorial choice to answer this particular query of the many received, as a surreptitious advertisement for the proposed scheme.[54] Not only was the group making connections across the country for support of labour disputes or discussion, but it was demonstrating that a united group had made individual sacrifices for the unity of all.

---

54   *Northern Star*, 2 October 1847.

Just as the *Star* was used as a noticeboard by individuals wishing to connect, or for advertisement of group membership, its wide circulation was used on a practical level to keep on top of administrative tasks of associations, such as illustrated previously. Indeed, of the 356 mentions of 'society' in the column over this ten-year period of activity, no fewer than fifty-nine distinct, self-identified 'societies' can be counted, in addition to the eighty individual self-identified 'associations'. Many examples of these groups can be counted not only in the letters to Readers and Correspondents, but within printed subscription lists for charity appeals; such as the 'Universal Suffrage Teetotal Association' of Leeds, who clearly united over a combination of lifestyle choices.[55] These various clubs included many 'working-men's' clubs; an alternative to the 'gentleman's clubs' of the higher echelons of society and acknowledged as such through their particular commitment to 'virtual' and 'improvement' activities as opposed to leisure. 'In' and 'out' groups served a performative function in upholding standards of activism and behaviour within a group, while seeming aloof and desirable to those in the 'out' group. To be a member of the self-identified collectives in the *Northern Star* was to adhere to a lifestyle, be it working-class activism, education and self-improvement, abstention from alcohol and tobacco, a trade, or a region. The community aspect of the *Northern Star* really amounted to more than the specific 'name generator' qualities of individual self-identities. Groups here had specific purposes to represent common interests of trade, of locality and of political or lifestyle group membership. These collectives were clearly identified as separate from individual distinctions and brought the idea of a relational position in their letters. Self-identified collectives wrote to voice a shared opinion within their group and build links with other groups: they sought not to distinguish themselves as individuals, but to connect with others. The use of a group identity furthermore reinforcd a unity of opinion and the many groups who formed the community of the Readers and Correspondents column formed a more structural foundation to the paper's readership. It furthermore demonstrates the communal reading practices of the paper and the times, truly emphasising the community of contributors for, and to, the paper.

What this chapter has illustrated is not only the variety of characters that made up the history of *Northern Star* and, therefore, the Chartist movement in general, but the ways in which the Readers and Correspondents column demonstrated the potential for community building within print media. Unlike a pamphlet, playbill, or flyer, newspapers and periodicals offered space for dialogue within and between literate communities on both sides of production. Not only this, but they offer us a way to see how these readers saw themselves: while more work is needed on the kinds of demographics who made up the *Northern Star* and other Chartist newspapers, through lenses such as gender and age and race, this chapter has shown what kind of values Chartists identified as important to themselves and important that others knew. While scholars are aware of the uses and importance of physical space with protest movements, the opportunity for using printed space to shape one's own identity and communicate with those of a similar political persuasion is undervalued by researchers, although its potential was abundantly clear to the editors, readers and correspondents of the *Northern Star*.

9 The *Freeman's Journal, Evening Packet* and
Saunders's News-Letter: Musical Identities,
Political Identities

The study of newspapers is integral to any historical study of musical life, as newspapers captured the contemporary perspective. Intensive use of newspapers for musicological research enables researchers to trace the activities and developments of musical life through the detailed accounts printed daily. This chapter will examine the musical and political identities of three Dublin newspapers: the *Freeman's Journal, Evening Packet* and *Saunders's News-Letter*. In examining the regular and consistent musical coverage as an example of their published output, the newspapers' idiosyncratic identities may be established. By taking a six-month period (January – June 1840) for intensive investigation, this chapter will demonstrate the role of the press as mediator, facilitator and enabler of activities within Dublin's divergent communities and demonstrate how each newspaper's political identity was reflected in its coverage of music.

Throughout history, music-making has been influenced and intertwined with wider social, cultural and political spheres. Newspapers are unique primary sources for the investigation of these relationships as their descriptions of contemporary culture and the constituent elements of cultural life are presented alongside commentary on the social and political matters which affected them. Newspaper analysis can, therefore, be used to provide a non-musical context to areas of musicological study; for example, Hughes' study of Attwood's *St David's Day* utilised the newspapers to accentuate the introductory narrative of Welsh politics and war in 1800, providing a social and political context for the composition.[1] Newspaper content can also be used to trace social and cultural patterns within musical life. Beausang used an in-depth study of newspapers to construct the narrative of a developing cultural and political identity within Dublin's music community.[2] Likewise, McHale's research on the temperance movement illustrated the value of using newspapers to determine contemporary opinion of a developing social movement.[3] Newspapers were written from a certain viewpoint and for a particular readership and, therefore, play a formative role in the contemporary perception of music-making. Their expression of musical content and the choice of musical subjects covered, together with the manner in which musicians and musical institutions used the newspapers, contributes to a clear comprehension of the dynamic between the musical public and the press. For example, the *Irish Times* published the minutes of the committee meetings of the Dublin Musical Society.[4] These minutes provide a valuable insight into the decision-making processes of the committee and also illustrate how the society considered the *Irish Times* readership to be the audience they drew support from.

Newspaper content in early Victorian Dublin was published anonymously, but was influenced directly by the editors, owners, consumers and advertisers of the newspapers. The content therefore reflects the reciprocal commercial relationship between the newspapers and their readers: the newspaper published content of interest to their readers, who

1   Meirion Hughes, 'Attwood's *St David's Day*: Music, Wales and War in 1800', in Rachel Cowgill and Julian Rushton, eds, *Europe, Empire, and Spectacle in Nineteenth-Century British Music* (Aldershot: Ashgate, 2006), 132–44.

2   Ita Beausang, 'From National Sentiment to Nationalist Movement, 1850–1900', in Michael Murphy and Jan Smaczny, eds, *IMS ix: Music in Nineteenth-Century Ireland* (Dublin: Four Courts Press, 2007), 36–51.

3   Maria McHale, 'Singing and Sobriety: Music and the Temperance Movement in Ireland, 1838–1843', in Murphy and Smaczny, eds, *IMS ix*, 166–86.

4   See Catherine Ferris, 'The Management of Nineteenth-Century Dublin Music Societies in the Public and Private Spheres: the Philharmonic Society and the Dublin Musical Society', in Paul Rodmell, ed., *Music and Institutions in Nineteenth-Century Britain* (London: Ashgate, 2012), 13–32.

in turn read the newspapers because the content appealed to them. While no records exist to illustrate the intentions of the editors or owners and, therefore, the influence they exerted on the content of the newspapers, researchers can ascertain the newspapers' idiosyncratic identities by observing their regular and consistent published output.

While little primary source material is available to assess the possible underlying motives of the newspapers in reporting on the music of early Victorian Dublin, research has sought to examine the musical press in London and Ireland throughout the nineteenth century. Murphy described two types of music journalist in the Irish press during the nineteenth century: the musically knowledgeable 'music critics' and the general, jack-of-all-trades journalist, 'penny-a-liners', who were concerned with recording events rather than judging and commenting on their value.[5] Hogan stated that during the period 1780–1830, 'newspapers did not employ regular music critics, but notices of concerts were written by musical amateurs who were members of their staff'.[6] It was not until later in the century that 'music criticism' by such critics as George Bernard Shaw began to be published. Langley's study of nineteenth-century opera in London in the newspapers specifically addressed the common misunderstanding of nineteenth-century music journalism by avoiding the phrase 'opera criticism', instead opting for 'writing on opera'.[7] She stated that 'criticism', in the modern sense of 'searching analytical discussions of nineteenth-century melodramatic structures', was not what constituted music journalism at the time.[8] This chapter demonstrates that Langley's insight into the coverage of opera in London newspapers can be applied to general music coverage in the early 1840s Dublin and shows that journalists were primarily concerned with reporting on events of interest to their readership.

5   Michael Murphy, 'The Musical Press in Nineteenth-Century Ireland', in Murphy and Smaczny, eds, *IMS* iv, 254

6   Hogan, *Anglo-Irish Music*, 117.

7   Leanne Langley, 'Italian Opera and the English Press, 1836–1856', *Periodica Musica*, 6 (1988), 10.

8   Langley, 'Italian Opera and the English Press', 10.

Murphy's examination of the musical press in Ireland referred to the motives underlying the newspaper press in general, throughout the nineteenth century. Dublin newspaper editors received two complimentary tickets from the manager of the Theatre Royal and Murphy concluded that this practice corrupted the resulting reviews:

> Critics had free access to all performances of Italian opera even when ticket prices were inflated for special occasions. In other words, music criticism was sponsored by the theatre managers and the paying public [...] As tax on advertising revenue was high in the first half of the century, the critic, as an employee of the paper, was under pressure to provide a return on the theatre manager's speculation by way of positive notices. Audiences were frequently reminded of their debt to the theatre managers whose name was kept before the public eye along with that of the state representative, usually the lord lieutenant and his entourage.[9]

However, this assumption is not borne out in this study of the newspapers during the early 1840s. A cursory glance at the negative observations regularly published by the *Saunders's News-Letter*, which was thoroughly dependent on advertising revenue, illustrates that the motives behind the editorial commentaries cannot be readily attributed to this ticket practice. It is perhaps more probable that the promoters supplied the newspapers with tickets in order to facilitate a review, as the newspapers could not afford to pay expensive ticket prices to provide journalists with access to the numerous nightly events.

The early nineteenth-century newspaper press in Dublin was defined by its relationship with the government. While the management of the press in Ireland was primarily the responsibility of the Chief Secretary and Under Secretary (although the Lord Lieutenant is also known to have contributed), the Chief Secretary's parliamentary responsibilities in London placed much of the practical responsibility with the Under Secretary, who was based year-round in Dublin Castle.[10] Newspapers during

9   Brian Inglis, *The Freedom of the Press In Ireland 1784–1841* (London: Faber and Faber, 1954), 123; Murphy, 'Musical Press', 254.
10   A. Aspinall, *Politics and the Press c. 1780–1850* (London: Home & Val Thal, 1949), 264.

this period each came to be defined by their allegiance or opposition to the administration in Dublin Castle, ranging from the staunch unionists to the liberals who advocated Catholic rights.[11] The government manipulated the press, both overtly and indirectly, creating a subservient relationship based on corruption.[12] In return for support of the administration's political ideology (and this of course changed with the election of each administration), a newspaper would receive financial assistance. Direct subsidies were made to the newspaper owners in the form of 'pensions' and 'allowances', terminology applied to justify payments as something other than bribery. These were financed by the government's £5,000 per annum 'secret service fund' and £4,000 savings of the Civil List, which were available for ministers to spend without accountability.[13] Newspapers in favour with the Castle would also receive the government's copies of the London newspapers (the expresses), thirty to forty hours earlier than the other newspapers received copies, establishing them as the most current source of news in the city and creating a dependency which the government could take advantage of.[14]

This aspect of the early Victorian Irish press – the corruption, political influence and dependent relationships with the administration – provides the context for an examination of the individual newspapers utilised in this study. The following section will successively assess the developing historical identities of the *Freeman's Journal*, the *Evening Packet* and *Saunders's News-Letter* and will, in the context of those histories, ascertain the musical identities of the newspapers as defined by their own published outputs. Given the considerable level of music coverage detailed in the press, a representative subset of six months (January to June 1840) has been selected for the purposes of this in-depth assessment of the individual newspapers' musical identities.

11	Stephen J. Brown, 'The Dublin Newspaper Press: A Bird's Eye View, 1659–1916', *Studies: An Irish Quarterly Review*, 25/97 (1936), 112.

12	Aspinall, *Politics and the Press*, 107–25, 134–47.

13	Aspinall, *Politics and the Press*, 109.

14	Aspinall, *Politics and the Press*, 148, 180.

The *Freeman's Journal* was published over a period of 161 years, although, as Brown asserted, 'so radical were the changes that took place at various periods in that long career, that its continuity was rather one of title than of anything else'.[15] It was established as a daily newspaper in 1763 by three Dublin tradesmen as the *Public Register or the Freeman's Journal*.[16] It soon became associated with the politician and pamphleteer Charles Lucas and developed an extreme Protestant character. However, by 1770, the *Freeman's Journal* had become a moderate supporter of Catholic relief and emphatic advocate of the nationalist cause, supporting the establishment of Henry Grattan's Irish parliament.[17] In 1783, the government purchased the newspaper and gave it to Francis Higgins (nicknamed the 'Sham Squire').[18] Through subsidies and pensions, the government paid Higgins to develop the newspaper into its mouthpiece, utilising a feigned sympathy with the nationalist cause in order to undermine it.[19] On his death in 1802, Higgins bequeathed the newspaper to Frances Tracy (speculated to be his daughter or the mother of his child).[20] Upon her marriage to Philip Whitfield Harvey, the paper was passed to him. Harvey continued to receive Higgins' government allowance and, during the Arthur Wellesley administration (1807–1809), he supported the government 'ineffectively, in obscurity', gaining access to the expresses only for a short period.[21] However, upon the appointment of William Wellesley-Pole as Chief Secretary in 1809, the attitude of the administration changed. Wellesley-Pole was unsympathetic to the Catholic cause and disagreed with the tactic of paying newspapers

15 Brown, 'Dublin Newspaper Press', 110–11.

16 Richard Robert Madden, *The History of Irish Periodical Literature from the End of the 17th to the Middle of the 19th Century* (London: T. C. Newby, 1867), II, 374; Laurel Brake and Marysa Demoor, eds, *Dictionary of Nineteenth-Century Journalism in Great Britain and Ireland* (London: The British Library, 2009), 230.

17 Madden, *History of Irish Periodical Literature*, II, 392; Brown, 'Dublin Newspaper Press', 111; Brake and Demoor, *Dictionary of Nineteenth-Century Journalism*, 230.

18 Brown, 'Dublin Newspaper Press', 111.

19 Brown, 'Dublin Newspaper Press', 111.

20 C. J. Woods, 'Higgins, Francis ("Sham Squire")', in James McGuire and James Quinn, eds, *Dictionary of Irish Biography*, <http://dib.cambridge.org/viewReadPage.do?articleId=a3999>, accessed 26 June 2018.

21 Aspinall, *Politics and the Press*, 116; Inglis, *Freedom of the Press*, 116.

for superficial support.[22] John Foster, the chancellor for the exchequer for Ireland, raised the advertisement duty and the *Freeman's Journal* was one of many newspapers which were 'cut adrift from the Castle, independent in spite of themselves'.[23] Despite this, Harvey maintained his pension and the *Freeman's Journal* took a moderate opposition position.[24] During the Robert Peel administration (1812–1818), which proactively sought to eliminate the opposition press entirely through excessive taxation and prosecutions, the *Freeman's Journal* exercised 'extreme editorial caution'.[25] Dublin Castle correspondence confirms that they were not able to manipulate Harvey, saying 'I fear he is too rich and we too poor to enter into terms'.[26]

The 1820s, while the moderate Marquis of Wellesley was Lord Lieutenant, saw a rise in the 'independent press', working without such government influence.[27] Subsidies (both direct and indirect) were reduced and there was little fear of prosecution.[28] New newspapers were initiated in support of the Catholic Association and Daniel O'Connell, but newspapers like the *Freeman's Journal*, which tried to 'advocate Catholic claims without committing themselves to unqualified support', were criticised as waverers, and readership suffered.[29] When Philip Whitfield Harvey died in 1826, the newspaper passed to his daughter, transferring upon her marriage to Henry Grattan (son of the parliamentarian), as part of her dowry.[30] During his ownership, the newspaper set a liberal pro-Catholic tone, printing full proceedings of the Catholic Association.[31] However, Francis Leveson-Gower, the Chief Secretary (1828–1830), attempted to

22 Inglis, *Freedom of the Press*, 120.
23 Inglis, *Freedom of the Press*, 128, 121.
24 Inglis, *Freedom of the Press*, 121.
25 Inglis, *Freedom of the Press*, 135–44, 150.
26 Aspinall, *Politics and the Press*, 116.
27 Inglis, *Freedom of the Press*, 166.
28 Inglis, *Freedom of the Press* 178.
29 Inglis, *Freedom of the Press* 176.
30 Felix M. Larkin, 'The Dog in the Night-Time: The *Freeman's Journal*, the Irish Parliamentary Party and the Empire, 1875–1919', in Simon J. Potter, ed., *Newspapers and Empire in Ireland and Britain: Reporting the British Empire c. 1857–1921* (Dublin: Four Courts Press, 2004), 110; Aspinall, *Politics and the Press*, 116.
31 Brown, 'Dublin Newspaper Press', 111.

dissuade the radical press by punishing liberals and Henry Grattan was prosecuted for libel (although he never went to jail).[32]

In 1831, the newspaper was purchased by its first Catholic editor, Patrick Lavelle, who emphatically supported Catholic Emancipation and the Repeal of the Union.[33] After publishing a letter of O'Connell's, the *Freeman's Journal* was described as 'the most violent of the Dublin papers' by the Chief Secretary Edward Stanley, who demanded its prosecution. Unfortunately for Stanley, a Castle newspaper printed the same letter on the same day and he was obliged to prosecute it also. The embarrassment resulted in the dismissal of both cases on a 'technicality'.[34] During the 1830s, the *Freeman's Journal* struggled, as an independent newspaper, to sustain commercial prosperity.[35] However, it was in a strong position to resist government manipulation due to its large advertisement revenue.[36] In 1840, O'Connell praised the *Freeman's Journal*, engaging it as a possible ally, and, in 1841, the newspaper was purchased by a group of O'Connell supporters, including the Protestant John Gray, who later became sole proprietor.[37] Gray was a moderate nationalist and supporter of the Repeal of the Union.[38] Three generations of the Gray family ran the *Freeman's Journal* for the subsequent fifty years and Brake and Demoor state that it 'reflected mainstream moderate nationalist opinion, describing the approach of Catholic Emancipation (1829) as "the triumph of freedom", but opposing Young Ireland in the 1840s and Fenianism in the 1860s'.[39]

It is interesting, in this context, to examine the musical profile and characteristics of *Freeman's Journal* from a study of the six-month period from January to June 1840. The primary, music-related focus of the *Freeman's Journal* was on the advertising, reviewing and previewing

32   Inglis, *Freedom of the Press*, 188–9.
33   Inglis, *Freedom of the Press*, 240.
34   Inglis, *Freedom of the Press*, 200.
35   Inglis, *Freedom of the Press*, 206.
36   Inglis, *Freedom of the Press*, 151.
37   Inglis, *Freedom of the Press*, 222; Brown, 'Dublin Newspaper Press', 118.
38   Brake and Demoor, *Dictionary of Nineteenth-Century Journalism*, 231.
39   Brake and Demoor, *Dictionary of Nineteenth-Century Journalism*, 230.

of operatic, concert and theatrical performances in the Theatre Royal, the Rotundo and the Theatre Royal, Abbey Street. The main concert series during this period were by the child prodigy Rossini Collins; the virtuoso Theodore Döhler; a new series of classical chamber concerts by Monsieur Rudersdorff; and three concerts by the city's leading performers and teachers, Henry Bussell, Samuel J. Pigott and Mrs Joseph Elliott.[40] A comparison with similar coverage published in other newspapers reveals that the *Freeman's Journal*'s coverage of the city's concert activities was incomplete and demonstrates that the concert promoters did not intend it to be the primary vehicle for making these concerts known to the public. On numerous occasions advertisements would be placed for one concert in a series, without reference to the others.[41] Opera performances were advertised, previewed and reviewed more frequently than other types of musical entertainment.

The formulaic style of the *Freeman's Journal*'s reviews of musical performances was always cautious and moderate, and the following is typical:

> The four 'Alpine Singers', who have succeeded in drawing such crowded houses to the theatre during the week, appeared again on yesterday evening in a national, vocal and instrumental concert, and gave several beautiful songs and pieces of their native Swiss music with considerable pathos and skill. 'The Frozen Alps', by Madame Schmidt, and the 'Tyrolienne', by Herr Augustine, were very interesting solos, and sung in a manner which elicited loud encores from the entire audience. Some extremely difficult variations on a theme of Paganini, which were performed on the single flageolet by Herr Hellwig, also appeared to us as particularly beautiful. The concerto pieces were 'The Snow on the Alps', 'The Swiss boy', and 'Recollections of our Native Land'.[42]

The attendance was always commented on (usually saying it was 'well-attended') and any important attendees would be listed, with their reactions

---

40   *Saunders's News-Letter*, 4 March 1840, 3; *Freeman's Journal*, 25 May 1840, 1; 31 March 1840, 2; 22 April 1840, 1; 8 May 1840, 1; 25 April 1840, 1.

41   The third of Mons. Rudersdorff's classical chamber concerts was advertised, without mention of the preceding two concerts in the series, *Freeman's Journal*, 31 March 1840, 2; Rossini Collins' 'second and last' concert was mentioned, without reference to her first, *Freeman's Journal*, 13 March 1840, 1.

42   *Freeman's Journal*, 7 March 1840, 2.

noted. The repertoire would be reported, together with superficial commentary on the manner in which it was performed. The use of adjectives was formulaic and restrained, and the calling for encores was always noted.[43]

During the period, the *Freeman's Journal* specifically highlighted the Irish performers and composers with pride. Of Mr Franks (the Irish-born principal tenor of the Theatres Royal Drury Lane and St James), it commented that 'as a vocalist, with some faults, we most admire him – as an Irishman, we are proud of him'.[44] Similarly, the newspaper employed an uncharacteristic verbosity in describing Michael William Balfe's ability as an Irish composer and performer:

> One of the healthiest evidences of a proper feeling of nationality in any community is a due appreciation of the work of those whose genius sheds a lustre on the land that gave him birth. The people of Dublin will, we trust, this evening, by an overflowing theatre, make a fit acknowledgment to the talents of their countryman [...] Justly proud of their national music, as Irishmen have always been, they owe it even to themselves to record the industry of him whose genius has added to the honours transmitted to us from those of old, and who infusing into the creations of modern art all the soul thrilling sweetness of our ancient strains, has won for himself the title of the Irish Italian.[45]

Due to its independent, yet pro-Catholic stance and wide readership, the *Freeman's Journal* was the main source of information on Catholic activity in the city. It featured unparalleled coverage of music in Catholic churches or concerts for the benefit of institutions run by Catholic orders. It noted the music performed during the consecration of new churches and 'nuns' ordination ceremonies, but, in particular, the coverage comprised

---

43 Examples of such usage can be found in Catherine Ferris, 'The Use of Newspapers as a Source for Musicological Research: A Case Study of Dublin Musical Life 1840–1844', PhD thesis, National University of Ireland Maynooth, 2011. See, in particular, Part II – 'Register of Musical Data on the Music Societies in the *Freeman's Journal*, the *Evening Packet* and the *Saunders's News-Letter*, 1840–1844' and examples on 258 ('Promenade Concert'), 274 ('New Music Hall – Promenade Concert') and 429 ('Philharmonic Society').

44 *Freeman's Journal*, 6 February 1840, 1; 14 February 1840, 2.

45 *Freeman's Journal*, 13 March 1840, 2.

advertisements, previews and reviews of charity events in the city: charity sermons (with choral performances) for the benefit of schools, orphanages, asylums and hospitals which took place in Catholic churches throughout the city.[46] Significantly, published descriptions of these essentially non-musical events refer to the repertoire and performers involved.[47] While it is unadvisable to imply an individual's religious beliefs due to their performances in such events, particularly due to the growing religious toleration in the city (and the attendance of Protestants at events in Catholic churches particularly), it is interesting to establish religious associations of such performers, as it allows conclusions to be drawn when they are referred to in other seemingly secular activities.[48] It is, furthermore, noteworthy that the pedagogical advertisements in the *Freeman's Journal* (which were a rarity, only three appearing during this period) were placed by Catholic musicians.[49]

Music trade advertisements in the *Freeman's Journal* were very limited, occasionally noting newly published works, such as Edward Bunting's *Ancient Music of Ireland* and a temperance song by Haydn Corri, dedicated to the Rev. Father Theobald Mathew.[50] Although the pro-Catholic identity of the *Freeman's Journal* would seem to align it with the temperance movement (which was multi-denominational, yet was supported most

---

46 *Freeman's Journal*, 21 January 1841, 1; 28 August 1841, 3; 9 March 1840, 1; 20 March 1840, 1; 22 January 1840, 1; 30 January 1840, 1; 29 April 1840, 2; 19 May 1840, 1; 7 January 1840, 1; 1 January 1840, 4; 18 March 1840, 2; 30 June 1840, 1.

47 *Freeman's Journal*, 30 January 1840, 1; 25 January 1840, 2; 15 June 1840, 3; 6 June 1840, 1; 30 January 1840, 1; 24 August 1840, 2.

48 Derek Collins, 'Music in Dublin, 1800–1848', in Richard Pine and Charles Acton, eds, *To Talent Alone, The Royal Irish Academy of Music 1848–1998* (Dublin: Gill & Macmillan, 1998), 15; Brian Boydell, 'Music 1700–1850', in T. W. Moody and W. E. Vaughan, eds, *ANHI iv: Eighteenth-Century Ireland 1691–1800* (Oxford: Clarendon Press, 1986), 608.

49 A personal advertisement by a Catholic governess offering to teach music and advertisements for classes by Haydn Corri (organist and choir conductor of the Church of the Conception, Marlborough Street), *Freeman's Journal*, 22 February 1840, 1–2; P. W. Gormley (organist and choir conductor of St Andrew's Church, Westland Row), *Freeman's Journal*, 6 May 1840, 1.

50 *Freeman's Journal*, 26 June 1840, 1; 6 April 1840, 2.

vehemently by the largely Catholic rural Irish communities), it also printed advertisements for public houses, one of which (the Ship Tavern, Coffee Room and Hotel at 5 Lower Abbey Street) specifically mentioned its daily musical performances by Mr Quinn, the 'celebrated Irish Harper'.[51]

The *Freeman's Journal* featured a considerable number of events (with musical elements) associated with the Lord Lieutenant, the representative of the British monarch. This correlates with the established political identity of the newspaper: pro-Catholic, yet subservient to the Castle and eager to please in order to protect the income generated by Castle-funded advertisements and avoid potential Castle-initiated legal action. These events included balls in Dublin Castle, festivities in Phoenix Park, events celebrating the Battle of Waterloo and the Queen's marriage.[52] It recounted that both military bands and non-military quadrille and waltz bands (directed by Dulang, Kelly and Scully) performed the music at such events.[53] Interestingly, Dulang personally utilised the *Freeman's Journal* to advertise his services for public and private balls, illustrating the perception that wealthy aristocratic organisers of such events comprised the readership of the newspaper.[54] This highlights the seemingly contrasting position that the newspaper maintained in supporting both the Catholic cause and Dublin Castle. It seems from further examination of the newspaper that its position was in support of the monarchy, rather than the administration, as can be seen from the transcription of 'A Loyal Song for 1840':

> What might, but a King's constitutional sway.
> Can dictate to faction, and make it obey?
> With equal abhorrence may England eschew
> The rule of the many – the yoke of the few –
> Ye Chartists, ye Tories, ye Commons, ye Lords,
> Ye Churchmen, ye Book-men, ye men of big words,
> Stand, stand by the balance of power, nor dream

51   *Freeman's Journal*, 9 May 1840, 1.
52   *Freeman's Journal*, 2 March 1840, 2; 26 May 1840, 3; 19 June 1840, 3; 11 February 1840, 3.
53   *Freeman's Journal*, 20 February 1840, 2; 17 March 1840, 2; 18 March 1840, 1; 22 February 1840, 1; 19 June 1840, 3; 24 February 1840, 2.
54   *Freeman's Journal*, 6 January 1840, 1.

The septre [*sic*] of England can ere strick the beam!
No! millions espouse the Queen's cause as their own,
With the old English feeling that stands by the throne.[55]

The *Freeman's Journal*'s coverage of aristocratic events was confined to those which took place in Dublin Castle. The general, everyday events attended by the aristocracy and upper middle classes were rarely featured, for example, occasional references to the pleasure garden entertainments at Portobello and the Rotundo, in the style of Ranelagh or Vauxhall in Britain, featuring concerts and background music performed by military bands.[56] Activities of the music societies, which were considered the dominion of upper middle-class Protestants, were not advertised or reviewed. The newspaper even printed a letter to the editor which expressed dissatisfaction with the establishment of Trinity College's University Choral Society and its acceptance by the university board.[57] It is interesting that the author chose to place this letter in the Catholic *Freeman's Journal* as all other advertisements, notices and reviews of University Choral Society activities featured in the Protestant *Saunders's News-Letter* and *Evening Packet*. Perhaps he perceived the newspaper as a means to rally support from outside of the University's allies.

This examination of six months of musical activity published in the *Freeman's Journal* illustrates that it was primarily concerned with reporting on charity events, opera and theatrical performances. Concert promoters in the city did not utilise it as the primary medium to communicate with their consumers. It provides valuable information on elements of Catholic music-making in the city during the period, particularly the incidental music performed during religious events, together with modest coverage of the activities of the Lord Lieutenant and aristocracy. The musical reviews were uncritically positive, moderate and inoffensive, focusing on the 'who, what, where' elements of performances, while also highlighting any nationalist elements.

55 *Freeman's Journal*, 4 January 1840, 2.
56 *Freeman's Journal*, 20 April 1840, 2; 15 May 1840, 1.
57 *Freeman's Journal*, 10 January 1840, 3.

The *Evening Packet* (1806–1862), originally published as the *Correspondent*, was founded by the Lord Lieutenant (the Duke of Bedford) as a Dublin Castle newspaper and was 'endowed with all the advantages the Castle could bestow'.[58] It was granted £100 annually from secret service money and proclamations fund, while also receiving sole access to the expresses.[59] Published three times a week, it quickly became established as the most current source of news in the city. The proprietors of the *Correspondent* believed that the government, as founders of the newspaper, were obliged to maintain its financial buoyancy and protect the proprietors from incurring personal debt.[60] However, during 1807, Chief Secretary Arthur Wellesley permitted the *Freeman's Journal* joint access to the exprenses for a short period. After complaints from the *Correspondent* (which threatened to become 'less to the Castle's taste'), the *Freeman's Journal's* access was revoked.[61] The *Correspondent* had the administration in such a manipulative stranglehold that, although the expresses were specifically for the Lord Lieutenant's use, he conceded that the newspaper could have first choice of the selection which was sent to him daily.[62] The resulting market dominance and weekly circulation figure of 7,500 emphasised the effect of the administration's explicit corruption to such an extent that concern was raised in parliament. The administration retorted that it was 'not practicable to send one set of papers to more than one place' and that the *Correspondent*, as the only evening paper, should receive them. Despite the feebleness of this response, the matter went no further.[63]

The *Correspondent* remained staunchly pro-Castle until William Wellesley-Pole became Chief Secretary in 1809.[64] He refused to pay newspapers for hollow superficial support and instead founded the *Patriot*

58   Inglis, *Freedom of the Press*, 239, 115.
59   Inglis, *Freedom of the Press*, 115.
60   Aspinall, *Politics and the Press*, 118.
61   Inglis, *Freedom of the Press*, 117.
62   Aspinall, *Politics and the Press*, 148.
63   Aspinall, *Politics and the Press*, 180.
64   Aspinall, *Politics and the Press*, 118.

to represent administration policies.[65] The *Correspondent* was practically forced into independence.[66] This break was further driven by Wellesley-Pole's unsympathetic position on the growing Catholic rights movement, which was supported by many of the *Correspondent*'s subscribers.[67] In the face of growing press opposition, the administration increased the advertisement tax and, although this had little effect on the *Correspondent*, the newspaper published vehement attacks on the 'tyranny of the tax-gatherer'.[68] The government (unsuccessfully) prosecuted the newspaper for libel.[69] During the Peel administration (1812–1818), the *Correspondent* returned to its previous position as a Castle newspaper. It received £2,640 a year in pensions and for the publication of both proclamations and government advertisements. This figure was greater than that received by any other newspaper including the *Patriot*.[70] However, the newspaper was noticeably less effusive in its support for the government than previously.[71]

The 1820s were a difficult period for the *Correspondent*, as the administration under the Marquis of Wellesley reduced the secret service fund and government advertisements.[72] As the *Correspondent* had built its foundation on such content, its reduction caused circulation figures to decrease dramatically.[73] During this period, there was significant internal division in government over the issue of Catholic rights and the Castle newspapers aligned with different Tory factions, the *Correspondent* supporting the 'conservative' Tories and the *Patriot* supporting the 'liberal' (pro-Catholic Emancipation) Tories.[74] Peel almost stopped the *Correspondent*'s government subsidies because of this, stating

---

65   Inglis, *Freedom of the Press*, 124.

66   Inglis, *Freedom of the Press*, 122.

67   Inglis, *Freedom of the Press*, 120.

68   Christopher Morash, *A History of the Media in Ireland* (Cambridge: Cambridge University Press, 2010), 66.

69   Inglis, *Freedom of the Press*, 132.

70   Inglis, *Freedom of the Press*, 145.

71   Aspinall, *Politics and the Press*, 190.

72   Inglis, *Freedom of the Press*, 178.

73   Inglis, *Freedom of the Press*, 178.

74   Inglis, *Freedom of the Press*, 182–3.

'if the *Correspondent* (which paper I never see) does abuse Mr Canning and other members of the administration, I think that abuse an excellent reason for withdrawing from it the favour of the Government'.[75] However, this withdrawal did not materialise.[76]

The *Correspondent* was renamed the *Evening Packet and Correspondent* in 1828 and re-established itself as an independent Protestant newspaper, with the stated aim of 'renewing the quest for ascendancy subscribers with a more vigorous opposition to emancipation'.[77] Although the Chief Secretary regularly threatened to withdraw financial support, it retained a small subsidy of £700 a year, without giving anything in return.[78] The administration reduced the proclamations and secret service money to all newspapers,[79] yet the *Evening Packet* continued to receive its pensions and government advertising. In 1840, it was acquired by the gothic novelist and journalist Joseph Sheridan Le Fanu at the same time as he took control of the *Warden* newspaper and became part-proprietor of the *Dublin Evening Mail*.[80] It continued to prosper as a tri-weekly newspaper, supported by the wealthy Protestant ascendancy and, in 1862, it merged into the *Dublin Evening Mail*.[81]

The *Evening Packet* presented a balanced, if modest, coverage of musical activities in Dublin, featuring concerts, auctions of musical goods, literature, trade and music lessons. Of particular interest are the reports of music at essentially non-musical events (such as dinners and balls), which provide insight into the audience of the newspaper.[82] One such report was published

75   Aspinall, *Politics and the Press*, 144.
76   Inglis, *Freedom of the Press*, 182–3.
77   Inglis, *Freedom of the Press*, 239, 183.
78   Inglis, *Freedom of the Press*, 239, 183.
79   Inglis, *Freedom of the Press*, 183
80   'Joseph Le Fanu', in *Probert Encyclopedia* <http://www.probertencyclopaedia.com/ cgi-bin/res.pl?keyword=Packet&offset=0>, accessed 2 November 2010; Robert Welch and Bruce Stewart, eds, *The Oxford Companion to Irish Literature* (Oxford: Oxford University Press, 1996), 306.
81   Inglis, *Freedom of the Press*, p. 206; Brake and Demoor, *Dictionary of Nineteenth-Century Journalism*, 181.
82   *Evening Packet*, 11 January 1840, 1; 22 February 1840, 1.

on the anniversary dinner of the Irish Metropolitan Conservative Society, a leading Dublin Tory organisation that encapsulated the complex political and religious dynamics of the time, by being a 'distinguished loyal Protestant Society', which also supported the Repeal of the Union.[83] Toasts during this dinner, which were followed by songs or airs, were expressly political: 'The glorious, pious, and immortal memory of King William', 'A speedy dismissal to her Majesty's Ministers' and 'The Lord Mayor and Loyal Corporation of Dublin, and may their rights and privileges never be transferred to a Popish body'. It was noted that the air of *The Boyne Water* was performed twice and other songs were performed by Dr John Smith and the Messrs. Magrath, Brooks and Sapio.[84] A report on a meeting of the society also referred to a proposal to erect a music hall in Dawson Street, 'in order that the Conservatives of Dublin, and Ireland, should have a place in which they could meet; for they all knew that they could not hold their meetings in the Round-room if the Corporation Bill passed'.[85] Although no further references to this proposed development were published, the report provides a valuable insight into the practical issues of music-making perceived by that group of Conservative Dubliners. The *Evening Packet* also transcribed proceedings of the High Sheriff Tomlinson's first official dinner, held in Radley's Hotel, Dame Street. Musical elements again featured between toasts, which were generally patriotic.[86] Events of the Freemasons were also featured, including a dedication of their new hall in the Commercial Buildings (with processional music and anthems) and an advertisement for the Masonic theatrical company, which noted the performance of a Masonic version of the national anthem.[87] It is apparent from the type of events covered that the *Evening Packet*'s audience comprised the upper middle and

---

83   *Evening Packet*, 11 January 1840, 1; Joseph Spence, 'Isaac Butt, Irish Nationality and the Conditional Defence of the Union, 1833–1870', in D. George Boyce and Alan O'Day, eds, *Defenders of the Union: A Survey of British and Irish Unionism since 1801* (London: Routledge, 2001), 68.

84   *Evening Packet*, 11 January 1840, 1.

85   *Evening Packet*, 10 March 1840, 2.

86   *Evening Packet*, 16 January 1840, 4.

87   *Evening Packet*, 24 March 1840, 1; 4 June 1840, 1.

aristocratic classes and this is consistent with its established political identity as a supporter of the Castle. The details published of the musical elements within fundamentally non-musical events provide valuable insights
into the role that music played in the everyday musical life of those classes.

Characteristically, therefore, the *Evening Packet* featured advertisements
and reviews for the balls in Dublin Castle and the Rotundo, events which
were previously noted in reference to coverage by the *Freeman's Journal*.[88]
Again targeting the organisers of these events, the quadrille and band
master Kavenagh placed advertisements in the *Evening Packet*, similar to
those published by Dulang in the *Freeman's Journal*.[89] These advertisements
infer a wealthy readership of the newspaper, comprised of the organisers
of state balls and those who were in financial positions to patronise musicians to perform in their homes.

Reviews of operatic, concert and music society performances featured
often in the *Evening Packet*, despite a lack of corresponding advertisements.
This suggests that the promoters of such events did not consider the *Evening
Packet* to be either a worthwhile financial investment (in comparison to
newspapers of higher circulation), or a useful or necessary medium between
them and their potential audience. Particularly notable are the rare reviews
of smaller and more private concerts, which were not referred to by the other
newspapers, specifically those held in Mrs Allen's Academy and Morrison's
Hotel.[90] The typical style of review in the *Evening Packet* is similar in its
formulaic content to the *Freeman's Journal*, but is distinctly more verbose
in its use of adjectives. This is evident in the following review of Monsieur
Theodore Döhler's performance:

> He is easy, polished, graceful, and impressive; and, after pouring forth a flood of
> intricate and involved passages, reverts to some simple melody with an earnestness
> that shows his soul is wrapped up in the subject. His playing appeals to the heart;
> and it is this peculiarity which more especially calls for our admiration.[91]

---

88   *Evening Packet*, 17 March 1840, 3; 22 February 1840, 1.
89   *Evening Packet*, 17 March 1840, 1.
90   *Evening Packet*, 11 April 1840, 3; 23 January 1840, 4.
91   *Evening Packet*, 23 May 1840, 3; Further examples in Ferris, 'The Use of Newspapers
     as a Source for Musicological Research', Part II 'Register of Musical Data on

It is important to establish this expressive use of adjectives as an archetype of the language used by the *Evening Packet* and this informs a comprehensive understanding of its editorial style. Döhler's performance (like all others reviewed) cannot, therefore, be interpreted as remarkable, as the language suggests, but rather as generally positive. The newspaper's positive outlook extended to its 'negative' commentary, which tended towards unsympathetic remarks, rather than direct admonishment. This is evident from the example of Signor Antonio Sapio's annual concert, which featured the band of the 97th regiment: the *Evening Packet* meekly commented that the band was 'rather too harsh for a concert-room'.[92]

The composition of the *Evening Packet*'s audience can be inferred from the patronising tone of its editorial commentary. It frequently remarked on the behaviour of the lower classes who were seated in the cheap seats ('the gods') of concert auditoria, particularly focusing on the etiquette of encoring. Of Mrs Waylett's performance, it noted that 'the applause was general, and the "gods" were unconscionable enough to insist on a repetition of each song, with which demand the fair vocalist complied with great good humour'.[93] During John Braham's engagement it remarked:

> At the conclusion of the opera there was a call for the veteran Braham, and another for Miss M'Mahon. The call, however, was evidently a got-up thing by a few persons, who, for the present, Terry, Bob, &c., shall be nameless [...] The object, we know, is to have the call reported in the papers, in order to give an artificial *eclat* to the performances, but the practice has been so shockingly abused of late that we can scarcely tolerate it when well-timed.[94]

---

the Music Societies in the *Freeman's Journal*, the *Evening Packet* and *Saunders's News-Letter*, 1840–1844', include 385 ('Metropolitan Choral Society'); 444–5 ('University Choral Society'); 451–2 ('Theatre Royal').

92   *Evening Packet*, 30 April 1840, 3. Such formulaic reviewing styles might, of course, allow a journalist to construct an account of the events from an advertisement or programme without attending. However, an indirect reference in an *Evening Packet* review to a change in the programme from the advertisement suggests that this practice was not common among *Evening Packet* reviewers. *Evening Packet*, 2 May 1840, 3.

93   *Evening Packet*, 28 January 1840, 3.

94   *Evening Packet*, 24 March 1840, 3.

The music trade advertisements in the *Evening Packet* were dominated by the music warehouse of Marcus Moses. He regularly placed long advertisements listing the contents of the warehouse in detail, including pianos of all makes, flutes, harps, guitars, seraphines and strings.[95] Moses also placed advertisements promoting newly published sheet music associated with recent popular performances in the city. This latter practice was also employed by M'Cullagh's 'Piano-Forte and Harp Warerooms', which often placed advertisements in this newspaper.[96] Although individual advertisements of new publications were common, editorial commentary on those publications was not. A notable exception to this was Hodges and Smith's publication of Edward Bunting's *Ancient Music of Ireland*. This review appears to have been written by a different author than the usual concert reviews as it featured in the 'Literature' section of the newspaper and illustrated the author's knowledge of similar publications and the contentious issue of authenticity in the transmission of historical Irish sources:

> The editor of 'The Ancient Music Of Ireland', has proceeded; and rejecting with scorn all modernised versions of our island melodies, he presents us with the varied strains of love and war, of woe and whiskey, in such a sort, that if his arrangements want that degree of polish which was so discernible in those of Sir John Stevenson, they are far superior to the latter in character, in originality of expression, in force, and in what the cognoscenti term, rhythm.[97]

Transcriptions of songs and hymns were printed in the *Evening Packet*, but unlike the *Freeman's Journal*, it seems they were included for their literary value rather than any underlying political message.

A number of advertisements made reference to the military, both in the performance of military music and as readers of the newspapers. M'Neile utilised the newspaper to inform the 'Commanding Officers of Regiments, his Friends and the Public' that his Military Musical Instrument Manufactory was moving premises.[98] There was also significant coverage of

95   *Evening Packet*, 4 January 1840, 3.
96   *Evening Packet*, 19 August 1841, 1.
97   *Evening Packet*, 27 June 1840, 3.
98   *Evening Packet*, 5 March 1840, 1.

military band performances in the newspaper, both as background music and in concerts in the pleasure gardens of Portobello and at the balls hosted by the Lord Lieutenant at Dublin Castle, the Commander of the Forces' celebration of the anniversary of Waterloo and St Patrick's Day celebrations.[99] This suggests that the readership of the *Evening Packet* included the distinguished ranks of the military based in Dublin.

During this period, the *Evening Packet* featured twelve advertisements for public and private auctions, which included musical goods. These auctions primarily comprised the effects of wealthy deceased gentlemen, including the late Judge Baron Smith.[100] Their residences were situated in many of the fashionable areas of the city and suburbs: Grafton Street, Fitzwilliam Square, Merrion Square, Mountjoy Square, North Frederick Street, Rathmines, Rathgar and Rathfarnham.[101] These auctions underline the social status of the *Evening Packet*'s readership, both as consumers of musical goods and as representative of the deceased's community. The newspaper, so closely associated with Dublin Castle, was read by the upper middle and aristocratic classes and so provides valuable and rare information on the social environment of the Irish urban elite, with its focus on military music-making, small concerts and the centrality of music in non-musical gatherings.

Saunders's News-Letter was a continuation of the *News-letter* published by R. Reilly in 1736, which merged with James Esdall's *News Letter* in 1746. On Esdall's death in 1755, it was purchased by Henry Saunders and became known as *Saunders's News-Letter*.[102] It was originally published thrice weekly, but became a daily paper in June 1777.[103] The political allegiances of the newspaper were alluded to in 1791, when the editor, James Potts, was

99   *Evening Packet*, 28 April 1840, 3; 21 May 1840, 1; 17 March 1840, 3; 20 June 1840, 3; 17 March 1840, 2.

100 *Evening Packet*, 11 April 1840, 3.

101 *Evening Packet*, 9 May 1840, 3; 18 April 1840, 1; 2 January 1840, 1; 16 May 1840, 1; 25 April 1840, 1; 13 June 1840, 1; 14 May 1840, 1; 11 April 1840, 3.

102 Brown, 'Dublin Newspaper Press', 110; Madden, *History of Irish Periodical Literature*, II, 254.

103 Madden, *History of Irish Periodical Literature*, II, 255.

physically attacked by the editor of the *Dublin Journal* (a zealous Castle newspaper) for publishing 'disloyal and seditious sentiments'.[104] In 1793, the newspaper was renamed *Saunders's News-Letter and Daily Advertiser*.[105] On James Potts' death in 1796, it was taken over by John Potts and the family continued to run the newspaper for the next seventy-nine years on 'Tory and genuine Protestant principles'.[106] During the 1798 rebellion, the advertisement space was reduced in favour of coverage of the Irish news and the newspaper's thoroughly hostile accounts are considered to be an important source for government and Orangemen's attitudes towards the rebellion.[107]

During the nineteenth century, *Saunders's News-Letter* became defined by its commercial and business content, focusing on advertisements and its editorial tone was moderate and neutral, generally avoiding controversy.[108] Its articles were frequently plagiarised from other newspapers and even those on Irish matters were extracted directly from the London press.[109] The editors claimed that this practice allowed them to fill the newspaper cheaply with high quality articles.[110] More importantly, this enabled the newspaper to propagate the appearance of neutrality and it was considered by the public and by the government to be independent.[111] However, Madden maintained that the 'moderate tone' of *Saunders's News-Letter* during the early nineteenth century was a façade used to manipulate readers according to the paper's underlying political allegiances.[112]

Saunders's News-Letter's 'independent' status, which was facilitated by its significant advertisement income, enabled it to retain financial

104 Madden, *History of Irish Periodical Literature*, II, 259.
105 Brake and Demoor, *Dictionary of Nineteenth-Century Journalism*, 558.
106 Brake and Demoor, *Dictionary of Nineteenth-Century Journalism*, 558; Madden, *History of Irish Periodical Literature*, II, 259.
107 Madden, *History of Irish Periodical Literature*, II, 259.
108 Brown, 'Dublin Newspaper Press', 110.
109 Brake and Demoor, *Dictionary of Nineteenth-Century Journalism*, 558.
110 Madden, *History of Irish Periodical Literature*, II, 262; Brake and Demoor, *Dictionary of Nineteenth-Century Journalism*, 558.
111 Inglis, *Freedom of the Press*, 147.
112 Madden, *History of Irish Periodical Literature*, II, 264.

independence from the government.[113] During the Peel administration, which attempted to systematically eliminate the opposition press through excessive taxations and prosecutions, *Saunders's News-Letter* remained unaffected. Its reputation as the city's leading commercial newspaper ensured that advertisements continued to be placed (despite the tax) and its avoidance of political issues caused little concern for the government.[114] The popularity of the newspaper increased to such an extent that, in 1814, the Dublin Conservative MP William Gregory utilised it for the publication of government proclamations, despite Peel's express orders that independent newspapers were not to be used.[115] The contemporary press expressed concern at the development, commenting that *Saunders's News-Letter* 'owes all its strength to its neutrality' and should 'not join the sycophants'.[116] As it consistently received the least government revenue of all the pro-Castle newspapers (after the *Correspondent, Patriot, Dublin Journal* and *Hibernian Journal*), it still maintained its perception of independence and continued to develop a market dominance in advertising.[117] In 1819, it asserted that it fulfilled advertisers' needs as a newspaper, 'which they know as sure to give the most extensive opportunities of laying their wants and wishes before the public'.[118] This position of strong neutrality and defined purpose enabled the newspaper to thrive during the rise of the independent press in the 1820s, while other new daily newspapers competed for readership.[119] Its financially independent status enabled its establishment as the country's most successful daily newspaper by the middle of the century.[120]

The musical coverage in *Saunders's News-Letter* was dense compared to the *Freeman's Journal* and the *Evening Packet*. The treatment of incidental music at non-musical events was similar to that of the *Evening Packet*,

113 Inglis, *Freedom of the Press*, 151.
114 Inglis, *Freedom of the Press*, 150.
115 Inglis, *Freedom of the Press*, 147.
116 Inglis, *Freedom of the Press*, 147.
117 Inglis, *Freedom of the Press*, 145; Aspinall, *Politics and the Press*, 139.
118 Inglis, *Freedom of the Press*, 155.
119 Inglis, *Freedom of the Press*, 176.
120 Brake and Demoor, *Dictionary of Nineteenth-Century Journalism*, 558.

featuring the dinners of the Irish Metropolitan Conservative Party, the
High Sheriff Tomlinson's Dinner, the Pembroke Club boating outing,
Freemason events, events at the Castle and balls at the Rotundo.[121] Quadrille
band leaders and court musicians used it to advertise their availability for
balls.[122] Ceremonial events were reported, but *Saunders's News-Letter* also
noted the performances of amateur bands in the St Patrick's Day celebrations that the other papers had not.[123] The military band performances in
the Portobello Zoological Gardens and the Rotundo Gardens, previously
mentioned in relation to the other newspapers, also featured in *Saunders's
News-Letter*, although it uniquely featured their weekly performances in
Mountjoy Square.[124] Garrison theatricals referred to in the *Evening Packet*
were also reviewed in *Saunders's News-Letter*.[125]

Both Catholic and Protestant denominations were represented
in coverage of religious musical activity.[126] However, the general musical activities of St Patrick's Cathedral and the Chapel Royal in Dublin
Castle received unparalleled coverage in *Saunders's News-Letter*, compared with the *Freeman's Journal* and the *Evening Packet*, thereby indicating that *Saunders's News-Letter* was the Anglican newspaper of note.
Advertisements were placed in *Saunders's News-Letter* for vacancies in the
choir at St Patrick's Cathedral and at the Chapel Royal.[127] The newspaper
featured a regular section commenting on the Lord Lieutenant's attendance
at weekly services in the Chapel Royal, which detailed the singers and the
anthem performed.[128] Dr John Smith was composer to the Chapel Royal
and *Saunders's News-Letter* reviewed a new anthem composed by Smith for
the occasion of the Queen's marriage.[129] Many of the anthems performed

---

121   *Saunders's News-Letter*, 10 January 1840, 1–2; 15 January 1840, 1; 2 June 1840, 2; 29
      April 1842, 3; 18 March 1840, 2; 29 February 1840, 3.
122   *Saunders's News-Letter*, 31 January 1840, 3; 25 January 1840, 3; 6 January 1840, 3.
123   *Saunders's News-Letter*, 18 March 1840, 2.
124   *Saunders's News-Letter*, 20 April 1840, 3; 15 May 1840, 3; 4 June 1840, 2.
125   *Saunders's News-Letter*, 25 January 1840, 2.
126   *Saunders's News-Letter*, 25 January 1840, 4.
127   *Saunders's News-Letter*, 6 January 1840, 4; 4 February 1840, 3.
128   *Saunders's News-Letter*, 10 January 1842, 2.
129   *Saunders's News-Letter*, 28 July 1841, 2; 17 February 1840, 2.

in these weekly Chapel Royal services were noted to have been by Sir John Stevenson and *Saunders's News-Letter* printed some discussions regarding the completion of a monument to the composer.[130]

The amount of pedagogical, music trade and private and public auctions covered by *Saunders's News-Letter* was substantial. There were advertisements by twenty-two music teachers, five schools (seminaries) and 175 governesses during the six-month period. The teachers included both relatively unknown musicians and well-known respected musicians, like Johann Bernard Logier, Dr John Smith, W. H. Buck and Mrs R. Mosley (all of whom had musical academies); performers/teachers like Mr Kavenagh, W. S. Conran, Antonio Sapio and Mons. Rudersdorff; and visiting Theatre Royal performers like Miss M'Mahon and Miss Williams, who offered their services as teachers while they were engaged in the city.[131] It is notable that both Catholic and Protestant teachers utilised *Saunders's News-Letter* to advertise due to its perceived independence, its standing as an advertisement-focused publication and its wide-reaching readership.[132] 175 governesses placed advertisements in *Saunders's News-Letter* offering to teach music as part of a general education – sixteen specified a preference for families of the Roman Catholic religion, compared to seventy-nine requesting positions within families of the Established Church.[133] While

---

130   *Saunders's News-Letter*, 24 January 1842, 2; 7 February 1840, 3; 2 June 1840, 2; 1 June 1840, 3.

131   *Saunders's News-Letter*, 25 January 1840; 4 January 1840, 3; 25 January 1840; 14 March 1840, 3; 25 January 1840; 7 May 1840; 25 January 1840; 5 June 1840, 3; 25 January 1840; 31 January 1840, 3; 25 January 1840; 31 January 1840, 3; 25 January 1840; 14 January 1840, 3; 25 January 1840; 11 March 1840, 3; 25 January 1840; 18 April 1840, 4; 14 February 1840, 3.

132   For example, Haydn Corri and Miss Harvey (organist of the Church of the Conception, Marlborough Street and of St Thomas's Church respectively) and professors such as John Smith (who was involved in the performance of music in the Protestant cathedrals). *Saunders's News-Letter*, 25 January 1840; 4 February 1840, 2; 25 January 1840; 21 May 1840; 31 *Freeman's Journal*, 22 February 1840, 1; *Saunders's News-Letter*, 25 January 1840; 2 January 1843, 3; 25 January 1840; 28 July 1841, 2; *Evening Packet*, 11 January 1840, 1.

133   *Saunders's News-Letter*, 25 January 1840; 8 January 1840, 4; 25 January 1840; 3 January 1840, 4.

there is an obvious focus on the Protestant community, it is interesting to note that *Saunders's News-Letter* was used by governesses of both denominations to communicate with their target audience.

The music trade advertisements were also much more varied, frequent and substantial than those published in either the *Freeman's Journal* or the *Evening Packet*. Six different pianoforte and music warerooms placed long, detailed advertisements in the newspaper.[134] Unique to *Saunders's News-Letter* were the advertisements for the 'cheap music warehouses' of Henry Shade and Samuel Burne, which offered the same instruments and music as other firms, but with a discount of 20 or 30 per cent.[135] The appearance of these cheaper alternatives, alongside the more traditional suppliers, demonstrates the wide audience of *Saunders's News-Letter* and indicates that it was read by both the upper classes and the lower classes with limited disposable income.

Over 200 advertisements for public and private sales were placed in *Saunders's News-Letter* during this period. Compared to twelve in the *Evening Packet* and two in the *Freeman's Journal*, this figure highlights the distinctive commercial nature of the newspaper. The detail provided allows conclusions to be drawn on the type and standard of musical goods and instruments owned by certain strata of society, through a comparison of the sellers' addresses (as neighbourhoods were generally inhabited by different classes) and the materials for sale (including string and brass instruments and particularly pianos by Broadwood, Clementi, Tomkinson, Ellard, Astor, Wolf, Goulding, Collard & Collard, M'Donnell, Mott and Co. – sold for prices ranging from five to eighty guineas).[136]

---

134   *Saunders's News-Letter*, 25 January 1840; 21 March 1840, 2; 25 January 1840; 25 March 1840, 3; 25 January 1840; 26 March 1840, 3; 25 January 1840; 6 April 1840, 3.

135   *Saunders's News-Letter*, 25 January 1840; 20 April 1840, 3; 25 January 1840; 28 April 1840, 2.

136   *Saunders's News-Letter*, 25 January 1840; 6 May 1840, 3; 25 January 1840; 7 January 1840, 3; 25 January 1840; 18 January 1840, 4; 25 January 1840; 8 May 1840, 3; 25 January 1840; 22 January 1840, 3; 25 January 1840; 24 January 1840, 3; 25 January 1840; 23 May 1840, 3; 23 January 1840, 3; 25 January 1840; 3 January 1840, 4; 25 January 1840; 15 February 1840, 4; 25 January 1840; 8 January 1840, 3; 25 January 1840, 9 May 1840, 3; 25 January 1840; 8 June 1840, 3; 25 January 1840; 30 March 1840, 3.

Saunders's News-Letter was the primary conduit for information on Dublin's musical clubs and societies and their Protestant upper-middle-class membership is reflected in the newspaper's readership. During the six-month period examined, the Anacreontic Society featured in three advertisements and reviews; the Philharmonic Society in three advertisements and one review; the Ancient Concerts Society in two advertisements; and the University Choral Society in two reviews.[137] The purpose of the advertisements was always to inform members of the next performance and/ or rehearsal and sometimes noted a ballot if new members were to join. *Saunders's News-Letter*'s coverage of engagements in the Theatre Royal was comparable to that of the *Freeman's Journal*. However, it published significantly more frequent, thorough and substantial previews and reviews of the rest of the city's concert activities, including those held in the Rotundo, the Theatre Royal Abbey Street, the Albion Hotel and Tavern and Morrison's Hotel. This coverage provides valuable insight into the comparative everyday musical activities and illustrates the purpose of the newspaper as a vehicle for everyday news for the newspaper's broad readership.[138]

The reviewing style in *Saunders's News-Letter* was vivid in its descriptions and its use of adjectives (though not as verbose as the *Evening Packet*), but it always gave the impression that the authors were knowledgeable in the subject area. It did not refrain from negative commentary, which the following extract demonstrates:

> Mr Wood sang very sweetly, but his style is bad, and his enunciation, although deserving praise for its distinctness, is too broad, and sometimes comes unpleasantly upon the ear.[139]

---

137   *Saunders's News-Letter*, 25 January 1840; 20 February 1841, 3; 25 January 1840; 12 March 1840, 3; 25 January 1840; 23 March 1840, 2; 25 January 1840; 25 May 1840, 3; 25 January 1840; 8 February 1840, 3; 25 January 1840; 13 March 1840, 3; 25 January 1840; 13 March 1840, 3; 25 January 1840; 16 May 1840, 3; 25 January 1840; 25 May 1840, 4; 25 January 1840; 9 May 1840, 3; 25 January 1840; 28 May 1840, 3; 25 January 1840, 6 April 1840, 2; 25 January 1840, 27 April 1840, 2.

138   *Saunders's News-Letter*, 22 May 1840, 3; 29 February 1840, 3; 25 May 1840, 3; 18 March 1840, 3.

139   *Saunders's News-Letter*, 21 April 1840, 2. Further examples in Ferris, 'The Use of Newspapers as a Source for Musicological Research. See in particular Part II – 'Register of Musical Data on the Music Societies in the *Freeman's Journal*, the *Evening Packet*

Notably, in the forty-two advertisements for Theatre Royal dramatic theatrical events, *Saunders's News-Letter* rarely specified the incidental musical works to be performed, stating only that 'in the course of the evening a variety of singing and dancing' was to be included.[140] This was a direct contrast to the corresponding advertisements in other newspapers, which provided more detail. This was unusual as it was common practice for promoters to publish the same advertisement in multiple sources and it raises questions as to why they chose to make the one in *Saunders's News-Letter*'s shorter and more succinct. It may perhaps suggest that advertising space in *Saunders's News-Letter* was more expensive than in other newspapers, but this would seem at odds with its defined purpose as an advertising medium and one associated with coverage of musical events.

The examination of six months of musical coverage in *Saunders's News-Letter* illustrates its depth, breadth and usefulness as a source. While its published output overlapped in many areas with the *Freeman's Journal* and the *Evening Packet*, it significantly overshadows both in the level of detail provided and the type of information covered. It represented the upper-middle-class and aristocratic music-making activities, but was also utilised as an advertising medium for the lower classes. The contemporary perception of its moderate political stance enabled its use by advertisers for both Catholic and Protestant purposes. Additionally, its unique editorial style, which indulged in negative commentary, provides a more discerning understanding of the subjects examined, compared to the uncritically laudatory dispositions of the other newspapers.

This study of the historical development of the *Freeman's Journal*, the *Evening Packet* and *Saunders's News-Letter* and the establishment of their individual musical identities has illustrated that the editorial style of each newspaper, while established and routine, was influenced by a defined bias through their focus on particular areas of musical life. While this has been examined for each individual newspaper above, it is difficult to comprehend in abstraction. It is important to have a clear understanding of

---

and the *Saunders's News-Letter*, 1840–1844' and examples on 244 ('Philharmonic Society'); 290–1 ('Mr Pigott's Concert'); and 326–27 ('Anacreontic Society').

140   *Saunders's News-Letter*, 13 May 1840, 3.

the differences between each newspaper's partisanship before the published content can be contextualised. An impression of the differences between each newspaper's bias is most clearly evident from a comparison of their reviews of a concert at the Rotundo on 13 May 1840.

Freeman's Journal, 14 May 1840:

CONCERT AT THE ROTUNDO
Mrs Joseph Elliott's annual concert of vocal music took place yesterday evening, at the Long Room of the Rotundo. The audience was highly numerous and fashionable – the attendance fully equalling what might be expected from the extraordinary assemblage of professional talent which was announced for the occasion. Mrs Wood made her first appearance in a concert room for this season, and seemed to have altogether recovered from her recent indisposition. She was in excellent voice, and sung Maeder's beautiful ballad, 'The unwilling bride', 'The Mermaid Cave', by Horn, and an air by Rossini, besides, taking part in several concerted pieces, and it is unnecessary to add that she was most enthusiastically applauded. Mrs Elliott also sung in a truly superior manner, and Miss Hayes appeared to us to surpass any of her former efforts that we have heard. – Messrs. F. and J. Robinson and Signor Sapio also took part in the concert. Among the airs and pieces more particularly beautiful were Balfe's airs, 'Lo, the early beam of morning', 'The last meeting', 'O'er Shepherd Pipe', 'The young soldier', and 'Time is on the wing'. 'Se la vita', from the Semiramide, by Miss Hayes and Signor Sapio, Stevenson's song and Chorus, 'Hark the Convent bells are ringing', by Mrs Elliott. 'Sulla tomba che rinserra', the favourite duetto from *Lucia di Lammermoor*, by Mrs Wood and Mr F. Robinson, and the grand finale to the first act of 'Il Don Giovanni', by all the performers.[141]

Evening Packet, 14 May 1840:

MRS. JOSEPH ELLIOTT'S CONCERT.
The musical treat announced in the advertisements of this lady's concert attracted a full and fashionable audience to the Rotunda last night. The performances, though entirely vocal, were of a rare quality, commanding the valuable services of Mrs Wood, and the assistance of Messrs. F. and J. Robinson, Signor Sapio, Miss Hayes, &c. Mrs Wood, though still suffering from the effects of her late illness, sung several times throughout the night with her usual ability. Among the pieces performed by her were 'Una voce poco fa', 'The unwilling bride', 'The mermaid's cave', and the duetto, 'Sulla tomba chi rinserra', the last of which she sung with Mr Francis Robinson, whose good

taste and mellow tenor voice give him ever such power in the realms of harmony. Mrs Elliott repeated the ballad of 'The blind man's bride', which we noticed on a late occasion, and sung several other pieces with effect. Mr F. Robinson gave two of Balfe's new ballads, one of which, 'The young soldier', was written expressly for him. 'Love and courage', by Mr Joseph Robinson, drew down an encore. Of all the songs which were sung throughout the evening we feel almost inclined to give the preference to the *old*, but not on that account *less pleasing*, ballad, 'John Anderson my joe', by Miss Hayes. Of this young lady we had the pleasure of speaking favorably in our remarks on Signor Sapio's concert, and certainly her execution of this song did not tend to alter our opinion; it was a most touching piece of harmony. The grand finale, from the 1st act of *Don Giovanni*, in which all the performers took part, concluded the entertainments, at a quarter before twelve o'clock.[142]

Saunders's News-Letter, 15 May 1840

MRS ELLIOT'S CONCERT. – Mrs Elliot gave a vocal Concert on Wednesday evening last, and was fortunate in securing for the entertainment of her visitors almost all the first musical talent in the city. Mrs Wood was there, and although still suffering from her late indisposition sang with great ability. Her singing, although without the accompaniment of her acting, is more pleasing in the concert room than on the stage. Her manner is more subdued, and she avoids those bursts delivered with all her power of voice, and sometimes going almost beyond it, which electrify rather than please. The duet (from *Lucia di Lammermoor*), which she sung with Mr Frank Robinson, was a charming specimen of the science and delicate feeling of both performers. Their voices blended together like one instrument, and they displayed a harmony of feeling which showed how equally they both understood the character of the music. 'The unwilling Bride' by Mrs Wood, received a well deserved encore. Spohr's song, 'Love and Courage', sung by Mr Joseph Robinson, was one of the most attractive performances of the evening. It is a thoroughly German characteristic composition, and the rich mellow base of the performer was adapted to give it with great effect. It too was favoured with an enthusiastic encore. A similar compliment was paid to Miss Hayes for the ballad, 'John Anderson my Joe', accompanied by her master, Signor Sapio. She sang it with delightful tenderness and expression. The concert, in short, was a very pleasing one, and the selections did great credit to Mrs Elliott. Her own song, 'Hark the convent bells are ringing', with the distant chorus, was one of the most pleasing and effective performances of the evening. The attendance was very fashionable, and the entertainments did not conclude until a quarter before twelve o'clock.[143]

---

142 *Evening Packet*, 14 May 1840, 3.
143 *Saunders's News-Letter*, 15 May 1840, 2.

All three reviews refer to the attendance, repertoire, performers and Mrs Wood's 'indisposition' or 'illness'. The *Freeman's Journal*'s style was awkward and fragmented, lauding insignificant formulaic praise onto the performers ('in excellent voice' and 'sung in a truly superior manner') and practically listing the pieces performed.[144] The *Evening Packet*'s writing style was more coherent, comparing the quality of the performers and placing the focus on the performance of the young Limerick performer Catherine Hayes.[145] *Saunders's News-Letter*'s style suggests the reviewer possessed considerable knowledge of both the performers' abilities and the repertoire performed ('a thoroughly German characteristic composition') and it provides an informed context for the performance.[146] This triangulation approach confirms the impression of the quality of the journalism of all three newspapers, given in the previous analysis of their individual styles.

Examinations of the religious or political aspects of Victorian music-making may find it worthwhile to utilise newspapers with corresponding allegiances. Specifically, in terms of music performed at religious ceremonies or the social events of political organisations, the Catholic/nationalist events were covered by the *Freeman's Journal*, Protestant/Conservative events were covered by the *Evening Packet* and *Saunders's News-Letter* featured both, although the Catholic events were in the extreme minority. Despite this assertion, it is valuable to employ a triangulation approach and examine other newspapers for contrasting or opposing opinions on these especially volatile subjects: for example, the music societies are generally accepted to be associated with the Protestant Ascendancy, which would direct the researcher towards *Saunders's News-Letter* and the *Evening Packet* for information and characteristically, that is where they received the most coverage. However, references in the *Freeman's Journal* highlight alternate views, exemplified by the aforementioned letter to the editor opposing the establishment of the University Choral Society, thereby providing valuable insight into the social dynamics surrounding the society's formation,

144   *Freeman's Journal*, 14 May 1840, 2.
145   *Evening Packet*, 14 May 1840, 3.
146   *Saunders's News-Letter*, 15 May 1840, 2.

which might have been overlooked had the *Freeman's Journal* not been examined.[147]

While the results of this study will encourage researchers to utilise the *Freeman's Journal*, *Saunders's News-Letter* and the *Evening Packet* for musicological research on the early Victorian period in Dublin, thematic examinations of single newspapers can often overlook the context of the wider music scene to the detriment of the integrity of the research, as these examples show. Without the knowledge that Haydn Corri performed at charity sermons in Catholic churches, the placement of his pedagogical advertisements in the *Freeman's Journal* and *Saunders's News-Letter* would overlook the religious inference on the identities of the newspapers. Likewise, understanding that the readership of the *Freeman's Journal* did not constitute the core audience for the city's music societies enables a contextualisation of the letter to the editor regarding the establishment of the University of Dublin Choral Society, which can therefore be seen as an attempt to rouse opposing support rather than challenge the society directly. It is not always possible or feasible for musicologists to examine and compare multiple newspapers, due to their dense nature. This study has offered a possible methodology in utilising a small number of individual newspapers, with a comprehension of their history, context, an awareness of their limitations and an understanding of the potential information which would remain undisclosed without supporting information from other newspapers.

147   *Freeman's Journal*, 10 January 1840, 3.

Notes on Contributors

JAMES BRENNAN is an MPhil/PhD student and visiting lecturer at Newman University, Birmingham. His thesis examines the political language used by the press in the West Midlands from 1918 to 1929 and thus scrutinizes the methods used by provincial newspapers to interact with voters in an age of mass democracy.

IAN CAWOOD, PhD, is Reader in Modern History at Newman University, Birmingham. He is the author of *The Liberal Unionist Party, 1886–1912: A History* (2012) and the editor of *Joseph Chamberlain: Imperial Statesman, National Leader and Local Icon* (2016).

VICTORIA CLARKE is a PhD student at the Schools of English and History, University of Leeds. Her thesis, entitled 'Reading and Writing the *Northern Star* in Britain, 1837–1848,' will be the first full-length study of the leading newspaper of the Chartist movement, and is funded by the White Rose College of the Arts and Humanities. Prior to her PhD, she completed an MA in Victorian Literature at the University of Leeds and a BA in English Literature with English Language and Linguistics at the University of Roehampton. She has previously worked as a research assistant on the AHRC Letterpress Project, based at the universities of Leeds and Birmingham City. Her research interests include print culture, radicalism, labour, masculinities, and fashion of the long nineteenth century.

JUDITH DAVIES gained her first degree in Politics and Russian Studies from the University of Wales, Swansea. She also holds a postgraduate diploma from the College of Librarianship Wales, Aberystwyth, and she worked as a librarian in Northamptonshire before taking early retirement in 2011. She has an MA in West Midlands History from the University of Birmingham. She is currently researching political, religious and social change in Dudley around 1815–1867 as she studies part-time for a PhD at the University of Birmingham and she also works as a volunteer for the Dudley Archives and Local History Service.

CATHERINE FERRIS, PhD, is Special Collections Music Cataloguer at the Dublin Institute of Technology. Her research focuses on Dublin music societies, the contextual history of everyday musical life in Dublin and the use of primary source materials for musicological research. Her research is published in *Brio* (2006), *Music and Institutions in Nineteenth-Century Britain* (2012) and the *Encyclopaedia of Music in Ireland* (2013). She is a founder member of the Research Foundation for Music in Ireland, chair of the IAML (UK & Irl) Documentation Committee and a member of the IAML (UK & Irl) Executive Committee. She is also editor of the online Dublin Music Trade database (<http://www.dublinmusictrade.ie>).

DUNCAN FRANKIS is a history teaching associate at the University of Birmingham. His research interests focus on the spread of ideas and knowledge during the eighteenth century. His PhD thesis examined the exchange of Newtonian mechanics between enlightened savants and working-class fabricants in Birmingham and how exclusive manufacturing knowledge and organisation of the Birmingham brass industry was used as leverage to gain political influence within Britain. This research is currently being turned into a book, podcast and documentary for History West Midlands. His other research and publications have explored Irish radicalism and race relations during the 1790s, as well as examining the 1823 Judgement of Death Act. Outside of academia, he has worked as a researcher for international development charities in Latin America, providing new evidence to highlight the extent and nature of gender-based crime in rural Honduran communities.

LISA PETERS, PhD, works in academic administration at the University of Chester. She is the author of *Politics, Publishing and Personalities: Wrexham Newspapers, 1848–1914* (2011). Her research focuses on the newspapers of North Wales and the border area. She is a member of the Print Networks conference committee.

SUE THOMAS is a PhD student at the University of Birmingham focusing on the development of radicalism in early and mid-nineteenth-century Birmingham, in particular the Birmingham radical George Edmonds. She taught for many years in further education, working with young adults and mature students who were returning to study. On retirement she went back to college and completed an MA in West Midlands History at the University of Birmingham.

HELEN WILLIAMS studied Russian as an undergraduate and later worked for the London Library, the British Library and the National Library of Scotland. She has worked on a number of projects relating to printing and the allied trades and was Programme Manager for the 500 years of printing in Scotland celebrations. She has been Honorary Secretary to the Scottish Printing Archival Trust since 2009 and has recently been awarded a PhD by Edinburgh Napier University for her thesis on the Scottish regional printing industry in the nineteenth century.

PAUL WILSON, PhD, is a researcher, typographer and writer whose work explores the intersections of language, landscape, community and communication. His current research involves the production of designed narratives of community and place and, in particular, investigates the potential for critically engaged typographies and language-acts, focusing on sites of class experience and situated knowledge at moments or points of change or transition. Much of his work orbits ideas and ideals of utopianism found in manifestations of the utopian action and has resulted in a broad range of activities: surveying the noticeboards found in the interior landscapes of Working Men's Clubs, mapping the route of the march which marked the closure of Britain's last deep coal mine and exploring the post-Brexit significance of the Esperanto-English dictionary held in Keighley Library, West Yorkshire. He is a lecturer in the School of Design at the University of Leeds.

Index

Printing History and Culture

Series Editors

Caroline Archer-Parré, Malcolm Dick and John Hinks

This series unites the allied fields of printing history and print culture, and is therefore concerned not only with the design, production and distribution of printed material but also its consumption, reception and impact. It includes the histories of the machinery and equipment, of the industry and its personnel, of the printing processes, the design of its artefacts (books, newspapers, journals, fine prints, and ephemera) and with the related arts and crafts, including calligraphy, type-founding, typography, papermaking, bookbinding, illustration, and publishing. It also covers the cultural context and environment in which print was produced and consumed.

This series is issued by the Centre for Printing History and Culture, a joint initiative between Birmingham City University and the University of Birmingham that seeks to encourage research into all aspects and periods of printing history and culture, as well as education and training in the art and practice of printing.

Published Volumes